Arts, Research, Innovation and Society

Creativity in general and the arts in particular are increasingly recognized as drivers of cultural, economic, political, social, and scientific innovation and development. In Art and Research, some of the principal questions to be explored by the ARIS project, are outlined: • Could and should Artists be Researchers? • How are the systems of the Arts and the Sciences connected and /or disconnected? • What is the position and status of the Arts in defining the terms "progress" and "development"? The Springer ARIS series explores – at the macro, meso and micro levels and in terms of qualitative as well as quantitative studies - theories, policies and practices about the contributions of artistic research and innovations towards defining new forms of knowledge, knowledge production as well as knowledge diffusion, absorption and use. Artistic research, artistic innovations and arts-based innovations have been major transformers as well as disruptors of the ways in which societies, economies, and political systems perform. Ramifications here refer to the epistemic socio-economic, socio-political and socio-technical base and aesthetic considerations on the one hand, as well as to strategies, policies, and practices on the other, including sustainable enterprise excellence considerations in the context of knowledge economies, societies and democracies. The series features research monographs, edited volumes, proceedings, Briefs, and textbooks, and may also include handbooks and reference works, and in-print as well on-line rich media encapsulations of ideas and insights, representing cutting-edge research and the synthesis of a body of work in the field.

More information about this series at http://www.springer.com/series/11902

Romola Adeola • Michael Gyan Nyarko
Adebayo Okeowo • Frans Viljoen
Editors

The Art of Human Rights

Commingling Art, Human Rights and the Law in Africa

Springer

Editors
Romola Adeola
Centre for Human Rights
University of Pretoria
Pretoria, Gauteng, South Africa

Michael Gyan Nyarko
Centre for Human Rights
University of Pretoria
Pretoria, South Africa

Adebayo Okeowo
Centre for Human Rights
University of Pretoria
Pretoria, South Africa

Frans Viljoen
Centre for Human Rights
University of Pretoria
Pretoria, South Africa

ISSN 2626-7683 ISSN 2626-7691 (electronic)
Arts, Research, Innovation and Society
ISBN 978-3-030-30101-9 ISBN 978-3-030-30102-6 (eBook)
https://doi.org/10.1007/978-3-030-30102-6

This Springer imprint is published by the registered company Springer Nature Switzerland AG
The registered company address is: Gewerbestrasse 11, 6330 Cham, Switzerland

Foreword

The Global Campus of Human Rights has a fascinating vision and programme of connecting the arts with human rights. Every year we organise a Summer School on Cinema, Human Rights and Advocacy in cooperation with the Venice Film Festival; we just published an art book on the commemoration of the 70th anniversary of the Universal Declaration of Human Rights entitled *Imagine Human Rights – Artists Celebrate the Universal Declaration*; we are editing, together with Musicians for Human Rights, a book on *Music and Human Rights*; we organise photo competitions on human rights and we aim to transform our Monastery of San Nicolo at the Lido of Venice into a "Human Rights Pavilion" in cooperation with the Venice Biennale. By means of freedom of artistic expression, human rights protect the arts against censorship and other measures aimed at restricting freedom of the arts. On the other hand, the universal language of the arts is the most powerful medium to communicate the universal values of human rights to a broad audience. The arts touch us more profoundly than the mere language of human rights as they speak to our innermost feelings and emotions.

The current book on arts and human rights in Africa, which is published by our Global Campus partners of the University of Pretoria, is a beautiful example for the power of arts to create debates that accommodate everyone, irrespective of learning stages and processes. When one thinks of Africa, within the scope of arts, one easily thinks of a place where arts finds its richness and splendour exported to various parts of the world as a modus operandi for communication and culture.

Africa is a place of arts. But more importantly, it is the home of richness both in the diversity of its artistic form and also in the depth of its quality. This book leverages on this pertinent form of expression in seeking to build knowledge formations on arts. The chapters are endowed with a plethora of seasoned perspectives. Through the various chapters, we learn about how to use arts to enhance human rights teaching and advocacy. For instance, in Chap. 3, we learn how we can leverage on photographic silhouettes in drawing attention to human rights violations including harmful cultural practices such as female genital mutilation (FGM). This book also seeks to strike a balance in teaching us to cautiously scrutinise usage of arts that may impact on human rights. Chapter 6 makes this important point in critically examining representation of black women in the media, considering three South African television shows.

The richness of this book both in form and content creates a notable optics for which we can confidently begin the debate both in Africa and globally on combining arts, human rights and the law.

Secretary-General, Global Campus of Human Rights
Professor of International Human Rights Law,
University of Vienna
Independent Expert Leading the United Nations
Global Study on Children Deprived of Liberty
Vienna, Europe

Manfred Nowak

Contents

Chapter 1
Arts, Human Rights and the Law in Africa: An Introduction

Romola Adeola, Michael Gyan Nyarko, Adebayo Okeowo, and Frans Viljoen

1 Introduction

While arts, human rights and law are well established fields that have emerged and developed through knowledge systems that are rich and extensive in engagement, their confluence has become a significant point of interest in recent years. Arts are as ancient as Africa's history. To understand Africa, and indeed, the culture of the continent, the role of arts is crucial. Prehistoric records reflect the use of rock arts in many parts of modern day Africa. As early as 8000 BC, arts were engraved on caves and even today gives us a sense of ancient African culture (Ofei 2008, p. 168). The Nok culture in Nigeria possesses notable terracotta sculptures with records doing as far back as 500 BC (Rupp et al. 2008, p. 284). Aside from the rich history of African Saharan trade, which was 'the vehicle for the transmission of ideas' (Isichei 1997, p. 218), African arts have been the vehicle of continental civilisation. In more recent years, the arts has become the mechanism for visual representation not only of African history but also communication of culture, feelings, power and knowledge. Across Africa, the arts has become a formidable expression of thoughts and a means of articulating reality in a form that simplifies truth and bolster resolve to advance change. In the human rights context, the arts has become a pertinent tool in expressing thoughts. In contemporary Africa, the potency of arts in human rights has been brought into light through various campaigns on the abduction of children by Joseph Kony in Uganda, the sale of migrants in Libya and the Bring Back Our Girls Campaign in Nigeria. While a plethora of examples abound on how arts has shaped the human rights narrative, scholarship on the intersection between arts and human rights law remains at its infancy. This book examines this intersectionality given the importance of arts in African expression. The arts serve as a formidable way of harvesting the voices of various groups. In recent years, it has become an important

R. Adeola (✉) · M. G. Nyarko · A. Okeowo · F. Viljoen
Faculty of Law, Centre for Human Rights, University of Pretoria, Pretoria, South Africa
e-mail: romola.adeola@up.ac.za

R. Adeola et al. (eds.), *The Art of Human Rights*, Arts, Research, Innovation and Society, https://doi.org/10.1007/978-3-030-30102-6_1

tool for engagement in view of the fourth industrial revolution and the power of visuals in representing pertinent issues. However, arts can also be used as to perpetuate dangerous stereotypes and propaganda machinery to entrench practices that violate human rights, usually of the most vulnerable in society. This book explores these intersectionalities within the African context. There are ten chapters in this book. The authors engage the subject of the arts from a plethora of perspectives: music, photographic silhouette, literature, photojournalism, soap operas, visual arts, sculpture and theatre. All ten chapters in this book were peer-reviewed in addition to the internal review process.

In Chap. 2, Babatunde Fagbayibo argues that in rethinking international legal pedagogy, it is useful to draw on the musical pieces of Fela Anikulapo-Kuti. Drawing on three musical pieces: "International Thief Thief", Beasts of No Nation", and "Teacher Don't Teach Me Nonsense", Fagbayibo proposes an alternative approach to teaching international law in a way that disrupts conventional international legal thinking and critiques the current international legal system. Leveraging on the critical mass of scholarship stemming from Third World Approaches to International Law (TWAIL), Fagbayibo leans towards the argument that it is important to re-image the optics of knowledge. Fagbayibo proposes three ideational issues that should underline the introduction of Fela's music into the teaching of international law in African universities: interdisciplinary, Afrocentricity and counterhegemonic-activist approaches. These perspectives, he argues, should "stimulate the discussions around the imperative of rethinking the pedagogy of international law, and thus encourage innovative thinking by educators."

In Chap. 3, Kaia L Magnusen critically engages Aida Silvestri's Unsterile Clinic in discussing the issue of Female Genital Mutilation (FGM) as a violation of human rights law including the right to health. Magnusen examines the reasons for the prevalence of FGM, notably, the socio-cultural narratives that foster its continuance. In discussing FGM as a violation of human rights, Magnusen draws on relevant regional human rights standards, in particular, the Protocol to the African Charter on Human and Peoples' Rights on the Rights of Women in Africa (African Women's Protocol) and the African Commission's *Guidelines on Combating Sexual Violence and its Consequences in Africa* which emphatically denounces FGM. Utilising photographic silhouettes from Eritrean-born Aida Silvestri, Magnusen demonstrates how artistic expression gives a voice to the voiceless and draws attention to the importance of combatting FGM. Magnussen emphasises that "[f]or viewers ignorant of the practice, the board presents an opportunity for them to educate themselves about the types of FGM thereby enabling viewers to have a more complete understanding of what the practice truly entails." She makes a strong case for engaging in artistic expressions in breaking the norm of silence on FGM, raising awareness and empowering women and girls to express their experiences given that "art therapy can provide an alternative method of expression."

In Chap. 4, Romola Adeola engages Adichie's *The American Embassy*—a literary text set in the military era of General Sani Abacha in Nigeria (1993–1998). Using this short story, Adeola argues that it is imperative to give due consideration to the traumatic experiences of asylum seekers in adjudicatory processes while determining the well-founded nature of an applicant's fear of persecution. A trauma-sensitive approach, she argues, "acknowledges the presence of trauma in the lived experience of an asylum seeker". In adopting a trauma-sensitive approach, an adjudicator becomes mindful of the fact that an asylum seeker may be affected by trauma in retelling her or his account. Given that trauma often characterises the refugee experience, especially in situations of conflict, Adeola argues that it is imperative for asylum-seekers to have access to psychosocial support. Recognising that the practical ramifications of the proposal may have financial costs, she argues that states should "pursue effective partnerships with international organisations and civil society in addressing the technical dimensions of this form of support."

In Chap. 5, Mohammed Elshamy uses photojournalism to visually capture human rights. With vast experiences across Africa, Elshamy demonstrates how this form of art can play a significant role in advancing human rights protection and unveiling violations for which responses are required. Drawing on the 2014 Ebola situation in West Africa, Elshamy illustrates how photojournalism contributes in raising attention to the issue. He shares powerful images that tell the story of the impact of visual representation, emphasising that "[t]hrough photojournalism, visual representations of the casualties from the Ebola virus was useful in prompting international response from aid groups and health organisations to countries in West Africa that were plagued with the disease." While noting that photojournalists can contribute to the furtherance of human rights in Africa, Elshamy notes that "it is important that free press is guaranteed."

In Chap. 6, Reshoketswe Mapokgole analyses the depiction of black women in soap operas. Analysing three SABC television shows (*Skeem Saam* on SABC 1, *Muvhango* SABC 2 and *Isidingo* on SABC 3), Mapokgole argues that the stereotypical representation of black women on SABC television reinforces the discrimination that they encounter within the South African society. She observes that black women are "represented as characters without agency". She draws on historical representation of black women in South Africa that is "both gendered and racialised". Using the Bechdel test, she demonstrates how these three SABC shows perpetuate stereotypical narratives contrary to South Africa's obligation under relevant international human rights instruments, notably women's rights treaties. She argues that the continuous representation of these stereotypes "inform harmful cultural and social practises." In conclusion, she makes the point that "films that are more diverse and offer new outlooks on the role of women make more money" and poses the salient question that "[i]f diverse and complex representations of women can create profit, what does this mean for the future of storytelling in the SABC?"

In Chap. 7, Josephat M Kilonzo engages the use of visual arts in telling history. Kilonzo recognises the potency of visual art in empowering people and serving as a "platform for victims of gross human rights violations to voice their views and concerns". He argues that art can serve as a useful means of advancing justice complementing other transitional justice mechanisms and telling the narrative of oppressed voices. Observing that there is "no single way of telling a story", he makes the salient point that "visual arts can be used to tell individual stories; stories of individuals struggles, pain and their past generally; and stories that may not be reflected in the grand narrative." Drawing on the Wagalla massacre, Malka Mari massacre and situations of sexual violence, Kilonzo demonstrates how memory is politicised and reflects on the importance of visual arts in providing justice and "countering the amnesia, denial, impunity and cover-ups by the state". Kilonzo concludes on a striking note that "[o]rdinary Kenyans are able to question the institutionalisation and normalisation of horrid human rights violations, structural violence and abuse of power through visual art". Through this chapter, Kilonzo offers a useful focal trajectory to commemorate history and preserve memory in protecting human rights and advancing transitional justice.

In Chap. 8, Elizabeth Lisot-Nelson engages the art works of Fasasi Abeedeen Tunde who uses sculptures to powerfully depict the plight of migrants at sea. Lisot-Nelson significantly explores the work of Fasasi in Italy. She demonstrates how Fasasi's art has been able to powerfully depict the visual imagery of what migrants' experience on the Mediterranean Sea and how it drives a moral imperative for global action. Lisot-Nelson tells the story of Fasasi from his voyage from Nigeria through the Sahara Desert until Libya through the Mediterranean Sea into Italy. Through powerful imagery and verbal recollections, Lisot-Nelson demonstrates the potency of art in communicating the plight of migrants at sea and in creating societal changes to improve human rights standards for migrants.

In Chap. 9, Albert O Oloruntoba examines the relevance of theatre to human rights protection in South Africa. This chapter examines how theatre has been engaged in shaping the human rights narrative in apartheid and post-apartheid South Africa. Notably, during apartheid South Africa, the works of playwrights including Athol Fugard, Gibson Kente, Dennis Walder and Percy Mtwa were used to spotlight human rights abuses and raise consciousness on the need for resistance to apartheid. Oloruntoba highlights the fact that post-apartheid, theatre has thematically expanded to include other significant social issues in contemporary South Africa including issues of gender and class. He narrows in on a post-apartheid theatrical expression: Mike Van Graan's *Green Man Flashing*. Oloruntoba uses this play to spotlight the issue of rape which has emerged as a significant problem. He unveils the politicisation of rape, social construction of gender and power dynamics that fuels injustice.

In Chap. 10, Ronald Kakungulu-Mayambala interrogates the role of music in the promotion of human rights in Uganda. He argues that music is important in shaping the human rights narrative in Uganda given its prevalence and the widespread acceptance of it in the popular culture. He stresses how prominent music artists have used music as a political tool in shedding light on human rights concerns in Uganda. He underscores the imperative of musical expression as a form of art through relevant international human rights standards. Notably, he references article 27 of the Universal Declaration of Human Rights (UDHR) which provides that everyone has the right "to enjoy the arts". He also makes reference to article 15(3) of the ICESCR, which spotlights the commitment of states to "respect the freedom indispensable for ... creative activity" which the Committee on Economic, Social and Cultural Rights (CESCR) has interpreted to include the right to "enjoy freedom of opinion, freedom of expression in the language or languages of their choice, and the right to seek, receive and impart information and ideas of all kinds and forms including art forms"

(CESCR 2009). However, he observes that there is a significant clampdown on musical expression which is at variance with Uganda's international human rights obligations.

Overall, the chapters in this book proceeds from an understanding that the field of arts is a significant method for advancing engagement on human rights law and given that it promotes "unconventional synapses-building between different fields of knowledge and approaches to knowledge production" (Bast et al. 2015, p. 3). As the ultimate test of international human rights law is at the domestic level (Viljoen 2012), engaging arts in raising awareness and building knowledge formations on human rights creates the space for significant engagements and opens up the possibility for a plethora of ways in which human rights research and advocacy can be advanced.

References

Bast G, Carayannis EG, Campbell DFJ (2015) In: Bast G, Carayannis EG, Campbell DFJ (eds) Arts, research, innovation and society. Springer, Cham, p 1

CESCR (2009) General comment No. 21, E/C.12/GC/21 21 December 2009. United Nation.

Isichei E (1997) A history of African societies to 1870. Cambridge University Press, Cambridge

Ofei KGK (2008) Black arts movement. In: Davies CB (ed) Encyclopedia of the African Diaspora: origins, experiences, and culture. ABC-CLIO, Inc., Santa Barbara, CA, p 167

Rupp N, Ameje J, Breunig P (2008) New studies on the Nok culture of central Nigeria. J Afr Archaeol 3(2):283–290

Viljoen F (2012) International human rights law in Africa. Oxford University Press, Oxford

Chapter 2
Critical Pedagogy of International Legal Education in Africa: An Exploration of Fela Anikulapo-Kuti's Music

Babatunde Fagbayibo

Abstract Fela Anikulapo-Kuti was a revolutionary who used his music as a weapon for tackling autocracy and global injustice. He advocated for pan-Africanism in socio-political and economic processes and fought against the marginalisation of the downtrodden. His non-conformist, radical stance resulted in numerous arrests, harassments and torture at the hands of successive military regimes in Nigeria. Fela's infectious beats and critically engaging lyrics, mainly sang in Pidgin English, continue to inspire multi-layered interests in his works. Beyond the commercial appropriation of his legacy, his intense and methodical delivery provides an important window to exposing students to critical understanding of the global system. While Fela's musical oeuvre generally speak to social consciousness, three of his songs are relevant to the critical teaching of international law: "Teacher Don't Teach Me Nonsense", "International Thief Thief", and "Beast of No Nations". These songs reflect some of the issues raised by critical movements, such as the Third World Approaches to International Law (TWAIL), thereby making them an important gateway to understanding the works of this school of thought. These issues include the hypocrisy of the international community regarding democracy, illicit financial flow from Africa, and the unequal structure of the United Nations (UN). This chapter discusses the ideational issues that should guide the introduction of Fela's music into the process of rethinking the pedagogy of international legal education in African law schools.

Keywords Fela Anikulapo Kuti · Critical pedagogy · Third World Approaches to International Law (TWAIL) · Paulo Freire · Afrocentric approach · Interdisciplinary · Dialogics · Teacher don't teach me nonsense · Beast of no nations · International Thief Thief

B. Fagbayibo (✉)
University of South Africa, Pretoria, South Africa
e-mail: fagbabo@unisa.ac.za

R. Adeola et al. (eds.), *The Art of Human Rights*, Arts, Research, Innovation and Society, https://doi.org/10.1007/978-3-030-30102-6_2

1 Introduction

For centuries, the intimate link between law and music has remained an integral part of human civilisation. In western civilisation, such link has its roots in ancient Greece, where "the function of laying down the law was entrusted to … sound pronounced with appropriate intonation and rhythm, in accordance with a rite celebrated by those on whom the gods had bestowed the gift of speaking the truths of life to men" (Cited in Mittica 2015, p. 30). Similarly, Thomas Hobbes noted that "in ancient time, before letters were in common use, the Lawes were many times put into verse, that the rude people taking pleasure in singing, or reciting them, might more easily reteine them in memory" (Cited in Grossfeld and Hiller 2008, p. 1150). As such, music provided not only a medium for gauging the tempo of the society but also an instrument for envisioning and implementing societal order. This background led to Plato's cautious assertion that "any musical innovation is full of danger to the whole state, and ought to be prohibited … when modes of music change, the fundamental laws of the state always change with them" (Plato 2008, p. 93).

In the African context, music has always played a significant role in societal configurations (Roux-Kemp 2014, p. 247; Soyinka 1985, pp. 544–549). Across ethnic groupings and societies in Africa, music served as a pedagogical mechanism for transmitting peoples lived cultural realities. In pre-colonial African Yoruba communities, music functioned as a dissenting tool for exposing misrule and dictatorial tendencies of a ruler. Olukotun (2002, p. 196) cites a Yoruba saying to prove this point: "I will have my say. The King does not say slay musicians". Furthermore, Soyinka (1985, p. 546) explained the juridical power of music in the following words:

> The combination of music and oratory in formal judicial structures may, however, be regarded as being yet another property of cultures in which music is not simply an isolated activity of the society, but an integral one. The Idoma of north-eastern Nigeria employed a tradition of judicial processes which utilized a semi-choric pattern within a predominantly theatric setting. Against a background of choric responses the contestants presented their cases like formal actors, moving out of the human, semicircular blackcloth and merging into the mass again. Gestures were deliberately theatrical, fully measured even for incongruous effects. The process would last for two days to a week. A litigation among the Watutsi involved similar theatricalities.

The role of music and musicians in contemporary Africa has been pertinent. Music provided the much-needed organisational capacity for resisting colonial rule, and the struggle for liberation and unity (Roux-Kemp 2014, Mapuwei and Orina 2013). In cases where music was, and is, seen as trying to "change the fundamental laws of the state", political elites have been swift to reprimand and persecute the musicians involved. One such example was the case of Fela Anikulapo-Kuti, the revolutionary Nigerian musician and originator of Afrobeat, whose entire music career exposed the many ills of the Nigerian ruling class, and the need for the downtrodden masses to resist bad governance. His non-conformist, radical stance resulted in numerous arrests, harassments and torture at the hands of successive military regimes in Nigeria. While the majority of his counter-hegemonic music centred on

Nigeria, his political posture was essentially pan-Africanist (Olorunyomi 2005, Olaniyan 2004).

In the context of his pan-Africanist approach to the international system, three of his songs are relevant to the critical teaching of international law. These are "International Thief Thief" (1979), "Teacher Don't Teach Me Nonsense" (1985), and "Beasts of No Nation" (1989). These songs reflect some of the issues raised by critical movements, such as the Third World Approaches to International Law (TWAIL), thereby making them an important gateway to understanding and disrupting the hegemonic nature of mainstream international law (Fagbayibo 2018). These issues include the hypocrisy of the international community regarding democracy and human rights, illicit financial flows from Africa, and the unequal structure of the United Nations (UN) (Bedjaoui 1979, pp. 23–63; Chimni 2006, p. 7; Mutua 2000, pp. 34–35; Okafor 2005, p. 178); Anghie 2000, p. 40; Gathii et al. 2013, pp. 9–13).

This chapter will discuss the specific ways in which the message of these songs can contribute to the process of enriching the pedagogy of international law in Africa. As Newman (2018, p. 4) rightly noted, "the use of popular music offers a writer a valuable device to render what could be quite dry and, otherwise dull, argument suddenly more interesting and thus engaging to the reader." In the context of an Afrocentric pedagogical approach, Nabudere (2003, p. 24) observed that the incorporation of performative arts into the curriculum could ensure "cognitive shifts in the way new knowledge is accessed and acquired". Similarly, Chimni (2006, p. 4) opined that music is one of the important tools that can assist in capturing the imagination of new participants in the international law arena. Similarly, movies and documentaries are used to teach in human rights and international law classes on subjects such as genocide. One example is the 2004 movie, "Hotel Rwanda", which has become a popular teaching tool on the subject of genocide, international human rights law and international humanitarian law (Amnesty International 2005).

This chapter argues that beyond the commercial appropriation of his legacy, Fela infectious beats, critically engaging lyrics, and intense methodical delivery, mainly sang in Pidgin English, all have the requisite ability to achieve the objective of sharpening the engagement of students with an international system that is in dire need of reforms. This chapter is organised as follows. The next section shows Fela oft-colliding relationship with the authorities in Nigeria, and his commitment to resisting the bad laws emanating from the state. The second section discusses the international law themes in his songs. The chapter concludes by exploring the ideational measures that should guide the introduction of Fela's music into the process of rethinking the pedagogy of international legal education in African law schools.

2 Fela and Law

Before discussing Fela's problematic relationship with authority and the law, it is important to first provide a brief biographical context. Fela Anikulapo-Kuti (1938–1997) was born in Abeokuta, South-West Nigeria, into a politically active and educated family. His mother, Olufunmilayo Ransome-Kuti had an impressive resume in her own right. She was a teacher, foremost women's right activist, the first woman to drive a motor car in Nigeria and formed part of the delegation that negotiated Nigeria's independence from the United Kingdom (Shonekan 2009, pp. 130–132; Simola 1999, pp. 99–104; Moore 2016, p. 15). Her activism was also international in character as she was able to engage with and travel in the 1950s to places like China (where she met with Mao Tse-tung), Poland, Yugoslavia, USSR and East Berlin (Simola 1999, p. 103). His father, Oludotun Ransome-Kuti was one of the founders of the Nigerian Union of Teachers (NUT) and was actively engaged in protesting against colonial education policies in Nigeria and the region of West Africa (Simola 1999, p. 102). Fela was influenced by his parents' activism, in particular the activities of his mother. As he noted to his biographer:

> The Nigerian Women's Union was a powerful organization. My mother founded it in the early '40s. As I got older, she started taking me around with her in the car to her campaign meetings … I admired her. My mother was quite heavy politically … I liked the way she took on those old politicians, all those dishonest rogues (Moore 2016, pp. 15–16).

Fela also recalled how he had accompanied his mother to visit Kwame Nkrumah (Moore 2016, p. 20). Interestingly, Shonekan (2009) argued that the revolutionary songs composed by the Abeokuta Women's Union, an organisation led by his mother to challenge colonial tax policies and other patriarchal attitudes, in terms of both approach and stylistic devices, heavily influenced Fela. Although Fela's outward display of political and ideological conscientisation only materialised upon his return from the United States of America in 1969, where Sandra Iszadore introduced him to black consciousness literature (Moore 2016, p. 61; Collins 2015, p. 37), his mother's strong impact remained a critical part of his outlook and position on pan-Africanism and the international system. Fela explained his mother's influence on his musical outlook in the following words: "In '66 I was playing highlife jazz with my Koola Lobitos band. Eventually I dropped that name too. 'Cause my mother had told me: "Start playing music your people understand, not jazz" (Moore 2016, p. 47). It should, however, be emphasised that before travelling to the U.S. in 1969, Fela's songs were devoid of radical and political undertones. His songs were essentially rooted in the jazzy "highlife", feel good music that was very popular in Nigeria and West Africa. Recounting a performance in Los Angeles in August 1969, on the day he met Sandra, Fela said, "The NAACP [National Association for the Advancement of Colored People] wanted me to play … So that's how I got to play there, not because I was political. I wasn't political. I just wanted to play, to make bread, to make myself a great artist" (Moore 2016, p. 59). In 1975, in line with his pan-Africanist ideal, Fela changed the "Ransome" part of his surname to "Anikulapo" (the one who has death in his pouch). As he explained, "My full name means: "He who emanates greatness, who has control over death and who cannot be killed by man" (Moore 2016, p. 113).

One of the key issues that defined Fela's music career was the extent to which he challenged normative rules and institutions. Femi Falana, one of Fela's lawyers in the 1990s, remarked that Fela was always prepared to challenge the state in the courts:

> Fela, for many of us, had propensity for criminality – for many people. But here was a guy, Fela, who would tell you, Femi, *I wan commit this offence Ah, no nao*. And he would say, 'No, I am going to breach the new colonial law, it's your business to defend me.' And as far as Fela was concerned, he would do it. And one thing I found very interesting was that he would have done his own work, all you then needed to do as a lawyer was just to look for the law to back up his own defence – a defence that you cannot challenge in any court. And that was how Fela got away with a lot of violations of the legal system (Cited in Ramon 2017).

In advocating a pan-African approach to justice and the law, Fela had asserted that:

> There is the need for the introduction of the use of indigenous languages or mother tongues as the medium of instruction in our society since it is the starting point of the revolution, such that in our courts of law an accused person may have the opportunity of understanding the judicial process. Community courts need to be set up in order to administer petty complaints so as to reduce remanding citizens in detention for long periods without access to justice. An administration of justice that would be corrective rather than punitive should also be devised. If prisons must be built, then they should be such that would be psychologically curative (Cited in Olorunyomi 2005, p. 36).

Olorunyomi (2005, p. 173) observed that such contestation was Fela's "regular polemical turf, where he tried to re-image the continent in relation to itself and others". Relatedly, Olaniyan (2004, pp. 81–83) posits that Fela's ideological matrix essentially rests on three components: Africanism (the quest for an authentic Afrocentric approach to socio-political and economic issues), solidarity with the oppressed lower class, and irrepressible libertarianism (guarantee of the widest realm of individual freedom is possible). He noted that without Fela's commitment to the cause of the poor, he would just have been another "Afro-cultural nationalist" (Olaniyan 2004, p. 81). As such, Fela was able to position both his personal conduct and music, which were in most cases intertwined, as a better, counterculture alternative to settled societal normative values. As far as Fela was concerned, laws must be subjected to the rigorous test of the principles of Africanism, and if it fails, there must be a resistance.

Fela's "irrepressible libertarianism" exposed him to incessant harassment in the hands of successive military regimes in Nigeria. From 1974 (when he was first arrested) until his death in 1997, his bohemian lifestyle, which openly promoted the recreational use of marijuana and sexual proclivities, served as a useful pretext for constant raids and arrests (Moore 2016, Olaniyan 2004, Olorunyomi 2005). As it proved difficult to tie his politically charged, name-and-shame textured songs to violation of any laws in the statute books, the authorities had to become more creative about their repressive approach. Even when he directly challenged the sovereign authority of the state by declaring a state within a state, the "Kalakuta Republic", the politico-military establishment never attempted to charge him with treason. Fela explained the rationale behind establishing "Kalakuta Republic" in the following words: "All African countries should open their doors to Africans from everywhere … So the idea of creating a place open to every African escaping persecution began taking shape in this mind" (Moore 2016, p. 87). In an interview with Collins (2015, p. 208) in the 1970s, he similarly noted:

> I found out that when I went [later] to East Africa that *kalakuta* is a Swahili word that means "rascal." So, if rascality is going to get us what we want we will use it. Because we are dealing with corrupt people we have to be "rascally" with them.

Similarly, when he decided to marry 27 women on the same day in 1978, which was a clear case of bigamy as he was still married to his legal wife, the state took no serious legal measures against him (Moore 2016, pp. 140–145). Rather, the authorities placed morality at the heart of its normative approach towards Fela, as he was portrayed as an anarchical reprobate that must be curtailed before destroying the moral firmament of the society. Few months before his death in 1997, Fela, alongside 107 people, was arrested by the Nigerian Drug Law Enforcement Agency (NDLEA) for the possession of large quantities of marijuana. He was handcuffed and paraded on national television as a criminal. The head of the NDLEA, Musa Bamaiyi, later told reporters that his agency had tried to give Fela counselling for his drug habits. He further noted that

> Fela has unleashed an unbridled reign of terror on the minds of unsuspecting youths long enough and the activities of his followers now call to question the ability of the agency to live up to expectations … [he has] held innocent souls hostage and with the gloom now pervading their lives, they are doomed if the agency fails in its sacred responsibility of rescuing their enslaved souls from his clutches (Olori 1997).

Fela later successfully sued the NDLEA for the violation of his fundamental rights to fair hearing, personal liberty and human dignity (Falana 2010, p. 99). The incessant violation of Fela's rights also extended to media censorship, as authorities ensured that his songs were banned from been played on all radio and television stations across Nigeria. In other bizarre cases, successive military governments tried to falsely link him to murder, armed robbery, foreign currency violation, and kidnapping, all in a desperate attempt to discredit him (Moore 2016, pp. 280, 290). One of the unintended consequences of this was that it clothed Fela's music with the authenticity of resistance, thus further cementing his popularity across the country and the African continent.

3 International Law Issues in Fela's Music

3.1 A "TWAILing" Fela

Fela's approach to international law is one situated within what Olorunyomi (2005, p. 173) referred to as his attempt to "re-image the continent in relation to itself and others". In this respect, Fela not only framed his music as a pedagogical tool for exposing the inherent errors of the global system, but also engaged in other political activities to further this goal. In addition to his music, Fela was able to advance his critical objection to the international system through a number of methods. In 1979, he formed a political party, Movement of the People (MOP), through which he wanted to contest the 1979 and 1983 presidential elections in Nigeria. However, the authorities refused to register the party on both occasions. In addition to advocating for a democratic system, entrenchment of pan-African ideals in national development and the promotion of unity of African peoples and its diaspora, the MOP manifesto espoused the:

> abolishing [of] imperialism, colonialism, racialism, tribalism and all forms of national and racial oppression and economic inequality among nations, races and peoples and to support all action for world peace (Olorunyomi 2005, under Appendices).

Fela also used his magazine, Young African Pioneers (YAP), and lectures across Nigerian universities to not only criticise the military regime in Nigeria but push for the reform of the global system from a pan-Africanist perspective (Olorunyomi 2005, pp. 33–80; Moore 2016, p. 119). He denounced the International Monetary Fund (IMF) as not serving Africa's interest and called for the creation of an African monetary system (Olorunyomi 2005). He also pointed out the complicity of multinational corporations in environmental and climatic degradation (Olorunyomi 2005).

Although Fela never self-identified as an ideological member of the TWAIL movement, it can be argued that many of his positions regarding the international system fit into some of the objectives of TWAIL. As Mutua (2000, p. 31) explained, TWAIL seeks to achieve three objectives:

> The first is to understand, deconstruct, and unpack the uses of international law as medium for the creation and perpetuation of a racialized hierarchy of international norms and institutions that subordinate non-Europeans to Europeans. Second, it seeks to construct and present an alternative normative legal edifice for international governance. Finally, TWAIL seeks through scholarship, policy, and politics to eradicate the conditions of underdevelopment in the Third World.

Gathii et al. (2013, pp. 11–12) similarly noted that:

> critical approaches to international law have therefore sought to re-imagine a revision of international legal norms in ways that challenge the hierarchies of international, national, and other modes of governance be they economic, political, social, gender and so on.

According to Okafor (2008, pp. 377–378; 2005, pp. 176–177), it is important to understand TWAIL as a broad approach or a school of thought that encompasses both theoretical and methodological dimensions that are grounded in similar ideas. As such, while the objective remains the overhauling of a rigidly Eurocentric conception of international law and the global system, proponents approach this from different perspectives. This include ideological framings such as Marxism, Feminism, Africanism and Post-structuralism (Okafor 2005, pp. 176–180; Mutua 2000, p. 37; Chimni 2006, pp. 23–26; Bedjaoui 1979). As already indicated above, Fela's critique of the international system was from an Africanist perspective. In spite of the differences in their methodological approach towards restructuring the international systems, there exists some consensus amongst "TWAILers". These include, but not limited to, issues such as (Okafor 2005, pp. 176–180; Mutua 2000, p. 37; Chimni 2006, pp. 23–26; Bedjaoui 1979):

- the democratisation of the decision-making structures of global institutions;
- the imperative of increasing the accountability of multinational corporations;
- prioritising the concerns of the poor and marginalised in governance and human rights discourses; and
- the need to reframe the conception of human rights and democratic governance in order to include the epistemic contributions of the developing world.

These themes featured in Fela's music, and is discussed below.

3.2 Musical Objection to the International System

In "Teacher Don't Teach Me Nonsense" (1985), Fela highlighted the hypocrisy of the West, who he sarcastically referred to as the "teacher", regarding democracy. He dismissed the western conception of democracy as "demonstration of craze/craziness". In this song, he provides an appraisal of the imposition of western style democracy on the developing world, which has led to inconsistency in practise and understanding:

Who be our teacher? **(Who is our teacher?)**
Na oyinbo **(It's the white people)**
(…)
Which kind election be dis? **(What kind of election is this?)**
People no go vote **(where people have not come out to vote)**
Dem come get big big numbers **(Yet the incumbent records massive voting numbers)**
(…)
Who teach us democracy? **(Who taught us democracy)**
Oyinbo teach us **(White people taught us)**
Oyinbo for Europe o **(White people from Europe)**
(…)
Me I no gree to copy Oyinbo style o **(I refuse to adopt white people's standard)**
Let us think say Oyinbo know pass me **(Let's assume that white people's knowledge surpasses mine)**
(…)
Oyinbo dem no tell army sef **(Why did the white people not tell the army)**
That for England, army no fit take over **(that in England, a military coup is an aberration)**
(…)
If good teacher teach something **(If a good teacher passes across knowledge)**
And student make mistake **(and the student makes a mistake)**
Teacher must talk so **(the teacher has an obligation to correct the mistake)**
But Oyinbo no talk so **(but white people have refused to say anything)** (Anikulapo-Kuti and The Egypt 80 1985).

In "International Thief Thief" (1979), he sang about the scourge of illicit financial flow from Africa, and the complicity of African elites in this act:

Many foreign companies dey Africa carry all our money go **(Many foreign companies operating in Africa illegally take our money out)**

Dem go write big English for newspaper, dabaru we Africans ***(Then they will write complicated English in newspapers to confuse us Africans)***
(…)
Dem go cause confusion, cause corruption, cause oppression, cause inflation ***([As a result of this] they cause confusion, corruption, oppression, inflation)***
(…)
Them get one style wey them dey use ***(They have a particular style of doing things)***
Them go pick one African man ***(They usually pick an African man)***
A man with low mentality
Them go give am million naira breads ***(Then they give him millions)***
To become of high position here ***(To assume well-connected, high positions)*** (Anikulapo-Kuti and The African 70 1979).

In "Beasts of No Nation" (1989), he sang about the unequal structure of the United Nations (UN):

Dem call the place United Nations ***(They call the place United Nations)***
Hear oh another animal talk ***(Listen to another animal talk)***
Wetin united inside United Nations? ***(What is united in United Nations?)***
Who and who unite for United Nations? ***(Who and who are united in the United Nations?)***
No be there Thatcher and Argentina dey ***(Is that not where you have Thatcher and Argentina)***
No be there Reagan and Libya dey ***(Is that not where you have Reagan and Libya?)***
Israel versus Lebanon/Iran versus Iraq
(…)
Disunited Nations
One veto vote is equal to 92 … or more ***(Where one veto vote is equal to 92 or more)***
What kind sense be dat? ***(Where's the sense in that?)***
Na animal sense ***(It is animal sense)*** (Anikulapo-Kuti and The Egypt 80 1989).

In these three songs, Fela was able to present complex dynamics under international law in a simple and effective manner. The arrangement of the lyrics speaks to Fela's perception of himself as a pedagogue, and his music as a pedagogical tool (Olaniyan 2004, pp. 148–149). In this respect, Olaniyan (2004, pp. 148–149) noted that:

> The political phase of Fela's musical practise is anchored by a predilection for teaching, explaining and sermonizing about local and global social relations and the myriad inequalities that often underpin them. In tracks such as "Teacher Don't Teach Me Nonsense," he foregrounds the pedagogical process and the politics of its content and form. I have given extended attention here to "I.T.T.," [International Thief Thief] one of the classics of that phase, as an example of Fela at his most pedagogically resourceful … It is not surprising that not only did he employ an array of devices deeply embedded in his music to advance his pedagogical agenda … but he also went on to explicitly thematise scenes of instruction and teacher-student relationship in his lyrics. He never wanted to be regarded as just a musician, even a political musician. He wanted above all to be regarded as a teacher, an educator, the one who lifts the veil of ignorance from the faces of oppressed black people worldwide and thereby empowers them to fight their oppressors.

As already indicated in the foregoing, Fela also used his YAP magazine and regular appearances on university campuses around Nigeria to give lectures to students on issues of African development, history and political economy (Olaniyan 2004, p. 149; Ramon 2017).

By framing the West as the "teacher" and Africa (including other states in the developing world) as the "student", in "Teacher Don't Teach Me Nonsense", Fela presented a picture of an unequal relationship, where one party places itself in a superior position, forcefully prescribing ideas and methods that are ill-suited for the political and economic interests of the other party. This is similar to concerns that have been raised over the years by scholars regarding how the global north champions its agenda through institutions such as the UN, IMF, and the World Bank, who then impose the parameters of what constitutes democracy and good governance on the developing world (Mkandawire 1999, p. 129; Bedjaoui 1979; Olukoshi 1999, p. 457). Furthermore, the western world continue to promote what Olukoshi (1999, pp. 456–457) referred to as "tropicalized version of democracy", a patronising measure that deliberately ignores autocratic actions of friendly dictators in the developing world, and uses a lower standard of assessment to measure democratic development (Mkandawire 1999, p. 127). This is an idea that promotes nominalism over substance, where the West, and its "global institutions", is content as long as such dictator(s) adopts its prescriptive policies. As Fela puts it in "Teacher Don't Teach Me Nonsense": *"Oyinbo dem no tell army sef (Why did the white people not tell the army) / That for England, army no fit take over (that in England, a military coup is an aberration)"* (Anikulapo-Kuti and The Egypt 80 1985).

"International Thief Thief" provides an illuminating and graphic explanation of how multinational corporations, in collaboration with African elites, illegally move money out of the continent. The fact that this is still a reality makes the message relevant. According to the Report of the "High Level Panel on Illicit Financial Flows from Africa", headed by the former president of South Africa, Thabo Mbeki, Africa loses at least US$50 billion annually due to Illicit Financial Flows (IFFs) (African Union and the United Nations Economic Commission for Africa 2015, p. 13). While Africa has received US$1.07 trillion in aid from 1970 to 2008, it lost an equivalent of the same amount during the same period to IFFs (African Union and the United Nations Economic Commission for Africa 2015, p. 13). Similar to Fela's assertions, the Report found that corruption remains a big enabler of IFFs as bribes are paid to custom officers, tax inspectors (which also includes job offers), and payments made to bankers and judges for the quick facilitation of illegal capital flow (African Union and the United Nations Economic Commission for Africa 2015, p. 50).

"Beasts of No Nation" shows how dominant interests determine intervention measures by the UN (Okafor 2005), and the continued exclusion of countries from the global South from critical decision-making structures. The reservation of the headship of global institutions such as the IMF and the World Bank, for Europeans and Americans respectively, is another indefensible part of the international system. Fela employs the terminology of "animal sense" to show how there is no possible rational basis for the existence of such unabashed level of inequality. He called the international community and the UN *"egbe kegbe"* (a bad society/group) (Anikulapo-Kuti and The Egypt 80 1989). As Shonekan (2009, p. 138) remarked, Fela successfully deployed direct speech and humour to address unethical practises of world leaders in this song. In the same song, he goes further to show how a compromised UN, and the global north, has no moral basis for preaching human rights:

And they wan dash us human rights ***(And they want to give/gift us human rights)***
Animal talk to human beings ***(Animals talking to human beings)***
Give them human rights ***([About] giv[ing] them human rights)***
Abeg o make you hear me well well x2 ***(Please listen to me very well)***
Human rights na my property ***(Human rights is my property)***
So therefore you can't dash me my property ***(So therefore you cannot give/gift me my property)***
(...)
Botha na friend to Thatcher and Reagan ***(Botha [Apartheid South African Prime Minister] is friends with Thatcher and Reagan)***
Botha na friend to some other leaders too ***(Botha is friends with some other leaders too)***
And together dem wan dash us human rights ***(And together they proclaim that they can give/gift us human rights)***
Animal can't dash us human rights ***(Animals have no capacity to give/gift us human rights)*** (Anikulapo-Kuti and The Egypt 80 1989).

Furthermore, these songs serve as a valuable mechanism for popularising and expanding the frontiers of the theoretical works of TWAIL scholars among teachers, students and others that are interested in the critical understanding of the international system. The next section considers the ideational issues that should underpin the introduction of Fela's music into the teaching of international law in African universities.

4 Bringing Fela to the Classroom: Some Specific Pedagogical Considerations

The idea of using Fela's music as a vehicle for enriching the teaching of international law is one that naturally lends itself to a number of considerations that challenge the current way of doing things. In bringing Fela's music into the classroom, three interrelated ideational issues are imperative: interdisciplinary, Afrocentric, and counterhegemonic-activist approaches.

The introduction of Fela's music into the teaching of international law is in itself a clear promotion of the essence of interdisciplinary engagement. It shows the confluence and relatedness of different disciplines, and how knowledge gained from one discipline can serve as a useful tool in solving the problem in another discipline. It further speaks to breaking away from the rigid colonial thinking that law has to be studied and understood, devoid of societal realities, in isolation (Ndulo 2014, p. 17). This conservative outlook has ensured that useful extra-textual sources such as performative arts and indigenous knowledge systems remain locked out of the teaching environment. In the context of the curriculum of international law, it has led to the non-questioning of the regurgitation of Eurocentric canons as the basis of international law, and also the non-consideration of a variety of sources (legal and non-legal) and works that dispute such fallacy (Fagbayibo 2019, pp. 175–179). As such, Fela's music has the potential of serving as a gateway to accessing the important works of critical scholars in international law, political science, history and international relations on the non-neutral basis of some of the principles underlining international law and the imperative of reforming the system. For example, on topics such as international institutions, non-state actors under international law, democracy and governance, students could first listen to the relevant Fela songs, read the different works that speak to the issues raised in the songs and then make a presentation and/or write a paper on the linkages and relevance to current situations. In addition, assignment and examination questions could be drafted in such a way that either presents an excerpt of Fela's song as a case study or students are asked to include the message learned from the song in their answers. A good example is the course outline developed by Amnesty International on teaching genocide through the movie "Hotel Rwanda". It is divided into four learning units: "Personal and Collective Responsibility; Hotel Rwanda: Counting on the Media, but who is Accountable; The International Community; and Hotel Rwanda: Resolution of Conflict" (Amnesty International 2005). Teachers could also experiment with inviting guest lecturers from other disciplines. Similarly, actors who are versed in indigenous knowledge systems could be invited to provide important contexts on history, politics and the role of music in changing the society (Nabudere 2003, p. 11).

The second ideational context is an Afrocentric perspective. Fela's music and politics are markedly situated within his firm belief in adopting an Africanist approach to addressing Africa's political and economic problems. By including his music in the teaching of international law, there is both an implicit and explicit understanding that the curriculum has to be grounded within an Afrocentric perspective. Asante described "Afrocentricity" as a process through which the "teachers provide students the opportunity to study the world and its people, concepts, and history from an African world view" (Asante 1991, p. 171). The idea is to dispel the notion that Eurocentrism is the single universal standard of knowledge and praxis. Therefore, Afrocentricity is a non-hierarchical approach that considers all civilisations as equal and capable of contributing important ideas and knowledge systems to the humanity pool (Asante 1991, p. 172; Nabudere 2003, pp. 19–20). Nabudere (2003, p. 17) observed that the nature of an Afrocentric education, unlike Eurocentrism, is one that conceptualises the intellectual arena as that of conjoined rather than disjointed knowledge systems. As I have noted elsewhere (Fagbayibo 2019, p. 186), an Afrocentric approach to the teaching of international law should reflect the following:

> Repositioning the discourse on international law in such a way that students have a sound grasp of African contributions (in particular the knowledge systems that informed the pre-colonial practise of international law and relations); the roles of other civilisations in shaping its underlining concepts; and how African thought systems can shape its relational engagement with the rest.

Fela's persuasive rhythmic beats and intense lyrics have the potential of easing both teachers and learners into achieving this task. The good thing is that his musical delivery is self-explanatory and helps break down complex dynamics. As such, it provides an ideal entrée for including the thoughts of critical scholars on centring pan-African knowledge systems in the pedagogical matrix.

Lastly, the introduction of Fela's music should be geared towards achieving a counterhegemonic-activist thinking from both teachers and learners. Fela's politics and music are rooted in resistance to all forms of injustice, and his music is peculiarly arranged in a way to teach and further engender action. This philosophy should guide the way in which students are exposed to the biased nature of the international system and the need to find ways of counteracting such discrepancies. In this respect, it is not sufficient to merely know about the nagging issues but more importantly to equip learners with the tool to be thought leaders and change agents.

This is only possible if students are given the space to critique and dissect issues learned, come up with likely approaches of transforming the status quo, and engage with the wider community on testing these ideas. In this regard, Paulo Freire's concept of *dialogics* is particularly relevant (Freire 2005, p. 92). He noted that:

> only dialogue, which requires critical thinking, is also capable of generating critical thinking … Education which is able to resolve the contradiction between teacher and student takes place in a situation in which both address their act of cognition to the object by which they are mediated. Thus, the dialogical character of education as the practise of freedom does not begin when the teacher-student meets with the students-teachers in a pedagogical situation, but rather when the former first asks herself or himself *what* she or he will dialogue with the latter *about*. And preoccupation with the content of dialogue is really preoccupation with the program content of education (Freire 2005, pp. 92–93).

As Giroux (2010, p. 716) observed, Freire's approach presents education as a tool for self-awakening and engagement that subject history to a critical dialogue as a means of "imagining a future that would not merely reproduce the present". According to Aronowitz (2009, ix) education, as understood in the *Freirean* context, encompasses three goals:

> self-reflection, that is, realizing the famous poetic phrase, "know thyself", which is an understanding of the world in which they live, in its economic, political and, equally important, its psychological dimensions. Specifically, "critical" pedagogy helps the learner become aware of the forces that have hitherto ruled their lives and especially shaped their consciousness. The third goal is to help set the conditions for producing a new life, a new set of arrangements where power has been, at least in tendency, transferred to those who literally make the social world by transforming nature and themselves.

Situating this within the context of using Fela's music as a teaching tool, the following measures are of pertinence:

- Exposing students to social actors who are at the frontline of activities aimed at reforming the skewed international system (Fagbayibo 2019, p. 187);
- Creating a network of student bodies within and outside the continent to exchange ideas and strategies on confronting global issues (Fagbayibo 2019, p. 187); and
- Encouraging students to be more politically active and conscious of the increasing interrelatedness between and among various national and international actions.

In essence, the idea is that students should use the knowledge gained as a weapon for addressing nagging global concerns.

5 Conclusion

African law schools have to be more open to interventions that can help disrupt the Eurocentric underpinnings of the teaching of international law. Music, poetry, literature, and films are some of the relevant extra-textual materials that continue to reflect the need to change the biased structure of the global system. Their inclusion in the curriculum holds immense benefits for students and lecturers alike. Not only does it widen their knowledge base, it provides them with relatable tools to awaken the consciousness to engage in social activism. It would also help reinforce the understanding that law does not, and cannot, exist in isolation. In other words, law should flow from the social reality and context of a society, and in turn seek to genuinely address real problems.

This chapter has attempted to show the intersection between Fela's music and international law, in particular the extent to which his music provokes the critical teaching of international law. It has shown how the themes raised in three of Fela's songs: "International Thief Thief", "Beasts of No Nation", and "Teacher Don't Teach Me Nonsense" reflect some of the critical concerns raised by movements such as TWAIL in exposing the biased nature of international law. These include issues such as the undemocratic nature of the decision-making system at the international level, complicity of multinational corporations in illicit financial flow from Africa, and the hypocrisy of the global north regarding the conception of democracy and human rights. This chapter proposes three ideational issues that should underline the introduction of Fela's music into the teaching of international law in African universities. These are interdisciplinary, Afrocentric and counterhegemonic-activist approaches. These proposals are by no means a "holy grail" prescription; rather they seek to stimulate the discussions around the imperative of rethinking the pedagogy of international law, and thus encourage innovative thinking by educators.

As Jaff (1986, p. 668) rightly observed about musicians:

> They have created true works of art by holding up a mirror to lawyers and to society so that we can see clearly "the most comprehensive truths" of our times, as well as of our profession. They have also transmitted feelings so that others can experience them.

In this respect, Fela has left us with critical materials to reflect on. The question is whether we are bold enough to channel them into changing the *status quo*.

References

African Union and the United Nations Economic Commission for Africa (2015) Illicit financial flows: Report of the high-level panel on illicit financial flows from Africa. https://www.uneca.org/sites/default/files/PublicationFiles/iff_main_report_26feb_en.pdf

Amnesty International (2005) Hotel Rwanda - Amnesty International USA. https://www.amnestyusa.org/files/rwanda_brochuredivided_0.pdf

Anghie A (2000) What is TWAIL: comment. Am Soc Int Law Proc 94:39–40

Anikulapo-Kuti F and The African 70 (1979) I.T.T International Thief Thief. LP Nigeria, Kalakuta no suffix
Anikulapo-Kuti F and The Egypt 80 (1985) Teacher don't teach me nonsense. LP Polygram PH2 004
Anikulapo-Kuti F and The Egypt 80 (1989) Beasts of No Nations. LP Kalakuta K008
Aronowitz S (2009) Foreword. In: Macrine S (ed) Critical pedagogy in uncertain times: Hopes and possibilities. Palgrave Macmillan, New York, pp ix–xi
Asante M (1991) The Afrocentric idea in education. J Negro Educ 60(2):170–180
Bedjaoui M (1979) Towards a new international economic world order. UNESCO, Paris
Chimni B (2006) Third World Approaches to International Law: a manifesto. Int Commun Law Rev 8(1):3–27
Collins J (2015) Fela: Kalakuta notes. Wesleyan University Press, Middletown
Fagbayibo B (2018) Fela's music can decolonise international law in African universities. The Conversation. https://theconversation.com/felas-music-can decolonise-international-law-in-african-universities-95816
Fagbayibo B (2019) Some thoughts on centring pan-African epistemic in the teaching of public international law in African universities. Int Commun Law Rev 21:170–189
Falana F (2010) Fundamental rights enforcement in Nigeria. Legal Text Publishing, Lagos
Freire P (2005) Pedagogy of the oppressed. Continuum, New York
Gathii J, Okafor O, Anghie A (2013) Africa and TWAIL. Afr Yearbook Int Law 20:9–13
Giroux H (2010) Rethinking education as the practice of freedom: Paulo Freire and the promise of critical pedagogy. Policy Futures Educ 8(6):715–721
Grossfeld B, Hiller J (2008) Music and law. Int Lawyer 42(3):1147–1180
Jaff J (1986) Law and lawyer in pop music: A reason for self-reflection. Univ Miami Law Rev 40(659):659–669
Mapuwei N, Orina G (2013) The role played by music in promoting peace and unity in East and Southern Africa: The case of Zimbabwe and Kenya. Dyke 7(2):110–127
Mittica M (2015) When the world was mousike: On the origins of the relationship between law and music. Law Hum 9:29–54
Mkandawire T (1999) Crisis management and the making of "choiceless democracies". In: Joseph R (ed) State, conflict and democracy in Africa. Lynne Rienner Publishers, Boulder, CO, pp 119–135
Moore C (2016) Fela: this bitch of a life: the authorised biography of Africa's musical genius. African Perspectives Publishing, Johannesburg
Mutua M (2000) What is TWAIL? Am Soc Int Law Proc 94:31–39
Nabudere D (2003) Towards the establishment of a pan-African university: a strategic concept paper. Afr J Pol Sci 8:1): 1–1):30
Ndulo M (2014) Legal education in an era of globalisation and the challenge of development. J Comp Law Afr 1:1–24
Newman D (2018) Law and justice in popular music: Murder ballads. Eur J Curr Lcg Iss 24:1): 1–1):16
Okafor O (2005) Newness, imperialism, and international legal reform in our time: a TWAIL perspective. Osgoode Hall Law J 43(1-2):171–191
Okafor O (2008) Critical Third World Approaches to International Law (TWAIL): theory, methodology, or both? Int Commun Law Rev 10:371–378
Olaniyan T (2004) Arrest the music! Fela and his rebel art and politics. Indiana University Press, Bloomington
Olori T (1997) Afrobeat king falls foul of drug enforcers. Inter Press Service. http://www.ipsnews.net/1997/04/music-nigeria-afrobeat-king-falls-foul-of-drug-enforcers/
Olorunyomi S (2005) Afrobeat! Fela and the imagined continent. French Institute for Research in Africa (IFRAN), Ibadan
Olukoshi A (1999) State, conflict, and democracy in Africa: The complex process of renewal. In: Joseph R (ed) State, conflict and democracy in Africa. Lynne Rienner Publishers, Boulders, CO, pp 451–465

Olukotun A (2002) Traditional protest media and anti-military struggle in Nigeria 1988-1999. Afr Affairs 101(403):193–211
Plato (2008) The republic (Translated by Jowett B). Cosimoclassics, New York
Ramon O (2017) Fela was my most interesting client – Falana. Punch Newspaper. https://punchng.com/fela-was-my-most-interesting-client-falana-2/
Roux-Kemp A (2014) Struggle music: South African politics in songs. Law Hum 8(2):247–268
Shonekan S (2009) Fela's foundation: examining the revolutionary songs of Funmilayo Ransome-Kuti and the Abeokuta Market Women's Movement in 1940s western Nigeria. Black Music Res J 29(1):127–144
Simola R (1999) The construction of a Nigerian nationalist and feminist, Funmilayo Ransome-Kuti. Nordic J Afr Stud 8(1):94–114
Soyinka W (1985) The arts in Africa during the period of colonial rule. In: Boahen A (ed) UNESCO General history of Africa, Africa under colonial domination 1880-1935, vol 7. Heinemann, Portsmouth, pp 539–564

Chapter 3
Photographic Silhouettes and Human Rights in Africa: Confronting and Deterring Female Genital Mutilation in Aida Silvestri's *Unsterile Clinic*

Kaia L. Magnusen

Abstract In 2016, Eritrean artist Aida Silvestri addressed female genital mutilation (FGM) in her solo exhibition, *Unsterile Clinic*. Silvestri interviewed and photographed East African-born women who were forced to undergo FGM. *Unsterile Clinic* presented photographic silhouettes of some of these women. Silvestri sewed beads and flowers to pieces of leather whose shapes resemble stylized vulvas in order to evoke the effects of the different kinds of FGM. She affixed the leather pieces to the mouth areas of the silhouettes to visualise the silencing of the women's voices. As children, their cries of pain and protest against the procedure went unheard and, as adult women, their shame and the taboo nature of the subject made the women reluctant to speak of it. Through *Unsterile Clinic,* Silvestri intends to bring greater awareness of FGM's harmful physical and psychological effects thereby encouraging individuals to take a stand against culturally sanctioned gender-based violence. Due to international migration, FGM does not only occur in Africa but has also been reported in Europe, North America, and Australia. Despite the widespread recognition of FGM as a violation of the rights of girls and women and various laws banning FGM in multiple countries, the World Health Organization estimates that millions of girls are still at risk of being subjected to the procedure. For Silvestri, this is unacceptable and the photographic work comprising *Unsterile Clinic* functions as a means for her to serve as an advocate for the abused, a voice for the silenced, and an educator for the unaware.

Keywords African Women's Protocol · Aida Silvestri · Female genital mutilation (FGM) · Photographic Silhouettes · Unsterile Clinic · Women's rights

---

K. L. Magnusen (✉)
University of Texas at Tyler, Tyler, TX, USA
e-mail: KMagnusen@uttyler.edu

R. Adeola et al. (eds.), *The Art of Human Rights*, Arts, Research, Innovation and Society, https://doi.org/10.1007/978-3-030-30102-6_3

1 Female Genital Mutilation (FGM)

The World Health Organization (WHO) indicates that female genital mutilation (FGM) "comprises all procedures involving partial or total removal of the external female genitalia or other injury to the female genital organs for non-medical reasons" (World Health Organization 2008). It is performed on girls ranging in age from infancy to 15. Adult women occasionally undergo the procedure but it is fairly uncommon for FGM to be performed on girls after the age of 15 (Groeneveld 2013; Yoder 2013).

The terminology used to designate the practice is contested. In addition to FGM, it is sometimes referred to as "female circumcision," "female genital cutting," "female genital modification," "female genital surgery," and "female genital mutilation/cutting" (The Public Policy Advisory Network on Female Genital Surgeries in Africa 2012; Mulongo 2014). Some Western anthropologists prefer the term "female circumcision" because that is the closest English translation of various indigenous words for the procedure (Yoder 2013). However, in Western cultures, the use of this term creates a false equivalence between male circumcision, in which the foreskin of the penis is removed, and FGM, which often involves more extensive tissue removal. Furthermore, the male and female external genitalia are completely different; when referring to FGM, the use of the word "circumcision" elides this distinction and severely underestimates the invasiveness of the procedure (Barrett 2014).

For scholars who prefer to use Western terminology but find the word "mutilation" too judgmental, the phrase "female genital cutting" is sometimes employed in an effort to convey neutrality. Those who strongly condemn the practice refer to it as "female genital mutilation" (FGM) because the term "mutilation" underscores the grievous harm it causes, reinforces the argument that it is a human rights violation, and distinguishes it from male circumcision (Yoder 2013; Serour 2013; Groeneveld 2013). For instance, WHO utilises the term "female genital mutilation" and its acronym while agencies such as UNICEF use the designation "female genital mutilation/cutting" (FGM/C) instead (Yoder 2013). In its condemnation of FGM as a "harmful practice," the Protocol to the African Charter on Human and Peoples' Rights on the Rights of Women in Africa (African Women's Protocol), refers to it as "female genital mutilation" (African Union 2003). This terminology accentuates the *Guidelines on Combating Sexual Violence and its Consequences in Africa's* designation of FGM as a form of sexual violence. Sexual violence is defined as "any non-consensual act, a threat or attempt to perform such an act, or compelling someone else to perform such an act on a third person" (African Commission on Human and Peoples' Rights 2017). In addition, Aida Silvestri, the artist who created *Unsterile Clinic*, uses FGM when discussing the procedure so that terminology will be employed here.

FGM has been classified into four types; three of these types contain subdivisions. Type I, the clitoridectomy, involves the partial or total excision of the clitoris and the prepuce; there are two subgroups within Type I (Jungari 2016; World Health Organization 2019). In some instances, only the prepuce is removed; this procedure is frequently called sunna ("tradition") (Green 1999). Type II, excision, refers to the complete or incomplete excision of both the clitoris and the labia minora; the labia majora may or may not also be removed. There are three subdivisions within Type II. Type III, infibulation, entails reducing the size of the vaginal opening by producing a cutaneous barrier over the area; this cutaneous covering is formed by cutting and repositioning either the labia minora, the labia majora or both (World Health Organization 2018b). In Type III, which is sometimes referred to as "pharaonic circumcision," the clitoris may or may not also be excised; within this type, there are two subgroups (Lax 2000; World Health Organization 2008). Type IV is a much more general category as it consists of "all other harmful procedures to the female genitalia for non-medical purposes" such as "pricking, piercing, incising, scraping and cauterization" (World Health Organization 2008). Inserting various substances into the vagina in order to "tighten" it is also included in this fourth category (Dorkenoo 1999). Given the broad nature of this category, introducing subdivisions to differentiate between these procedures would be a logical step.

According to the United Nations Children's Fund (UNICEF), at least two-hundred million females in thirty different countries have been subjected to FGM (UNICEF 2016). Many of the girls and women who have been cut live in 27 African countries plus Iraq and Yemen (UNICEF 2015). In Africa, FGM is especially widespread in North-East Africa and in some countries in West Africa. It is particularly prevalent in Djibouti, Egypt, Eritrea, Somalia, and the Sudan. 59 percent of all women in Africa who have undergone FGM reside in one of these five countries. The percentage of women who have been subjected to Type III, infibulation, is higher in these countries than elsewhere in Africa. In West Africa, FGM is prevalent in Gambia, Guinea, Mali, and Sierra Leone (Yoder 2013). FGM has also been documented in Indonesia, Malaysia, India, Oman, Saudi Arabia, and the United Arab Emirates and among some indigenous groups in Colombia (UNICEF 2016; Ross et al. 2015). FGM, specifically introcision, which involves the cutting of the perineum to enlarge the vaginal opening, has been reported among aboriginal Australians (Rushwan 2013). Due to international migrations, FGM is also found among immigrant populations in the United States, Europe, Canada, Australia, and New Zealand (Jungari 2016). Some girls from FGM-practicing communities who reside in Western countries are taken back to their countries of origin to undergo FGM (Berg and Denison 2013).

The origin of the practice of FGM is unknown. Herodotus, the ancient Greek historian, noted that FGM was being performed in Egypt as early as 500 B.C.; thus, it predates both Christianity and Islam (El-Damanhoury 2013). FGM is not limited to one specific ethnic or religious group. Followers of various religions, including Islam, Judaism, Christianity (Catholicism, Protestantism, Coptic Christianity), and traditional animist belief systems, and even nonbelievers perform FGM (Dorkenoo 1999; El-Damanhoury 2013). However, there is no Christian scriptural basis for FGM; the Bible does not mention FGM (Dorkenoo 1999).

FGM is not included in the Qur'an but some Muslims perceive it as being authorised by Islam and, thus, it is regarded as an indicator of religious devotion (Berg and Denison 2013). For some Sunni Muslims, the belief that FGM is a *Sunnah*, a practice sanctioned by Mohammed, stems from a *hadith*, a saying accredited to Mohammed, in which he came upon a woman performing excision and instructed the practitioner to continue but not to cut too deeply (El-Damanhoury 2013; Alhassan et al. 2016). The four schools of Islamic law differ in their doctrines pertaining to FGM. For those who follow the Shafi'i doctrine, FGM is considered obligatory; the other three schools recommend but do not require it. However, some Muslims oppose this understanding and regard FGM as violating Islamic precepts (Berg and Denison 2013).

Despite FGM not being expressly commanded by any particular religion, the practice persists and is often regarded by practicing communities as a significant cultural tradition that is worthy of being preserved. In communities in which FGM is considered a normative practice, it tends to be enforced through social pressures and various mechanisms of community enforcement. The widespread collective enforcement that exists within FGM-practicing communities results in pressure to continue the practice leading to the perception that FGM is compulsory in order to avoid bringing shame to oneself, one's family, and one's community.

Amongst these communities, FGM is closely aligned with beliefs pertaining to female sexual morality and marriageability. FGM weakens female sexual desire and, thus, is regarded as a means of preventing promiscuity and preserving premarital virginity. Virginity is a requirement for marriage in many FGM-practicing cultures; thus, as FGM supposedly acts as a guarantee of premarital female virginity, it is often a prerequisite for marriage (Berg and Denison 2013). In addition, FGM is widely regarded as ensuring a wife's marital fidelity by curtailing female hypersexuality thereby reducing the risk of a wife committing adultery (Catania et al. 2016). While reducing female desire, FGM, particularly infibulation, is believed to enhance male sexual pleasure because a "tight" vagina supposedly increases male enjoyment of the sex act (Mackie 1996). While not necessarily accurate, the notion that men prefer infibulated women to uncut women persists (Berg and Denison 2013).

Misinformation about the clitoris seems to play a role in the perception of supposedly wanton female sexuality. Some ethnic groups consider the clitoris to be a male element in the female body and this perceived maleness is regarded as threatening (Finke 2006). The fairly common belief that, if left uncut, the clitoris will grow into a penis or a penis-like appendage is related to this idea and is used to justify clitoridectomies (Obermeyer 1999; Lax 2000). This perceived danger is also found in the erroneous beliefs that a baby will die if he or she comes into contact with the mother's clitoris during delivery or that an uncut clitoris will harm a man during sexual intercourse (Finke 2006; Abdulcadir et al. 2011).

Some societies view FGM as a rite of passage whereby a girl becomes a woman and, thus, eligible for marriage (Berg and Denison 2013). As a result, the idea that FGM is a prerequisite for entering into womanhood and the notion that it ensures marriageability reinforce each other. FGM is sometimes also associated with feminine genital hygiene. Some groups perceive intact female genitalia as being unclean, malodorous, or ugly whereas cut genitals are regarded as clean and aesthetically pleasing (Berg and Denison 2013; Mackie 1996). This belief also pertains to marriageability because having attractive, clean genitalia would, presumably, result in a more advantageous marriage whereas the alternative would likely contribute to the idea that an uncut woman would not make an acceptable wife. Thus, the deeply embedded nature of the tradition of FGM is reinforced.

2 Aida Silvestri's *Unsterile Clinic*

In 2015, Eritrean artist, Aida Silvestri began to research the practice of female genital mutilation. Motivated by her own experience, Silvestri interviewed and photographed East African women in London who also underwent FGM. As part of the project, she spoke with women from Eritrea, Ethiopia, the Sudan, Somalia, Kenya, Mali, Gambia, and Djibouti ("Aida Silvestri: Unsterile Clinic," 2018). After further investigation into the practice, Silvestri realized that, in the UK, many cases of FGM are undiagnosed until a woman becomes pregnant or goes into labour. Consequently, she decided to create *Unsterile Clinic* in order to raise awareness about the types of FGM and the severity of its effects among those who have endured it so they can seek appropriate medical attention before they find themselves in an emergency situation. She also wanted to educate those in FGM-practicing communities so parents might reconsider carrying out the procedure on their daughters. In addition, she hoped to embolden health care workers to speak openly with patients affected by FGM and to bring awareness to those in the general population who might be ignorant of the procedures that fall under the umbrella term of female genital mutilation (Silvestri 2015; "Aida Silvestri: Unsterile Clinic" 2018).

For *Unsterile Clinic,* Silvestri worked with National Health Service (NHS) clinics in order to adapt the types of FGM and the subcategories within them from the classifications utilized by WHO (Berg and Denison 2013). Although the artist's categories are similar to those employed by WHO, her distinct classification system is more nuanced and includes a larger number of subgroups. WHO's classification system only includes two subcategories for Type I (clitoridectomy), whereas Silvestri's categories for *Unsterile Clinic* enlarge this to three subgroups. Silvestri expands WHO's subgroups for Type II (excision). *Unsterile Clinic* includes eight subcategories which offer a greater level of nuance regarding the amount of cutting, stitching and tissue removed. Silvestri alters and adds one subcategory under Type III (infibulation). In her classification, Silvestri does not alter WHO's classification of Type IV (Silvestri 2015).

Unsterile Clinic presents larger than life-size photographic silhouettes of women Silvestri interviewed. The women's faces are in opaque shadow so the outlines of the heads, necks, and hairstyles are apparent against the stark white backgrounds but their facial features cannot be discerned. The artist affixed pieces of leather, whose shapes resemble stylized vulvas, to the mouth areas of the silhouettes. The details of the leather pieces vary and correlate with the type of FGM experienced by the women depicted. On the leather pieces, Silvestri sewed round white beads to represent the clitoris, black beads evocative of flowers to denote the urethra, and small white flowers to suggest the vaginal opening. The delicacy of these materials is offset by the violence implied by the use of cut animal flesh—the leather—onto which they are sewn. The suggestion of violence that is present in the mixed media appliqués in *Unsterile Clinic* reflects the explicit condemnation of FGM as a form of sexual violence that is found in the *Guidelines on Combating Sexual Violence and its Consequences in Africa* (African Commission on Human and Peoples' Rights 2017). As sewing is often thought of as "women's work," the gendered nature of violence of FGM is accentuated. This highlights the fact that FGM is a form of gender-based violence (African Commission on Human and Peoples' Rights 2017). In *Unsterile Clinic,* Silvestri deliberately aestheticized the cut and stitched leather pieces so the viewers, some of whom may have undergone FGM, would not be overwhelmed or further traumatized by the brutal subject matter. For the leather pieces, the artist deliberately utilized a range of colours to suggest the variety of the participants' skin tones, ethnic origins, and religious and national affiliations (Silvestri 2015).

The placement of the leather pieces on the mouth areas of the silhouetted figures visualizes the silencing of the women's voices and represents Silvestri's belief that she has "given voice to the voiceless" (Autograph ABP 2016). As children, their cries of pain and protest went unheard and, as adult women, their shame and the taboo nature of the subject made them reluctant to speak about having undergone FGM or to criticize the practice. In order to further provide the depicted women with a voice, each photo-work is paired with a long caption featuring a text poem based on the testimony of the women represented. For instance, *Type 1 B—Clitoridectomy* (Fig. 3.1) is accompanied by the following text poem, "Type I B – Clitoridectomy":

> I was ten years old / My grandmother and I went to visit relatives / There were lots of girls playing / They gave me food and treats / I could hear singing from afar / The singing got louder as the women got closer / One lady asked the girls to sit next to their grandmothers / Three ladies including my grandmother held me down / I didn't know why / I started to scream / Other girls started to scream / It felt like a screaming choir / While one of the ladies covered my mouth / Another took my pants off / And another grabbed my private parts / She used a razor / Promised she wouldn't cut much / The pain was so strong / I felt it from my chest down to my toes / I was left there to bleed / During weeing it burned like hell / I didn't like my relatives anymore / I didn't like my grandmother anymore / I was crying and wanted to go home / I missed my mother / I was told I had to stay at the new house until I healed / My cut was infected / The healing process was long / I had a keloid scar / A big scar tissue instead of the promised half clitoris / My boyfriend didn't understand why he couldn't touch me / I loved him / I wanted him but I couldn't feel anything / I used to get jealous when my friends talked about orgasms / Sex became a chore / I was happier without it / I was single for a very long time / I am happier now with my new husband and my new private parts / I had a reconstruction (Silvestri 2015).

The silhouetted woman seen in *Type I B* has an afro and wears a garment with a bow on her right shoulder. Even though the specific details of her face cannot be seen, the unique aspects of her hairstyle and clothing individualize her and distinguish her from the other silhouetted women of *Unsterile Clinic.* The title of this work indicates that the silhouetted woman in question underwent excision that involved the removal of her prepuce, and the partial removal of both her clitoris and

Fig. 3.1 Type I B. New commission ©Aida Silvestri. Courtesy Autograph, London (2016)

labia minora (Autograph ABP 2016). The text poem displayed next to this image explicitly recounts the woman's experience of this procedure which further particularizes this work. It confronts the viewers with both the immediate and the long-term physical and psychological effects of the type of FGM visualized by the brown and pink sculptural leather piece affixed to her visage.

The text poems are installed next to each respective photo-work so they almost seem like speech bubbles next to the silhouetted women; through this text, the women "speak" to the viewers. The photo-works are placed at the viewer's eye level so the viewers are immediately confronted with each woman's silhouette and testimony. By reading each text poem and visually engaging the photo-work with which it is paired, the viewers enter into a kind of dialogue with each silhouetted woman. Their unique silhouettes hint at each woman's distinct hairstyle and clothing; the coloured leather suggests each woman's skin tone. Although the women's identities are not known, they do not remain complete strangers for the viewers. The photo-works act as stand-ins for the women themselves and the evidence of their physical, psychological, and emotional trauma is visualized by the sculptural forms affixed to their silhouetted faces. By visually engaging the photo-works and reading the text, the viewers are unable to claim ignorance of FGM and deleterious aftermath. Although the viewers are probably not responsible for what happened to the silhouetted women, *Unsterile Clinic* confronts them with the distressing realization that their ignorance is someone else's suffering. Awareness implies accountability and

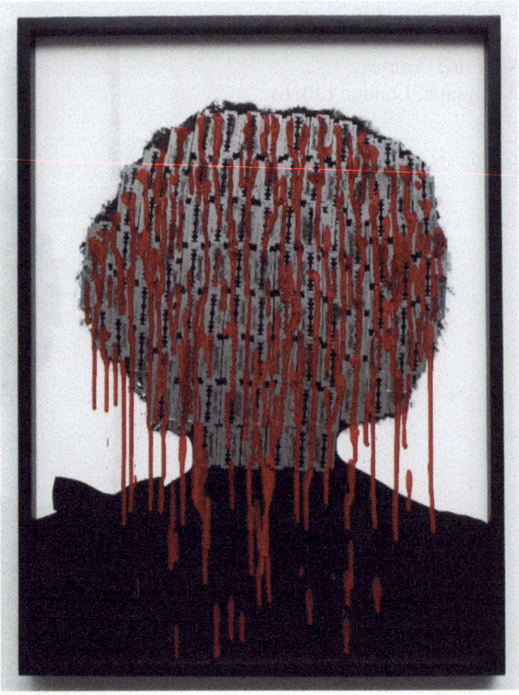

Fig. 3.2 Type I B-Distance. New commission ©Aida Silvestri. Courtesy Autograph, London(2016)

viewers can either use their raised consciousness to affect meaningful change or they can turn away from the photo-works, the women they represent, and the problem of FGM.

The woman seen in *Type I B—Clitoridectomy* reappears in *Type I B—Distance* (Fig. 3.2). However, in this image, vertically aligned razor blades are arranged over the space of the woman's face and hair; they end approximately halfway down the woman's neck. Over the razorblades, bright red paint, which mimics blood, has been applied to the photo and appears to drip down the image. The stark contrast of the drippy, red blood-like substance against the precise outlines of the black silhouette on the white background is visually jarring and provides a provocative counterpoint to the implied violence of the other silhouetted images. This image confronts the viewers with a disconcerting visualization of the violence committed against not just the silhouetted woman in question but against all of the women featured in *Unsterile Clinic* in particular and against women who have undergone FGM in general. Silvestri's inclusion of multiple razor blades reminds the viewer that numerous females continue to be subjected to FGM.

The face of the woman in *Type I B—Distance* has been completely concealed by razor blades and blood. This visually manifests the idea that, as a form of sexual violence, FGM can be regarded as "a form of torture… or can constitute cruel, inhuman or degrading treatment" (African Commission on Human and Peoples' Rights 2017). The obliteration of the woman's face by instruments of violence and the

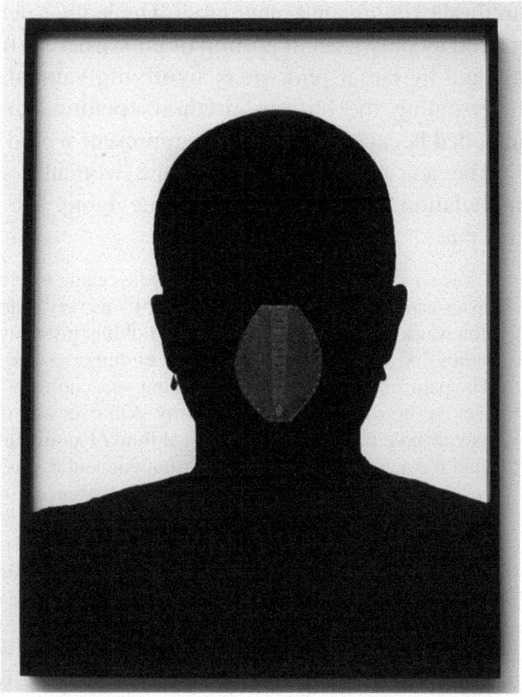

Fig. 3.3 Type III C. New commission ©Aida Silvestri. Courtesy Autograph, London (2016)

bloody evidence of their physical effects emphasises the serious bodily harm and the gross violation of women's rights that occur when FGM is carried out. The woman's visage is so obscured that, at first glance, the image almost appears abstract. The viewer's initial perception of this work as nonfigurative further stresses the dehumanization that is a tragic consequence of FGM.

Another photo-work, entitled *Type III C* (Fig. 3.3), depicts the silhouette of a woman with either a shaved head or very closely cropped hair who wears small, dangling teardrop shaped earrings. The brown piece of leather that has been affixed to her mouth area is characterized by a vertical line of stiches that culminate in a small pink teardrop that echoes the shape of her earrings. Her teardrop-shaped earrings function on a symbolic level to convey not only the actual tears she likely cried during the procedure but also the subsequent physical anguish she suffered as a result of having been cut. There is a perverse irony in the fact that the small, pink vaginal opening also approximates a teardrop-shape because FGM and its subsequent effects on her life and health were, as the text-poem indicates, the cause of so much pain and sadness.

This silhouetted woman underwent the most severe form of FGM, infibulation, so the pink portion of the leather represents the incredibly narrow vaginal introitus after it has been covered by the repositioned labia majora and the resulting scar tissue, which is evoked by the slight colour variation in the leather. As the title indicates, the woman also endured the removal of her prepuce, clitoris, external urethral opening, and inner labia. The leather piece attached to her visage is characterized by only a small portion of pink whereas the other women's leather pieces are marked by larger pink areas signifying vaginal tissue. Also, the beads and flower representing the clitoris, urethral opening, and vaginal opening have not been included because the parts they represent would be covered over by scar tissue.

The text-poem placed near the woman's silhouette, entitled "Type III C – Infibulation" testifies to the extreme agony she suffered both during and after she was cut:

> I was six or seven years old / Four ladies came to visit / I was told today was the day /My sister was taken away, she went first / I was very scared hearing her scream / The anticipation was killing me / My mother was holding my arms / I was tied up and held down by four ladies / A well-respected traditional circumciser and midwife / Performed the procedure / The pain was unbearable / Everything was cut away by a razor and then stitched / I could feel the needle piercing through my skin over and over / I was deformed and left with a narrow hole for urine and menstrual fluid / Passing urine for the first time felt more painful than the actual ritual/ My first sexual encounter was a very long, excruciating and unsuccessful process / It was slow; it had taken around a month for me to lose my virginity / It had taken me a while to conceive / I was diagnosed with the worst kind of FGM during my first pregnancy / At seven months I had a reversal procedure I was told I was opened up / The birth of my child was a traumatic event / I had an episiotomy and the baby was pulled out with forceps / More pain / More bleeding / More scarring (Silvestri 2015).

In addition to graphically describing the actual process of infibulation, the text-poem indicates that, during her pregnancy, the woman underwent a surgical procedure known as defibulation in which the scar tissue that seals the vaginal opening is cut open in order to expose the vagina and urethral opening (Abdulcadir et al. 2016). The text-poem also notes that, in order to successfully give birth, the woman's vaginal orifice had to be surgically enlarged by means of an episiotomy, a procedure in which an incision is made in the perineum to prevent posterior tearing of the vaginal opening into the rectal area as the baby's head delivers (Rodriguez et al. 2016). As a direct result of the complications caused by FGM, an event that should have caused tremendous joy, instead, was marked by psychological trauma. Indeed, the references to additional "pain," "bleeding," and "scarring," recall the original FGM the woman experienced as a young child (Silvestri 2015). Knowing that the cutting she forcibly underwent as a child was the cause of her increased suffering during childbirth, seemingly forced her to relive the physical pain and mental anguish caused by her initial childhood ordeal.

The viewer reads about this silhouetted woman's suffering as conveyed through the text-poem but the stitched piece of leather attached to the photo-work does not explicitly visualize the corporeal distress experienced by the woman as she gave birth or when she was cut as a child. Instead, the viewer is left to imagine the bloody, traumatic circumstances of her labour and to establish a correlation between it and the FGM that caused her childhood suffering and was also the root cause of the unnecessarily difficult and painful complications she suffered during childbirth. In light of the woman's account about being deinfibulated in order to give birth, the stitched piece of leather, which has not been cut, evokes reinfibulation, the resuturing of the scar tissue caused by infibulation, some women undergo after delivering a child. The text poem does not indicate that the silhouetted woman in question underwent reinfibulation but the intact stiches on the leather, perhaps, suggest the restitching that is a painful reality for between 6.5 and 10.4 million women throughout the world (Abdulcadir et al. 2016). Thus, *Type III C* and the corresponding text-poem not only confront the viewer with the severity of the long-term consequences of FGM but they also suggest that the physical and psychological problems caused by FGM are so extensive that they cannot all be fully represented by the works included in *Unsterile Clinic.*

In addition to the photo-works, when *Unsterile Clinic* was installed at Autograph ABP in London in 2016, Silvestri included a large board with additional leather pieces featuring labels to indicate the types being displayed and text to elaborate on the extent of the cutting entailed by each type. For comparison purposes, the board, which was placed in a display case, also included a leather version of intact female genitalia. The parts of this leather piece were also labelled so the viewers could determine what had been cut away or covered over in the subsequent leather pieces referencing the various types of FGM. This board served an educational purpose as it presented specific information about the types of FGM Silvestri identified and visualized in her photo-works. By explaining these types via both text and images in a clear, objective manner, the artist was able to instruct viewers about the cutting and tissue removal that occurs when a girl or woman endures FGM.

For viewers who have undergone FGM, the board provides them with easily comprehensible information and visual aids to enable them to fully understand the nature and extent of the cutting they experienced. The presence of the silhouetted portraits of other women subjected to FGM and the accompanying text-poems that reveal their experiences convey to viewers affected by FGM that they are not alone and that they do not need to be afraid of speaking about what happened to them or of seeking appropriate medical or psychological care. For viewers from FGM practicing communities, the combination of the informational board, the text-poems and the photo-works might, perhaps, prompt them to reconsider FGM and to re-examine the myriad factors perpetuating the continuation of a practice that causes so much physical and mental anguish to so many girls and women. For viewers ignorant of the practice, the board presents an opportunity for them to educate themselves about the types of FGM thereby enabling viewers to have a more complete understanding of what the practice truly entails.

3 Health and Human Rights

Although the perceived value of FGM is still deeply ingrained in some communities, it is widely regarded as a violation of human rights. In 1979, WHO endorsed abolishing the practice of FGM and, subsequently, the many campaigns against FGM stressed the health risks associated with it. In the early 1990s, the emphasis shifted from the negative health consequences of FGM to the human rights violations of the practice (Barrett 2014). In June 1993, the World Conference on Human Rights officially recognized FGM as a human rights violation (Groeneveld 2013). At that time, it was also categorized as a form of violence against women (Shell-Duncan 2008). Article 21 of the African Charter on the Rights and Welfare of the Child addresses what it terms "Protection against Harmful Social and Cultural Practices" (Organization of African Unity 1990). Although FGM is not specifically mentioned in this section, it indicates that that "harmful social and cultural practices affecting the welfare, dignity, normal growth and development of the child..." should be eliminated (Organization of African Unity 1990). Similarly, the African Women's Protocol includes FGM under Article 5: Elimination of Harmful Practices. It states that FGM "negatively affects the human rights of women" and expressly calls for the legal prohibition of FGM and its medicalization (African Union 2003). Regardless of whether or not FGM is perceived as a traditional practice, the Protocol makes it clear "that any practice that hinders or endangers the normal growth and affects the physical and psychological development of women and girls should be condemned and eliminated" (African Union 2003). Although the specific practices are not mentioned, this point undoubtedly pertains to FGM and other practices that violate the human rights of females in Africa. In an effort to end the practice of FGM, twenty-six countries throughout Africa and the Middle East have passed laws against it; an additional thirty-three countries with migrant populations originating from countries in which FGM is practiced also have legal statutes pertaining to FGM (World Health Organization 2018a).

FGM violates the right to health because it has no known health benefits (Groeneveld 2013; Ismail et al. 2017). The negative health consequences of FGM vary depending on the extent of the cutting, the kind and sterility of the instruments used, the anatomical knowledge of the person doing the cutting, and the conditions of the location in which the cutting occurs. As suggested by the title of Silvestri's work, the conditions in which FGM is performed are often unhygienic. In traditional situations, the cutting is performed in suboptimal lighting conditions, without effective antiseptic preparation of the surgical site and with cutting instruments, including kitchen knives, razorblades, or scissors, crude tools such as shards of cut class, sharpened rocks, or human fingernails that have not been properly sterilised (Jungari 2016; Odukogbel et al. 2017; Groeneveld 2013). FGM often occurs without anaesthesia so, despite being held down, the person undergoing it would, presumably, struggle which would affect the ability of practitioner to make precise cuts (Groeneveld 2013). After the cutting, the girl is probably not given antibiotics which, combined with poor hygiene post-procedure, such as binding a girl's legs together, would increase the risk of infection (Jungari 2016). In FGM rituals, the same unsterile cutting instrument could be used on as many as 15–20 girls (Monjok et al. 2007). In instances in which the same unsterilised cutting tools are used on groups of females, there is an increased risk of transmitting blood-borne illnesses such as human immunodeficiency virus (HIV) and hepatitis (Monjok et al. 2007; Serour 2013). In some instances, blood poisoning, known as septicemia, may occur (Jungari 2016). Neurogenic shock caused by intense pain and hemorrhagic shock caused by heavy bleeding are common problems associated with FGM (Green 1999).

If the external urethral opening has been partially or totally excised, as may occur in variations of Types II and III, a variety of urinary tract issues would likely occur. If stricture occurs, then painful micturition, known as dysuria, prolonged urination, and the inability to completely empty the bladder could result. The risk of urinary tract infections and bladder infections would also increase. Bladder infections can cause high fevers and even sepsis and could result in infection or hydrostatic pressure ascending up the ureters which could result hydronephrosis, in which kidneys are damaged by the back pressure of obstructed outflow, or pyelonephritis (kidney infection). Additionally, ureteral fistulas could occur to other regions of the vulva or even into the vagina which could result in additional problems. Even if the urethral opening has not been excised, for girls who have undergone Type III, infibulation, the retention of urine may be a significant issue due to partial obstruction of the urethral opening by the scar tissue. As the urine is expelled slowly in drops rather than in a stream, micturition may take 10–15 min or, according to some infibulated women, even hours to complete (Kelson 1998). The formation of keloids could result in the further obstruction of the urinary canal which could cause additional problems with urination. In addition, micturition can be painful so some girls will try to avoid it. Incomplete bladder emptying, whatever the cause predisposes to urinary tract infections and the placement of a catheter would be complicated by a urethral stricture. Infibulated women may also suffer from menstrual difficulties because the tiny vaginal opening may result in the retention of menses (Green 1999). The prevention of proper menstrual flow may cause severe dysmenorrhea (Abdulcadir et al. 2016). In serious cases, especially if the menstrual flow is heavy or if a clot forms that further occludes the vaginal introitus, hematocolpos, a condition in which menstrual blood accumulates in the vagina, may occur (Jungari 2016).

In addition, FGM, especially Type III, is known to cause obstetric complications. During pregnancy, urinary tract infections (UTIs) remain a common problem for women who have undergone FGM. In addition, depending on the type of FGM, performing vaginal examinations and inserting a speculum can be difficult. Women who were subjected to Type III require deinfibulation in order give birth vaginally. Despite this, prolonger labor is still a concern and the need for a caesarian section, especially among those who underwent Type III, increases. Type III more than doubles a woman's likelihood of needing an episiotomy. Perineal tearing is also more likely to occur to women with FGM. FGM also puts women at a greater risk for primary postpartum haemorrhage which can result in maternal death. There also seems to be a correlation between FGM and fetal distress and infant perinatal death (Gayle and Rymer 2016). If an infibulated woman suffers a miscarriage, unless she is deinfibulated, the foetus may remain inside her body and cause serious complications, including infection (Rushwan 2013).

Despite the complications that might arise due to the unsanitary conditions in which FGM is often performed, the so-called "medicalisation" of this practice is not an acceptable alternative and was jointly condemned by WHO, the United Nations Children's Fund (UNICEF) and the United Nations Population Fund (UNFPA) in 2009 (Rushwan 2013). The medicialisation of FGM is also unequivocally denounced by the African Women's Protocol (African Union 2003). The term "medicalisation" is employed when health care providers carry out FGM (Jungari 2016). When health care professionals perform FGM, presumably, the setting and tools are sterilised and the practitioner would, theoretically, have a greater knowledge of human anatomy. However, medicalisation does not necessarily reduce later gynaecological and obstetric problems and, despite medicalisation, FGM remains a violation of health and human rights (Serour 2013). The *Guidelines on Combating Sexual Violence and its Consequences in Africa* clearly denounces FGM as a form of sexual violence so doctors who perform any form of FGM wilfully commit and normalise sexual violence against women and girls.

Medicalisation undermines laws banning FGM and provides it with a false legitimacy as it implies the approval of a practice that has absolutely no known medical or health benefits (Ismail et al. 2017). This misleading appearance of legitimisation could result in the misbelief that FGM is innocuous or beneficial to health. Furthermore, if medical professionals are paid to perform any type of FGM, this gives the impression that the practice is condoned by the larger medical community (Jungari 2016). In some cases, particularly in countries that have outlawed FGM, health professionals charge high fees to carry out FGM or re-infibulation. Consequently, those who perform the procedure have a monetary stake in seeing the practice perpetuated despite the harm it causes. These professionals have a conflict of interest because performing FGM or re-infibulation violates medical ethics and sacrifices the well-being of the patient for personal financial gain. Medical ethics indicates that medical professionals should "do no harm." As FGM inarguably causes unnecessary bodily harm, as well as psychological and sexual harm, the medicalisation of the practice should be strongly condemned and those who engage in it should be held accountable for their unethical behaviour (Serour 2013).

Ritual or symbolic nicking is sometimes proposed as an alternative to FGM (Abdulcadir et al. 2011). Although this would be less physically harmful than other types of FGM, it would still be classified as Type IV FGM. As there is no medical or religious justification for it, it would be unethical for doctors to perform this as a compromise. The ritual nicking of a female child's clitoris seems to concede some validity to misinformed sexual beliefs about the clitoris and might actually undermine attempts to legally ban FGM and subvert attempts to institute initiation rites that do not involve cutting.

FGM also violates women's sexual rights and sexual health (Amado 2004). In addition to the immediate and long-term physical injuries caused by FGM, sexual dysfunction is also a common problem for women who have been subjected to FGM. A recent study of sexually active Egyptian women with FGM Type I or Type II determined that there is a correlation between impaired female sexual function and FGM. According to the Female Sexual Function Index (FSFI), the women who had undergone FGM experienced higher incidences of sexual dysfunction in the areas of desire, arousal, lubrication, and orgasm than uncut women. In addition, the study found that dyspareunia, painful intercourse, was more common among women who had been subjected to FGM than those who had not and that women who had FGM had sexual intercourse less often than the uncut women (Ismail et al. 2017). As Type III is the most severe form of FGM, the side effects pertaining to sexual dysfunction, would, presumably, be even more serious for women who have undergone this variation of the procedure.

The negative side-effects of FGM can also include psychological problems and psychosomatic diseases (World Health Organization 2008; Jungari 2016). Behavioural disturbances may occur in children who are subjected to FGM, especially if the child represses her trauma. If a child has little awareness of what undergoing FGM actually entails, then after the procedure, she may feel that her parents have violated her trust and her relationship with them could be negatively affected (Dorkenoo 1999). Later in life, women who underwent FGM, especially infibulation, may experience psychological complications including depression, anxiety, and post-traumatic stress disorder (PTSD) (Knipscheer et al. 2015). Psychosexual complications such as fear of sexual intercourse and frigidity may occur in some woman and may contribute to marital conflicts (World Health Organization 2008; Dorkenoo 1999).

The Declaration of the Rights of the Child, accepted by the United Nations General Assembly in 1959, is sometimes invoked to support the argument that FGM violates the human rights of children (Shell-Duncan 2008). Principle 2 of this Declaration states that children should be provided with the opportunities "to develop physically, mentally, morally, spiritually, and socially in a healthy and normal manner and in conditions of freedom and dignity" and that "the best interests of the child shall be the paramount consideration" (United Nations General Assembly 1959). This is supported by the provisions included in article 21 of the African Charter on the Rights and Welfare of the Child. This particular section recommends that "customs and practices prejudicial to the health or life of the child" and "those customs and practices [that are] discriminatory to the child on the grounds of sex or other status" should be abolished; arguably, FGM pertains to both of these items (Organization of African Unity (OAU) 1990). Furthermore, the inability of children to give informed, meaningful consent to FGM provides justification for condemning the practice and for asserting that it violates children's rights (Mackie 2003). The counterargument to this position is that parents have a right to make decisions on behalf of their children who have not yet reached the age of consent. As FGM is culturally sanctioned by some groups and is regarded as being socially and economically beneficial to the girl and her family, it could be argued that parents who choose FGM for their daughter are acting in her best interest as defined by their specific culture (Shell-Duncan 2008).

The problem with the cultural relativizing of a child's best interests as they pertain to FGM become apparent if one substitutes an equivalent practice for FGM. Gerry Mackie notes the similarities between FGM, specifically infibulation, and the Chinese practice of foot-binding. Despite the negative health complications, foot-binding was carried out on female children and was strongly associated with female chastity, marriageability, and family honour. Bound feet were perceived as being aesthetically pleasing and were believed to contribute to more satisfying sexual relations. It was viewed as a prerequisite for a suitable marriage. A variety of factors, including increased educational and employment opportunities and anti-foot-binding societies, ultimately resulted in the abandonment of foot-binding (Mackie 1996).

As with FGM, the good intentions of loving parents can still cause irreparable damage to children. Today, condemning foot-binding is largely uncontroversial despite the fact that it was a valued cultural tradition when its practice was widespread. If the denunciation of foot-binding is not maligned as an example of Western cultural imperialism, then it seems specious to smear opponents of FGM with this accusation. Denouncing a particular practice within a culture is not automatically an indicator of neo-colonialist intentions and seeking culturally informed ways to alter factors that result in parents believing they have no real choice but to select FGM for their daughters is not necessarily evidence of ethnocentrism.

4 The Role of Art in Eradicating the Practice of FGM

The *Guidelines on Combating Sexual Violence and Its Consequences in Africa* affirm the need for awareness raising campaigns to causes, effects, and consequences of sexual violence (African Commission on Human and Peoples' Rights 2017). Programmes designed to encourage the abandonment of FGM should be adapted to specific audiences and must consider nuanced ethnic, cultural, religious, social, and regional traditions and distinctions. For some Africans, the Western condemnation of FGM has been perceived as an assault on African cultural values and traditions and the continued practice of FGM has become a kind of nationalist symbol. Attempts to stop it have been censured for supposedly being culturally imperialist and anti-African (Green 1999). Consequently, educating communities about the health problems associated with FGM and allowing individuals to make their own decisions about it might result in a quicker end to the practice than demanding outright cessation ("Changing Tradition of Female Genital Mutilation (FGM) Across Africa," 2013).

Mackie describes the practice of FGM as a "belief trap" in which perceived costs of not engaging in FGM are so great that they do not want to risk noncompliance; thus, FGM has become self-regulating (Mackie 1996). The congruity between the female belief that men would not marry an uncut woman and the male belief that an uncut woman would be an unfaithful wife has resulted in FGM becoming a "self-enforcing convention" (Mackie 1996). With regard to ending the practice of foot-binding in China, Mackie indicates that educational campaigns centred around the benefits of unbound feet and the damage caused by bound feet were constructive. He also emphasises the role played by societies opposed to foot-binding in which members publicly pledge not to bind their daughters' feet or permit their sons to marry women with bound feet. Due to education and the influence of these societies, as the value ascribed to natural feet increased, the preference for bound feet decreased and, ultimately, natural feet became widely accepted and preferred (Mackie 1996).

Using a similar model, villages could be encouraged to collectively take public pledges not to subject females to FGM and to establish local anti-FGM societies that could act as marriage markets (Oboler 2001). Similarly, uncut women are shamed so publicly celebrating the marriages of uncut women might be one way to challenge the social stigma associated with not undergoing FGM (Finke 2006). To further encourage communities to praise rather than condemn uncut females, male religious and community leaders who are against FGM could explicitly communicate that FGM is not required by any religious doctrine and provide extra support for uncut girls and their families (Bitong 2005).

The basic principle of Mackie's argument, the disruption of the belief trap, would need to occur in order for the widespread abandonment of FGM to happen. To this end, educational interventions that are tailored to specific populations and address the human rights violations and health risks associated with all types of FGM and dispel false beliefs about female genitalia, sexuality, and hygiene are important aspects of the necessarily multifaceted approach to ending FGM. The African Women's Protocol acknowledges that "harmful cultural and traditional practices ... are based on the idea of the inferiority or the superiority of the sexes, or on stereotyped roles for women and men;" to combat such practices, initiatives must be enacted to "modify the social and cultural patterns of conduct of women and men through public education, information, education and communication strategies" (African Union 2003). Partnering with local groups would allow international agencies to more successfully mediate with indigenous communities in order to more effectively challenge, and ultimately alter, erroneous beliefs and stereotypes that "legitimize and exacerbate the persistence and tolerance of violence against women" (Althaus 1997; African Union 2003).

Utilising the visual and performing arts could be a useful strategy for communicating with FGM practicing communities. Silvestri's *Unsterile Clinic* provides a visually compelling way to engage viewers in order to convey the degree of suffering caused by FGM. The photo-works and their accompanying text poems provide viewers with factual information and first-hand testimony from women who were subjected to FGM so the viewers are forced to intellectually and emotionally evaluate the practice. In order to raise awareness about FGM, various events, such as talks, tours, and performances, were held in conjunction with the 2016 exhibition of *Unsterile Clinic*. Being able to interact with the artist, healthcare workers, academics, and advocates enabled the diverse audience to become active participants in an informed dialogue (Autograph ABP 2016).

The unique interchange that was facilitated by the exhibition of *Unsterile Clinic* and the events that coincided with it successfully empowered victims of FGM by providing them with the opportunity to educate themselves about the details of the various types of FGM, the physical and psychological consequences of FGM, and the steps they can take to seek and receive the support they need. However, rather than putting the onus of obtaining medical or psychological assistance solely on the victims, the events placed victims in direct contact with healthcare professionals and advocates who could, presumably, make further recommendations for the victims. Additionally, the exhibition, the talks, and the performances emphasised that the victims are not alone in their suffering and they should not be afraid to share their experiences. By breaking the culture of silence that often surrounds the practice of FGM and by stressing that it is possible to effect meaningful change, the exhibition and its attendant events helped to embolden those in attendance to work, in their own ways, to end sexual violence against women and girls.

By using the events that occurred at the 2016 exhibition of *Unsterile Clinic* as a model, effective awareness-raising campaigns could be enacted and even combined with additional support mechanisms for FGM victims, including "health services, legal and judicial support, emotional and psychological counselling [and] vocational training" (African Union 2003). Female artists in various communities could be commissioned to create artwork about FGM that would specifically engage the visual language of their local communities. Ideally, these artworks would incorporate the personal experiences of not only the victims of FGM but also of healthcare professionals and others who can attest to the physical and psychological damage caused by FGM. As with Silvestri's works, poetry or other testimony written by victims could be incorporated with the artworks or displayed near these. These artworks or reproductions of them and any accompanying poetry or text could then be incorporated into age-appropriate educational programmes for young people and into training received by professionals in government and in the private sector. When engaged in a context that fosters informed dialogue, the artworks would potentially communicate the experiences of FGM victims on a deeper level than simply listening to a lecture or reading through a pamphlet. Thus, incorporating the visual arts into awareness-raising campaigns could be a successful strategy for combatting violence against women. In conjunction with employing the visual arts, other arts-based approaches, such as utilising local theatre troupes to perform plays addressing the negative effects of FGM, might also prove successful in educating communities and initiating discussions about the practices.

The visual and performing arts communicate information in powerful ways that cannot be achieved through other educational means so their unique contribution to efforts aimed at eradicating FGM should not be ignored. For instance, the arts can also play crucial roles in the judicial process. With regard to the judicial process, the section devoted to "special measures for the participation and protection of children victims or witnesses of sexual violence," in the *Guidelines on Combating Sexual Violence and its Consequences in Africa* specifically indicates that numerous legal hearings and extensive questioning might further traumatise children who have experienced sexual violence (African Commission on Human and Peoples' Rights 2017). As a result, the *Guidelines* stipulate that "alternative methods of expression, such as art, should be used to encourage the child to express himself/herself (drawing, theatre, etc.)" (African Commission on Human and Peoples' Rights 2017). When used in this context, the arts can facilitate the participation of child victims and witnesses in the legal process while protecting them from suffering additional psychological trauma. This participation may contribute to the appropriate sentencing of perpetrators of sexual violence.

Furthermore, the arts can help victims of FGM work through their trauma. For example, art therapy can be used as a vehicle for those who have experienced sexual violence to communicate and process both their conscious and unconscious emotions. Some victims have difficulty verbally expressing their thoughts and emotions and some find words inadequate to convey the depth of their physical and psychological pain. In such cases, art therapy can provide an alternative method of expression. In addition, the concrete form of the art can also aid victims in acknowledging and reflecting on their emotions in order to regain confidence and feel more empowered. Thus, art therapy could be incorporated into support services for FGM survivors and could be used in conjunction with verbal and cognitive-based therapies to aid victims in the process of recovering from this traumatic experience (Chong 2015).

As the perpetuation of FGM seems to coincide with social, economic, and legal inequalities, working to diminish this imbalance would potentially encourage groups to turn away from the practice. If females are provided with increased educational and economic opportunities, they will be less dependent on marriage for financial security. As one female, Somali immigrant to the United States remarked, "If my daughter finishes school, learns how to drive a car, and gets a job, she doesn't need a man whether she is circumcised or not" (Upval et al. 2009). While not representative of all groups, this assertion suggests that, for some parents, FGM is mentally aligned with financial stability. If education provides the means for females to achieve financial independence, some parents might be amenable to their daughters pursuing education in lieu of undergoing FGM.

Many traditional excisors are older, uneducated women who are financially compensated for performing FGM (Bitong 2005; Mackie 2003). As long as their financial security depends upon the continuation of FGM, they will likely be disinclined to cease their work. If, however, they were able to receive education and training for a different occupation, perhaps even one with higher wages, their financial incentive to continue practicing FGM would be diminished.

Lastly, when combined with the measures discussed above, legislation seems to act as a deterrent. Although legal measures and their enforcement vary across the countries in which FGM is practiced, the presence of anti-FGM legislation emphasises that the practice violates human rights (Muthumbi et al. 2015). Legislation reinforces initiatives that underscore the adverse health effects of FGM and also provides legal justification and support for those who chose not to subject their daughters to the practice (Ruiz et al. 2017). Locally-based approaches to ending FGM are probably more successful in effecting meaningful change regarding the perception of FGM, but when combined with educational measures and social programmes, legislation is an important supporting tool for eradicating FGM (Aberese Ako and Akweongo 2009).

5 Conclusion

FGM is deeply rooted in certain ethnic groups that it is unlikely to disappear on its own. Despite its cultural entrenchment, FGM is an injurious practice that compromises the health and violates the rights of women and girls around the world.

Although the practice still occurs, there are indications that it is becoming less prevalent in certain places (Aberese Ako and Akweongo 2009). Thus, despite its persistence, there is still hope that FGM might be eradicated in the future. In order to successfully combat this practice, it is important that the norm of silence traditionally surrounding it continues to be broken (Mackie 2003). Providing girls and women with increased educational and economic opportunities will help rectify the gender imbalance in FGM practicing societies which will alleviate some of the pressure females face to accept and perpetuate this harmful practice. By calling attention to the health dangers and human rights violations of FGM via avenues such as education, awareness raising, social programmes, arts-based initiatives, including exhibitions like Aida Silvestri's *Unsterile Clinic,* and legislation, important strides are being made toward the goal of its global eradication. Hopefully, with continued persistence and the efforts of Silvestri and others, that objective will one day be realised.

References

Abdulcadir J, Margairaz C, Bouvain M, Irion O (2011) Care of women with female genital mutilation/cutting. Swiss Med Wkly 140:1–8. https://doi.org/10.4414/smw.2011.13137

Abdulcadir J, McLaren S, Boulvain M, Irion O (2016) Health education and clinical care of immigrant women with female genital mutilation/cutting who request postpartum reinfibulation. Int J Gynecol Obstet 135:69–72. https://doi.org/10.1016/j.ijgo.2016.03.027

Aberese Ako M, Akweongo P (2009) The limited effectiveness of legislation against female genital mutilation and the role of community beliefs in Upper East Region, Ghana. Reprod Health Matters 17(34):47–54. https://doi.org/10.1016/S0968-8080(09)34474-2

African Commission on Human and Peoples' Rights (2017) Guidelines on combating sexual violence and its consequences in Africa, pp 1–51

African Union (2003) Protocol to the African Charter on Human and Peoples' Rights on the rights of women in Africa. African Union, Maputo, Mozambique, pp 1–32. http://www.achpr.org/files/instruments/women-protocol/achpr_instr_proto_women_eng.pdf

Alhassan YN, Barrett H, Brown KE, Kwah K (2016) Belief systems enforcing female genital mutilation in Europe. Int J Hum Rights Healthc 9(1):29–40. https://doi.org/10.1108/IJHRH-05-2015-0015

Althaus FA (1997) Female circumcision: rite of passage or violation of rights? Int Fam Plan Perspect 23(3):130–133. https://doi.org/10.2307/2950769

Amado LE (2004) Sexual and bodily rights as human rights in the Middle East and North Africa. Reprod Health Matters 12(23):125–128. https://doi.org/10.1016/S0968-8080(04)23119-6

Autograph (2018) Aida Silvestri: Unsterile Clinic. https://autograph.org.uk/exhibitions/unsterile-clinic. Accessed 27 Aug 2018

Autograph ABP (2016) Aida Silvestri: *Unsterile Clinic. Exhibition report.* Autograph ABP, London

Barrett H (2014) Female genital cutting: crossing borders. Geography 99(1):20–27

Berg RC, Denison E (2013) A tradition in transition: factors perpetuating and hindering the continuance of female genital mutilation/cutting (FGM/C) summarized in a systematic review. Heath Care Women Int 34(10):837–859. https://doi.org/10.1080/07399332.2012.721417

Bitong L (2005) Fighting Genital Mutilation in Sierra Leone. Bull World Health Organ 83(11):806–807

Catania L, Mastrullo R, Caselli A, Cecere R, Abdulcadir O, Abdulcadir J (2016) Male perspectives on FGM among communities of African Heritage in Italy. Int J Hum Rights Healthc 9(1):41–51. https://doi.org/10.1108/IJHRH-07-2015-0023
Changing tradition of female genital mutilation (FGM) across Africa (2013) Reproduct Health Matters 11(22):200
Chong CYJ (2015) Why art psychotherapy? Through the lens of interpersonal neurobiology: the distinctive role of art psychology intervention for clients with early relational trauma. Int J Art Ther 20(3):118–126. https://doi.org/10.1080/17454832.2015.1079727
Dorkenoo E (1999) Combating female genital mutilation: an agenda for the next decade. Women Stud Q 27(1/2):87–97
El-Damanhoury I (2013) The Jewish and Christian view on female genital mutilation. Afr J Urol 19(3):127–129. https://doi.org/10.1016/j.afju.2013.01.004
Finke E (2006) Genital mutilation as an expression of power structures: ending FGM through education, empowerment of women and removal of taboos. Afr J Reprod Health 10(2):13–17
Gayle C, Rymer J (2016) Female genital mutilation and pregnancy: associated risks. Br J Nurs 25(17):978–981. https://doi.org/10.12968/bjon.2016.25.17.978
Green D (1999) Gender violence in Africa: African women's responses. St. Martin's Press, New York
Groeneveld AE (2013) Female genital mutilation: tradition versus human rights. Afr J Urol 19:134–135
Ismail SA, Abbas AM, Habib D, Morsy H, Saleh MA, Bahloul M (2017) Effect of female genital mutilation/cutting types I and II on sexual function: case-controlled study. Reprod Health 14(1):1–6. https://doi.org/10.1186/s12978-017-0371-9
Jungari SB (2016) Female genital mutilation is a violation of reproductive rights of women: implications for health workers. Health Soc Work 41(1):25–31. https://doi.org/10.1093/hsw/hlv090
Kelson GA (1998) Female circumcision in the modern age: should female circumcision now be considered grounds for asylum in the United States? Buffalo Hum Rights Law Rev 4:185–209
Knipscheer J, Vloeberghs E, van der Kwaak A, van den Muijsenbergh M (2015) Mental health problems associated with female genital mutilation. BJPsych Bull 39(6):273–277. https://doi.org/10.1192/pb.bp.114.047944
Lax RF (2000) Socially sanctioned violence against women: female genital mutilation in its most brutal form. Clin Soc Work J 28(4):403–412. https://doi.org/10.1023/A:1005119906627
Mackie G (1996) Ending footbinding and infibulation: a convention account. Am Sociol Rev 61(6):1004–999-1017
Mackie G (2003) Female genital cutting: a harmless practice? Med Anthropol Q 17(2):135–158. https://doi.org/10.1525/maq.2003.17.2.135
Monjok EE, Essien J, Holmes L Jr (2007) Female genital mutilation: potential for HIV transmission in sub-Saharan Africa and prospect for epidemiologic investigation and intervention. Afr J Reprod Health 11(1):32–44
Mulongo P, Hollins Martin C, McAndrew S (2014) The Psychological Impact of Female Genital Mutilation/Cutting (FGM/C) on Girls/Women's Mental Health: A Narrative Literature Review. J Reprod Health Infant Psychol 32(5):469–485. https://doi.org/10.1080/02646838.2014.949641
Muthumbi J, Svanemyr J, Scolaro E, Temmerman M, Say L (2015) Female genital mutilation: a literature review of the current status of legislation and polities in 27 African countries and Yemen. Afr J Reprod Health 19(3):32–40
Obermeyer CM (1999) Female genital surgeries: the known, the unknown, and the unknowable. Med Anthropol Q 13(1):79–106. https://doi.org/10.1525/maq.1999.13.1.79
Oboler RS (2001) Law and persuasion in the elimination of female genital modification. Hum Organ 60(4):311–318. https://doi.org/10.17730/humo.60.4.2h3kh9nqckhrer03
Odukogbel A-TA, Afolabi BB, Bello OO, Adeyanju AS (2017) Female genital mutilation/cutting in Africa. Transl Androl Urol 6(2):138–148. https://doi.org/10.21037/tau.2016.12.01
Organization of African Unity (OAU) (1990) African Charter on the rights and welfare of the child. CAB/LEG/24.9/49. https://www.ifrc.org/docs/idrl/N971EN.pdf. Accessed 5 Apr 2019

Rodriguez MI, Seuc A, Say L, Hindin MJ (2016) Episiotomy and obstetric outcomes among women living with type 3 female genital mutilation: a secondary analysis. Reprod Health 13:1–7. https://doi.org/10.1186/s12978-016-0242-9

Ross CT, Campiño PJ, Winterhalder B (2015) Frequency-dependent social transmission and the interethnic transfer of female genital modification in the African diaspora and Indigenous populations of Colombia. Hum Nat 26(4):351–377. https://doi.org/10.1007/s12110-015-9234-7

Ruiz IJ, Martínez PA, Giménez LG (2017) Eradicating female genital mutilation; a viable reality. Raising awareness in the men involved. Procedia Soc Behav Sci 237:784–791. https://doi.org/10.1016/j.sbspro.2017.02.122

Rushwan H (2013) Female genital mutilation: a tragedy for women's reproductive health. Afr J Urol 19(3):130–133. https://doi.org/10.1016/j.afju.2013.03.002

Serour G (2013) Medicalization of female genital mutilation/cutting. Afr J Urol 19(3):145–149. https://doi.org/10.1016/j.afju.2013.02.004

Shell-Duncan B (2008) From health to human rights: female genital cutting and the politics of intervention. Am Anthropol 110(2):225–236. https://doi.org/10.1111/j.1548-1433.2008.00028.x

Silvestri A (2015) Artist statement on *Unsterile Clinic*

The Public Policy Advisory Network on Female Genital Surgeries in Africa (2012) Seven things to know about female genital surgeries in Africa. Hast Cent Rep 42(6):19–27

UNICEF (2015) Female genital mutilation/cutting: a statistical overview and exploration of the dynamics of change. UNICEF Data and Analytics Section, New York, pp 1–6

UNICEF (2016) UNICEF's data work on FGM/C. *FGM/C brochure*. UNICEF Data and Analytics Section, New York, pp 1–2

United Nations General Assembly (1959) Declaration of the rights of the child. 20 November 1959. A/RES/1386(XIV). http://un-documents.net/a14r1386.htm. Accessed 28 Aug 2018

Upval MJ, Mohammed K, Dodge PD (2009) Perspectives of Somali Bantu refugee women living with circumcision in the United States: a focus group approach. Int J Nurs Stud 46(3):360–368. https://doi.org/10.1016/j.ijnurstu.2008.04.009

World Health Organization (2008) Eliminating female genital mutilation: an interagency statement UNAIDS, UNDP, UNECA, UNESCO, UNFPA, UNHCHR, HNHCR, UNICEF, UNIFEM, WHO. Geneva, Switzerland: WHO Press, World Health Organization. https://www.unfpa.org/sites/default/files/pub-pdf/eliminating_fgm.pdf. Accessed 28 Aug 2019

World Health Organization (2018a) Classification of female genital mutilation. Sexual and reproductive health. http://www.who.int/reproductivehealth/topics/fgm/overview/en/. Accessed 27 Aug 2018

World Health Organization (2018b) Female genital mutilation: fact sheet. http://www.who.int/en/news-room/fact-sheets/detail/female-genital-mutilation. Accessed 28 Aug 2019

World Health Organization (2019) Classification of female genital mutilation. Sexual and reproductive health. http://www.who.int/reproductivehealth/topics/fgm/overview/en/. Accessed 28 Aug 2019

Yoder PS, Wang S, Johansen E (2013) Estimates of female genital mutilation/cutting in 27 African countries and Yemen. Stud Fam Plan 44(2):189–204. https://doi.org/10.1111/j.1728-4465.2013.00352.x

Chapter 4
Literature and Human Rights in Africa: Making a Case for a Trauma-Sensitive Approach in Proving Persecution in Asylum Processes through Adichie's *The American Embassy*

Romola Adeola

Abstract The right to seek and enjoy asylum is recognised in international law as a cardinal principle in the safeguard for persons in need of international protection. Drawing on the discretion of states to grant asylum, the right to seek and enjoy asylum is contained in several in a plethora of international soft norms and underscored in international refugee law through the principle of non-refoulement. In the process of seeking asylum, an applicant would need to demonstrate the fact that there was a fear of persecution which is well-founded in the country of origin. This process may entail retelling a factual situation which has psychosocial implications given the sensitivity of the particular situation and its consequences on the mental health of the asylum-seeker. Using Chimamanda Ngozi Adichie's *The American Embassy*, this chapter makes the case for trauma-sensitive approach to be utilised in the course of proving persecution in asylum processes.

Keywords Chimamanda Ngozi Adichie · The American Embassy · Short stories · Asylum · Refugees · Trauma · Literature · Credibility

1 Introduction

The right to seek and enjoy asylum, guaranteed under international law, draws on the discretionary power of states to grant asylum to persons in need of international protection. In seeking asylum, the asylum-seeker is generally required to provide support in the asylum process – of a well-founded fear of persecution on the ground

R. Adeola (✉)
Faculty of Law, Centre for Human Rights, University of Pretoria, Pretoria, South Africa

R. Adeola et al. (eds.), *The Art of Human Rights*, Arts, Research, Innovation and Society, https://doi.org/10.1007/978-3-030-30102-6_4

of race, religion, nationality, membership of a particular social group or political opinion (UN Refugee Convention 1951, art 1(A); OAU Refugee Convention 1969, art 1(1)).

This process may entail retelling a factual situation which has psychosocial implications given the sensitivity of the particular situation and its consequences on the mental health of the asylum-seeker. It is within this context that this chapter is located. Leveraging on Chimamanda Ngozi Adichie's *The American Embassy* (Adichie 2009, p. 128), this chapter argues that asylum-seeking processes need to give due consideration to such traumatic experiences. This chapter utilises Chimamanda Ngozi Adichie's *The American Embassy* as it offers a prism through which to flesh out the impact of trauma on the evidentiary process of seeking asylum and more importantly, spotlight the need for a trauma-sensitive approach in asylum processes. *The American Embassy* is a short story contained in Adichie's collection "The Thing Around Your Neck".

This chapter is divided into four parts. The first part discusses the right to seek and enjoy asylum under international law, examining the content of the right under relevant international standards. The second part examines the burden of proof in asylum processes exploring the international legal standards and application by states. The third part considers the concept of trauma as a psycho-social problem. The fourth part examines the imperative for a trauma-sensitive approach to asylum seeking processes leveraging on Chimamanda Ngozi Adichie's *The American Embassy* and considers how the trauma-sensitive approach can be utilised in practice for the protection of asylum seekers and in the furtherance of a rights-based approach to asylum in international law.

2 The Right to Seek and Enjoy Asylum

Recognised in international law, the right to seek and enjoy asylum draws on the discretion of states to grant asylum. The right to 'seek' asylum requires that individuals should not be prevented from seeking asylum, either through restrictive policies or interceptions that serve as deterrence to the process. Moreover, the right to 'enjoy' asylum requires that asylum seekers, upon being granted asylum, are afforded adequate rights-based protection in the state. As such, when asylum is granted, a state must provide a conducive environment for its enjoyment. Article 14(1) of the Universal Declaration of Human Rights provides that all persons have a 'right to seek and to enjoy in other countries asylum from persecution' (Universal Declaration of Human Rights 1948, art 14(1)). This right is reaffirmed in other soft norms (UN Declaration on Territorial Asylum 1967, art 3(1); Principle Concerning Treatment of Refugees 1966, art 3). In international refugee law, the essence of this right is further underscored in the principle of non-refoulement which prohibits states from returning refugees to territories where their freedoms would be threatened (UN Refugee Convention 1951, art 33(1); OAU Refugee Convention 1969, art 2(3)).

It is imperative to emphasise that alienage is at the core of refugee protection (Hathaway and Foster 2014, pp. 17, 23). While Adichie's literary text omits this detail given that the woman (in the story) is not outside the country of persecution—a requirement under international refugee law—the text is yet employed in this chapter to underscore the imperative for a trauma-sensitive approach in asylum processes. As such, the aim of utilising Adichie's *The American Embassy* is to demonstrate how asylum seekers may struggle and encounter difficulties due to conceptions or other forms of restraints, in retelling trauma to ground their claims of a well-founded fear of persecution.

3 Burden of Proof in Asylum Processes

In principle, the burden of proving persecution in an asylum process is with an applicant who is requesting asylum. In the determination process, the applicant has to establish that she/he has a well-founded fear of persecution. This will require the asylum seeker to prove to the adjudicator, in the process of status determination, that there are contextual and personal experiences that give rise to factual circumstances on which a well-founded fear of persecution emerges. Based on the existence of this well-founded fear of persecution, the person is unwilling or unable to avail herself/himself of the protection of the state of origin. It is imperative to emphasise that the applicant is not required to prove her/his claim beyond reasonable doubt. Essentially, the applicant is solely to establish her/his claim to a reasonable degree. In essence, the claim of the asylum seeker of a well-founded fear of persecution should be to 'a reasonable degree, that his continued stay in his country of origin has become intolerable to him for the reasons stated in the definition, or would for the same reasons be intolerable if he returned there' (UN High Commissioner for Refugees 2011, para 41). On the strength of the evidence, an adjudicator makes a decision on the asylum process. In arriving at this conclusion, the adjudicator will need to determine that the applicant's claim is indeed credible on the basis of the evidence presented.

The issue of credibility is a pertinent aspect of refugee status determination as it is a significant component in ascertaining the truth 'especially where applicants for protection lack documentary proof that their claimed experiences have in fact occurred' (McDonald 2014, p. 116; UN High Commissioner for Refugees 2011, para 41). Going by the ordinary meaning of the term, credibility means 'believability', 'likelihood' and 'acceptability' (Oxford Dictionaries n.d.). While it is not a criterion for refugee status, credibility is integral to ascertaining that an applicant has a well-founded fear of persecution (Gyulai et al. 2013, p. 22). In assessing credibility, the standard is not for the adjudicator to be 'fully convinced that all factual assertions are true' (UN High Commissioner for Refugees 1998, para 12). Rather, the adjudicator should be guided by whether 'the applicant has presented a claim which is coherent and plausible, not contradicting generally known facts, and therefore, is on balance, capable of being believed' (UN High Commissioner for Refugees

1998, para 11). This evidentiary position has been established in legal jurisprudence. In *Tantoush v Refugee Appeal Board*, the South African High Court (SAHC) emphasised that credibility 'for the purpose of establishing whether … [an applicant] has a well-founded fear of persecution must be weighed looking at the inherent probabilities, the presence or absence of external or internal contradictions, its consistency or otherwise with the other evidence, his candour and overall performance in testifying, and so on.' (Tantoush v Refugee Appeal Board 2007, para 102).

From international legal texts and jurisprudence, there are five useful indicators in assessing credibility, namely, internal consistency, external consistency, demeanour, plausibility and sufficiency of details. Internal consistency relates to the coherence in the testimony of the applicant regarding the background and personal experiences. As a general requirement, an asylum seeker's story must cohere and not be contradictory. The asylum seeker's account should not undermine the credibility of her/his claim. With regards to external consistency, there must be generally known facts that lends credence to the testimony of the applicant. This indicator will, in principle, seek to establish the coherence between the asylum seeker's claim and the country of origin information. Demeanour relates to the overall conduct and manner in which the asylum-seeker presents his claim. The essence of this indicator resonates from the relevance of mannerism and conduct that may be telling in ascertaining the veracity of a claim. Plausibility contemplates that the claim of the applicant is probable or inherently possible. This indicator generally relates to the rationality of the claim. Moreover, sufficiency of details primarily seeks to foster a detailed understanding of the claim.

However, it is imperative that these requirements are not construed strictly against an asylum seeker. For instance, internal consistency may be affected by a series of factors, not least, the applicant's vulnerability and memory. Also, external consistency may be predicated on the availability of information on the country of origin to substantiate the claim. Likewise, predicating the negation of a claim on demeanour may be problematic given that it is not a reliable source of ascertaining credibility. Demeanour may differ based on a host of factors. Placing a reliance on this as a pertinent indicator may cause an adjudicator to err and consequentially result in an injustice. Plausibility may also be contextually relative. As such, the fact that an applicant's claim may not be plausible in country of refuge does not imply that it is not plausible in her/his country of origin. Context is imperative. In addition, an asylum seeker may also not be sufficiently detailed and this may be due to a plethora of reasons.

Overall, the point that resonates from the preceding paragraph is the fact that a credibility assessment should not take place in abstraction. It is not a straightforward legally determinable process although it must resonate from the object and purpose of law, significantly international refugee law. Given that the assessment is essentially on a case-by-case basis, it is often challenged by a plethora of issues including extra-legal factors such as language, geographical background, cultural contexts, gender, education and trauma. And it is imperative to emphasise that adjudicators should be mindful of these factors and not 'assume that the way they think is also the way the asylum-seeker thinks' (Kälin 1986, p. 234). What this chapter is essentially concerned with is the issue of trauma. Leveraging on Chimamanda Ngozi Adichie's *The American Embassy*, the next section discusses how trauma may affect an asylum process and why it is imperative that a trauma-sensitive approach is adopted in an asylum process in furtherance of a right-based approach to status determination under international refugee law.

4 Trauma as a Psycho-Social Problem

In contextualising a trauma-sensitive approach in status determination, it is imperative to interrogate trauma as a psycho-social problem experienced by asylum-seeker. From the start, it is imperative to emphasise that trauma is a condition that can be experienced by anyone. The word 'trauma' derives from the Greek term for 'wound' and can be physical and psychological in nature (Krippner et al. 2012, p. 2). Trauma is a 'direct personal experience of an event that involves actual or threatened death or serious injury, or other threat to one's physical integrity; or witnessing an event that involves death, injury, or a threat to the physical integrity of another person; or learning about unexpected or violent death, serious harm, or threat of death or injury experienced by a family member or other close associate' (American Psychiatric Association 2000, p. 463; Briere and Scott 2015, p. 9). Garland describes trauma as an event that 'overwhelms existing defences against anxiety in a form which also provides confirmation of those deepest universal anxieties' (Garland 1998, p. 11). While there might be conceptual variations in understanding trauma (Harms 2015, p. 6), a recurring undertone is the fact that '[t]he damage done, more often than not, is neither trivial nor temporary' (Garland 1998, p. 11). It is imperative to understand trauma as a disintegration of the coherent self. Put differently, trauma renders powerless the psychic defence that may stabilise the sense of the coherent self (Bernstein 2005, p. 91). Maček explains that in trauma, the psychic defence 'cut[s] off this experience [trauma] from any integrative psychic process' (Maček 2014, p. 4). Given that its impact may be 'subtle, insidious or outright destructive' (Substance Abuse and Mental Health Services Administration 2014, p. 59), paying significant attention to its manifestations is important.

Closely linked to the discussion in this chapter is the notion of trauma as an emotional response that 'takes place when the very powers that we are convinced will protect us and give us security become our tormentors: when the community of which we considered ourselves members turns against us or when our family is no longer a source of refuge but a site of danger' (Edkins 2003, p. 4). Put differently, trauma derives from a disruption between expectations of protection and security on the one hand and the actual factual situation of denied protection and security on the other hand. Taking a slightly nuanced approach, van der Kolk observes that trauma 'occurs when one loses the sense of having a safe place to retreat within or outside oneself to deal with frightening emotions or experiences. This results in a state of helplessness, a feeling that one's actions have no bearing on the outcome of one's life.' (van der Kolk 1987, p. 32).

What often makes trauma 'traumatic' is often its gravity, duration, repetition, proximity, coping, history, unexpectedness and support (Baker 2010, p. 60). Gravity relates to the context. It encapsulates the severity of the traumatic experience. The greater the trauma, the more plausible it is for the person experiencing the situation to be embroiled in an emotional crisis. Duration relates to the time frame in which the experience occurs. The duration of trauma may exacerbate the intensity of the experience and deepen emotional fractures. While repetition may render the trauma insidious, proximity may impact stress levels. Moreover, the individualised response to such experiences may also exacerbate its gravity. Depending on the nature of trauma, coping will differ based on variables such as age, developmental stage and dependency. Moreover, the histories of trauma may exacerbate its impact. Sudden, unexpected events may trigger the magnitude of the episode. The absence or availability of support mechanisms affects resilience and depending on the mechanisms available, the intensity may be protracted.

There is a plethora of stressors that can trigger trauma. These stressors may be direct, witnessed or learnt about (Cougle et al. 2012, p. 13). Direct stressors may include: mental and physical abuse, war, forced displacement, domestic violence, natural and human-made disasters, terrorist attacks, kidnappings, torture, sexual abuse and physical assaults (Cougle et al. 2012, p. 13). Examples of witnessed stressors include observing the unexpected death of an individual due to attack, accidents, grave injuries due to violent attack, war, accidents or disasters. Learned stressors including knowing about a violent attack on an individual, unanticipated loss of a close family member or friend (Cougle et al. 2012, p. 13). As a result of these stressors, an individual may experience post-traumatic stress disorder (PSTD). PTSD is often the form in which stress is externalised. These may be through avoidance, anxiety and reliving the traumatic event. Avoidance often manifests through dissociation from social circles. This may result in emotional numbness and break in relationship ties (South African Depression and Anxiety Group 2006). An individual displaying this symptom may withdraw from family, friends, colleagues as a means of coping with the traumatic experience. However, such avoidance, while seeming as a temporary relief, interferes with 'successful processing of the trauma memory, habituation of negative emotions associated with the trauma memory, and extinction of fear responses conditioned to internal or external trauma reminders' (Pineles et al. 2011, p. 2). Anxiety is often displayed through a state of hyperarousal (Hick 2003, p. 103) which manifests through insomnia, hypervigilance, irritability and loss of concentration (Scher et al. 2008). Moreover, PTSD may also occur through intrusive traumatic memories that manifest through flashbacks, dreams and nightmares (Hick 2003, p. 103).

For asylum seekers, direct, witnessed and learned stresses are factual traumatic realities that place them at a higher risk of PTSD. Arguably, an eminent feature of the refugee experience is the trauma that triggers the need for international protection (Weaver 2016, p. 122). Drawing on the refugee definition, this stems from the notion of fear of persecution which will almost always be characterised by a stressor. For instance, witnessing wars, genocidal acts or the deaths of a loved one through violent attacks by state or non-state agents can create fear of persecution. While knowing about the circumstances that give rise to a request for asylum is imperative to status determination, adjudicators need to be mindful of the trauma and its attendant risks. As such, a trauma-sensitive approach should be adopted.

Drawing on Chimamanda Ngozi Adichie's *American Embassy* (Adichie 2009, p. 128), the next section discusses how trauma may affect an asylum process and why it is imperative that a trauma-sensitive approach is adopted.

5 The Imperative for a Trauma-Sensitive Approach

The use of literature in law has gained significant momentum in the literature (Wigmore 1922; Cardozo 1931; White 1973; Posner 1986; Edney 2004; Uffelman 2008; Schultz and Ost 2018). Scholarly research has notably established the pertinence of literature in shedding light on key legal subjects. This section leverages on Adichie's *The American Embassy* in the context of asylum in view of the importance of literature as a premise for understanding the imperative for a trauma-sensitive approach in the furtherance of a rights-based approach.

The story is set in Lagos, specifically at an American Embassy during the military era of General Sani Abacha (1993–1998). In the opening paragraph, a woman waits in line to enter the American embassy in a long queue of about 'two hundred that trailed from the closed gates of the American embassy all the way past the smaller, vine-encrusted gates of the Czech embassy' (Adichie 2009, p. 128). Through a series of flashbacks, the plot unfolds the reason for her presence at the American embassy. She had come to the embassy to request asylum.

Her husband, a journalist, had become a prominent voice against the Abacha-led administration. Through editorial pieces in *The New Nigeria*, he details the atrocities of the Abacha-led administration. His latest piece, entitled "The Abacha Years So Far: 1993 to 1997" would jeopardise his security and that of his family (the woman and their son, Ugonna). At first, the woman had not been perturbed about the piece because her husband 'had written nothing new, only compiled killings and failed contracts and missing money' (Adichie 2009, p. 137). This was popular knowledge. However, 'a day after the paper came out, BBC radio carried the story on the news and interviewed an exiled Nigerian professor of politics who said her husband deserved a Human Rights Award' (Adichie 2009, p. 137). Through an anonymous call, her husband got wind of the fact that the Head of State was 'personally furious' and that soldiers were coming to arrest him. Although he had previously been detained 'for two weeks' (Adichie 2009, p. 135), the caller informed him that this was to be 'his last arrest, he would never come back' (Adichie 2009, p. 137). He leaves Nigeria afterwards having been sneaked out through the border into Benin Republic with the help of his co-editor who leveraged on his contacts. He would travel to the United States and apply for asylum upon arrival in New York since his American visa was still valid (Adichie 2009, p. 138). The woman 'told him not to worry, she and Ugonna would be fine, she would apply for a visa at the end of the school term and they would join him in America' (Adichie 2009, p. 138). But on that night, three men, whom she believed were 'government agents' (Adichie 2009, p. 140) burst into her house (Adichie 2009, pp. 131–138) and one of them killed her son (Adichie 2009, p. 132).

While the plot centres around the woman's ordeal, the scene at the American embassy brings to fore other prominent issues such as the difficulties and frustrations in visa applications (Adichie 2009, pp. 130, 138, 139, 141), police brutality (Adichie 2009, p. 131) and the use of children in begging (Adichie 2009, p. 130). However, of relevance to the discussion in this chapter is the woman's ordeal highlighted above and significantly, the exchange with the visa interviewer (Adichie 2009, p. 139). The interview opens with the interviewer requesting the woman to retell her story (Adichie 2009, p. 139). Before coming to the embassy, she had been told by 'people who had helped with her husband's escape and with Ugonna's funeral, who had brought her to the embassy' (Adichie 2009, p. 134), that she should not falter in answering questions. She had been told to speak about her son, but not to 'overdo it, because every day people lie to them to get asylum visas, about dead relatives that were never even born' (Adichie 2009, p. 134). However, when it was time to relay this to the interviewer, she was laconic with the details: '[h]er son had been killed, that was all she would say' (Adichie 2009, p. 139) as she was not prepared to have Ugonna 'hawked' for 'a visa to safety' (Adichie 2009, p. 139).

When the interviewer had asked for proof that government agents were involved, she replied that she had buried her evidence: referring to Ugonna's body (Adichie 2009, p. 140). However, the interviewer insisted on proof given that there were clashes between ethnic groups and private assassinations taking place and as such there was a need for 'some evidence of the government's involvement' and evidence that she was in danger if she stayed in Nigeria. But the woman was not willing to giving this information and 'had the urge to ask the visa interviewer if the stories in *The New Nigeria* were worth the life of a child' (Adichie 2009, p. 140). And even while the interviewer had assured her that the 'United States offers a new life to victims of political persecution' (Adichie 2009, p. 140), the mental impact of the event on her was unveiled in how she mentally conflated what new life means with how her son's existence redefined her son. This is captured in the fact that it 'was Ugonna who had given her a new life, surprised her by how quickly she took to the new identity he gave her, the new person he made her' (Adichie 2009, p. 140). This was mostly captured in the words: 'Ugonna's mother' (Adichie 2009, p. 140). All through the interview, a recurring theme was the cleavage between her experience and what she perceives as the interviewer's inability to relate with it (Adichie 2009, p. 140). This is climaxed in her thought just before leaving the Embassy refusing to divulge further details or heed the interviewer's call when eventually she turned to leave (Adichie 2009, p. 141).

While the setting in which asylum adjudicatory processes takes place may differ, this literary text unveils the importance of taking into account the lived experiences of an asylum seeker. In the literary text, the process of retelling the experience, which justifies the well-founded fear of persecution, appeared overwhelming for the woman as with the insistence on evidence by the visa interviewer. Consequently, the woman abandoned her request for asylum. Counterfactually however, a trauma-sensitive approach to the asylum process may have stimulated a different reaction from the woman. The woman had three restraints: details on her son's death, the new life as intrinsic to her son's existence and the perception that the visa interviewer could not relate to her ordeal. However, it would have been different if there were trauma-sensitive methods. This brings to the fore, the pertinent question: what is a trauma-sensitive approach? And how should this be implied in an asylum process?

In simple parlance, a trauma-sensitive approach is a victim-centred approach. It is an approach that is guided by the need to avoid arousing negatively the lived traumatic experience of an asylum-seeker. A trauma-sensitive approach is one which considers the victim's trauma as the commencement point for advancing international protection. In other words, a trauma-sensitive approach acknowledges the presence of trauma in the lived experience of an asylum seeker, considering the fact that it is imperative to adjudicate the asylum-seeker's claim based on the understanding of her/his stress which induces the need for international protection. There is support for arguing for this approach. Over the last decade, empirical research has actively begun to establish patterns of trauma among asylum seekers and the need to address these issues through coping measures (Renner and Salem 2009; Slobodin et al. 2018). This chapter argues that from the process of adjudication of asylum, it is imperative that psychosocial support is provided. Where factual circumstances of an asylum seeker's claim attest to the likelihood of trauma, psychosocial support must be present. This support must be geared towards ensuring that the victim is shielded from the mental consequences that may arise from having to proof the well-founded nature of the fear of persecution.

Linked to the practical ramification of this proposal is the question of resources. This links back to the argument that the resources of a state are often limited and there is need for prioritising interventions for asylum seekers and refugees. In addressing this issue, it is imperative for states to leverage on the technical support of international organisations and civil society involved in providing psychosocial support. Through effective partnership, actualising such approach will become a reality.

6 Conclusion

This chapter argues the need for a trauma-sensitive approach in the asylum process to ensure that individuals seeking asylum based on a well-founded fear of persecution are protected from the mental consequences of retelling traumatic experiences. This chapter recommends that psychosocial support should be provided in the adjudicatory process. The relevance of this stems from the fact that, in the absence of psychosocial support, asylum seekers may experience difficulties in retelling the traumatic experience. Engaging Adichie's *The American Embassy*, this chapter accentuates this fact. Overall, there is need for states to pursue effective partnerships with international organisations and civil society in addressing the technical dimensions of this form of support.

References

Adichie CN (2009) The American Embassy. In: Adichie CN (ed) The thing around your neck. Harper Collins Publishers, London
American Psychiatric Association (2000) Diagnostic and statistical manual of mental disorders. American Psychiatric Association, Washington, DC
Baker R (2010) Understanding trauma: how to overcome post-traumatic stress. Lion Book, Oxford
Bernstein JS (2005) Living in the borderland: the evolution of consciousness and the challenge of healing trauma. Routledge, New York
Briere JN, Scott C (2015) Principles of trauma therapy: a guide to symptoms, evaluation, and treatment. Sage Publications Inc, California
Cardozo B (1931) Law and literature and other essays and addresses. Harcourt Brace and Company, New York
Cougle JR, Kilpatrick DG, Resnick H (2012) Defining traumatic events: research findings and controversies. In: Beck JG, Sloan DM (eds) The Oxford handbook of traumatic stress disorders. Oxford University Press, Oxford
Edkins J (2003) Trauma and the memory of politics. Cambridge University Press, Cambridge
Edney R (2004) Literary concepts and the plea in mitigation. Deakin Law Rev 9(1):183–195
Gyulai G, Kagan M, Herlihy J, Turner S, Hárdi L, Udvarhelyi ET (2013) Credibility assessment in asylum procedures – a multidisciplinary training manual. Hungarian Helsinki Committee, Budapest
Garland C (1998) Thinking about trauma. In: Garland C (ed) Understanding trauma: a psychoanalytical approach. Routledge, New York
Harms L (2015) Understanding trauma and resilience. Palgrave Macmillan, New York
Hathaway JC, Foster M (2014) The law of refugee status. Cambridge University Press, Cambridge
Hick T (2003) Post traumatic stress disorder and the law. http://dissertation.com/books/158112208X. Retrieved May 2019
Kälin W (1986) Troubled communication: cross-cultural misunderstandings in the asylum-hearing. Int Migration Rev 20(2):230–241
van der Kolk BA (1987) Psychological trauma. American Psychiatric Publishing Inc, Washington, DC
Krippner S, Pitchford DB, Davies J (2012) Post-traumatic stress disorder. Greenwood Press, California
Maček I (2014) Engaging violence: trauma, memory and representation. Routledge, New York
McDonald D (2014) Credibility assessment in refugee status determination. National Law School of India Rev 26(2):115–126
Organization of African Unity (OAU) (1969) Convention governing the specific aspects of refugee problems in Africa
Oxford Dictionaries (n.d.) Credibility. https://en.oxforddictionaries.com/definition/credibility. Retrieved May 2019
Pineles SL, Mostoufi SM, Ready CB, Street AE, Griffin MG, Resick PA (2011) Trauma reactivity, avoidant coping, and PTSD symptoms: a moderating relationship? J Abnorm Psychol 120(1):240–246. https://doi.org/10.1037/a0022123
Posner R (1986) Law and literature: a relation reargued. Va Law Rev 72(8):1351–1392
Bangkok Principles on the Status and Treatment of Refugees (1966)
Renner W, Salem I (2009) Post-traumatic stress in asylum seekers and refugees from Chechnya, Afghanistan and West Africa: gender differences in symptomatology and coping. Int J Soc Psychiatry 55(2):99–108. https://doi.org/10.1177/0020764008092341
Scher CD, McCreary DR, Asmundson GJG, Resick PA (2008) The structure of post-traumatic stress disorder symptoms in three female trauma samples: a comparison of interview and self-report measures. J Anxiety Disord 22(7):1137–1145. https://doi.org/10.1016/j.janxdis.2007.11.012. Retrieved May 2019

Schultz T, Ost F (2018) Shakespearean legal thought in international dispute settlement. J Int Dispute Settlement 9(1):1–27
Slobodin O, Ghane S, De Jong JTVM (2018) Developing a culturally sensitive mental health intervention for asylum seekers in the Netherlands: a pilot study. Intervention 16(2):88–94
South African Depression and Anxiety Group (2006) Posts-traumatic stress disorder: treatment and referral guide (Compiled by the Scientific and Advisory Board Members of the South African Depression and Anxiety Group, and reviewed by the MRC Research Unit on Anxiety and Stress Disorders). http://www.sadag.org/images/brochures/PTSD%20Brochure.pdf. Retrieved May 2019
Substance Abuse and Mental Health Services Administration (2014) A treatment improvement protocol: trauma-informed care in behavioural health services. Substance Abuse and Mental Health Services, Maryland
Tantoush v Refugee Appeal Board (2007) ZAGPHC 191
Uffelman J (2008) Hamlet was a law student: a "dramatic" look at emotion's effect on analogical reasoning. Georgetown Law J 96(5):1725–1729
United Nations Declaration on Territorial Asylum, UN Doc A/6716 (1967)
United Nations High Commissioner for Refugees (1998) Note on burden and standard of proof in refugee claim (16 December 1998)
United Nations High Commissioner for Refugees (2011) Handbook and guidelines on procedures and criteria for determining refugee status under the 1951 convention and the 1967 protocol relating to the status of refugees (December 2011)
United Nations Convention relating to the Status of Refugees 189 U.N.T.S 137
Universal Declaration of Human Rights, UN Doc A/810 (1948)
Weaver HN (2016) Between a rock and a hard place: a trauma-informed approach to documenting the traumatic experiences of Tamil refugees. J Hum Rights Soc Work 1:120–130. https://doi.org/10.1007/s41134-016-0013-0. Retrieved May 2019
White JB (1973) The legal imagination: studies in the nature of legal thought and expression. Little Brown and Co, Boston
Wigmore JH (1922) A list of one hundred legal novels. Illinois Law Rev 17:26–41

Chapter 5
Photojournalism and Human Rights in Africa: Stories from the Field

Mohammed Elshamy

Abstract In this chapter, the research attempts to briefly demonstrate the impact and effectiveness of photojournalism by describing the lived experience and surrounding cultural, historical, and political contexts of certain events that took place in several African countries, including Sierra Leone, and Liberia. In Sierra Leone and Liberia, through the lived experience as a photojournalist and through in-depth research and analysis, I come to the conclusion in this work that while photojournalism can prove useful in promoting immediate impact, whether in the form of donations or government action (albeit minimal), it may not always impact or provoke the government's or the international community's seeking of justice. Regardless, photojournalism in Africa is essential in providing an agenda and laying a framework to seek justice for human rights abuses and promote progress. Photojournalism is a crucial player in witnessing history in Africa, and it functions as a key player in pushing forward human rights issues. In this chapter, I focus on the role of photojournalism in highlighting the Ebola situation in Sierra Leone and Liberia, relaying personal experience as a photojournalist in Africa.

Keywords Africa · Ebola · Sierra Leone · Liberia · Disease · Wear Africa · Photojournalism · Human right · Impact · Accountability

1 Introduction

Africa is a massive continent with various regions. North Africa differs dramatically from West or East Africa, Central or Southern Africa. Western media does not often correctly and fairly cover the continent and rarely does it justice in reporting.

M. Elshamy (✉)
Independent documentary photographer, New York, USA

R. Adeola et al. (eds.), *The Art of Human Rights*, Arts, Research, Innovation and Society, https://doi.org/10.1007/978-3-030-30102-6_5

Africa is made up of 55 countries, with more than 500 different languages and hundreds of other cultures, tribes and subcultures. Each subcontinental region and even each country has its unique political, social and economic circumstances that make press coverage far from an easy job, especially given that autocratic political regimes still govern many African countries. This political atmosphere makes the task of any photojournalist not just challenging, but sometimes life-threatening. Every country has its own unique story and history.

In this chapter, I attempt to briefly demonstrate the impact and effectiveness of photojournalism by describing the lived experience and surrounding cultural, historical, and political contexts of certain events that took place in several African countries, including Sierra Leone and Liberia. In Sierra Leone and Liberia, through the lived experience as a photojournalist myself and through in-depth research and analysis, I come to the conclusion in this work that while photojournalism can prove useful in promoting immediate impact—whether in the form of donations or government action (albeit minimal)—it may not always impact or provoke justice from the government or international community. Regardless, photojournalism in Africa is essential in providing an agenda and laying a framework to seek justice for human rights abuses and promote progress. Photojournalism is a key player in witnessing history in Africa, and it functions as a key player in pushing forward human rights. In this chapter, I focus on two countries I have worked in, namely Sierra Leone and Liberia, relaying personal experience as a photojournalist across the African continent.

Photojournalism could easily be debated as the toughest platforms of photography for its long-lasting if not permanent mental health effects and death risk. Unlike other forms of photography, without degrading the importance of other forms of photography, photojournalism is known to have physical and psychological costs (Feinstein 2017). According to the prominent media watchdog, the Committee to Protect Journalists, “1955 journalists and media workers have been killed between 1992 and 2018 with motive confirmed or unconfirmed” (The Committee to Protect Journalists 2018).

Photojournalists are the most exposed to risks-of-life risks and are also sometimes asked to “work for no pay” or for the mere compensation of “exposure” (Chandler 2017; Sanschagrin 2010). Photojournalism in Africa can easily come off as a complex industry. Journalism in Africa still faces obstacles and major crackdowns including the shutdown of TV stations, arrests of photographers, and confiscation of media equipment, in addition to harassment, intimidation, and other forms of censorship or forced self-censorship (Clarke and Duggan 2018; The United Nations Human Rights Council Working Group on Arbitrary Detention 2016; Al Jazeera camera equipment seized 2011).

Even lack of resources can pose as a form of censorship and limit the ability of African jouranlists to perform their duties. Simon Allison, an African journalist, testified to this in 2013, arguing that a “shortage of money and skills leaves local reporters struggling to compete with big western media outlets” (Allison 2013). An unsolicited and unaddressed disadvantage is that native African journalists are seeking to do in-depth, risky, and necessary work must either overcome or bear with as they work.

Today, the coverage of Africa in Western media is filled with images of violent conflict and chaos, devoid of any context or nuance (Somalia's capital Mogadishu hit by a huge explosion, BBC, 2018). The result is an inaccurate depiction of events in one of the most critical regions in the world. We hear more stories of devastation in Africa as opposed to stories of growing economies or democratic transitions.

As a national of Egypt—a country that neglects the art form that sheds light on the injustices happening around the world—I did not enjoy the freedom of pursuing my passion of photojournalism to my fullest potential for fear of incarceration. On a personal level, I have witnessed first-hand the dangers of misrepresentation and innacurate reporting during times of conflict in my country. During the 2011 revolution, when millions took to the street to protest the 30-year autocrat Hosni Mubarak, Egyptian state television broadcasted videos showing Egypt's streets virtually empty. The pro-Mubarak media denounced the 2011 protesters as people under foreign influence or operating on behalf of foreign entities (spies, basically) (Zayed and Hammond 2011). When, in fact, they were Egyptian thriving for democracy.

Growing up in times of turmoil, I realised that most media platforms were biased. Although understanding this as an inevitable fact, I did not want to document my narrative—instead, I wanted to show the very complicated situations that get lost in single narrative sound bites. Living in the age of falsified stories and conflict, I realised that there is a need for more photojournalists that can be the difference in reflecting the human experience and promoting human rights in these conflict zones.

As photojournalists, we are always making choices. We have to choose whether to label an event a "conflict" or "war" or whether to label a group of people "protesters" or "rioters." We have to decide which photos to take, who and what is included in the frame, and who never appears. The exposure I received working throughout Africa has heightened my sense of appreciation for the importance of photojournalism and the promotion of human rights as a core value in conflict reporting. I wanted to dedicate time to advancing photojournalism across Africa. I have covered major global stories such as the Ebola outbreak in West Africa; the military coup in Egypt; civil war in South Sudan; the humanitarian crisis in Darfur; Boko Haram extremism in northern Nigeria; the refugee crisis in Europe and most recently, the presidential elections in the United States of America and the growing xenophobia and immigration crisis.

As I show in this chapter, I am confident that despite the high numbers of human rights abuses taking place in Africa, and the comparative lack of awareness of them, human rights situation can improve with photojournalists witnessing the events.

Photojournalism is a tool, and it could be the strongest and most useful in times of turmoil. Photojournalism itself documents human rights abuses across Africa and promotes it in some cases. Nevertheless, photojournalism will only reach its full potential of impact when there is a political and social justice atmosphere that holds those who violate human rights accountable, as it compels the African Union and other Western states to face blatant, undeniable abuses perpetrated by military coups or those who commit war crimes. Photojournalism robs decision and policy makers from ignorance and forces them into accountability—there is no denying suffering when it is caught on camera.

In catching, for example, the starvation in Darfur, Sudan, now former President Omar al Bashir has a target on him that even other world leaders have a responsibility to acknowledge. When traveling to South Africa—albeit with the failure of sending him to the ICC—former President al Bashir was under scrutiny as much as the South African government to hold him accountable for crimes the whole world knows of mainly in part to media and more specifically, visual media and photojournalism.

Nathan Nunn, an economics professor, in his study of the effect of Africa's slave trade on subsequent economic development, was unequivocal in his assessment: "The African countries that are the poorest today are the ones from which the most slaves were taken" (Nunn 2008).

Photography reveals a truth that is so raw that it brings a new meaning to the phrase: "The power of visual imagery is well known, enshrined in such familiar sayings as "seeing is believing" and "a picture is worth a thousand words" (Slovic, Västfjäll, Erlandsson and Gregory 2017). Paul Slovic, Daniel Västfjäll, Arvid Erlandsson, and Robin Gregory reveal during their study published in Proceedings of the National Academy of Sciences that: "Iconic photos stir our emotions and transform our perspectives about life and the world in which we live" (Slovic, Västfjäll, Erlandsson and Gregory 2017).

In the history of Africa, human rights violations seem never to have stopped. Moreover, with the silence of leadership, photojournalism is the only witness to these violations that shall not die despite the time. I believe that it is by perfecting this method of truth-telling, it will be possible to change the dire circumstances that plague the world today.

Below, I outline cases in which photojournalism plays vital roles in advancing human rights. The two countries explored in this chapter are, as I have mentioned above, drawn out from my experience as a photojournalist, i.e. directly as an eye-witness.

2 Ebola

In the spring of 2014, a few reports emerged of suspected cases of the Ebola virus in Guinea (Center for Disease Control 2018). The Ebola virus causes an acute, serious illness which is often fatal if untreated. Ebola virus disease (EVD) first appeared in 1976 in two simultaneous outbreaks, one in what is now, Nzara, South Sudan, and the other in Yambuku, Democratic Republic of Congo. The latter occurred in a village near the Ebola River, from which the disease takes its name.

Ebola is a severe, often fatal illness, with a death rate of up to 90%, and is a member of the filovirus family that started spreading in an area that lacked developed medical infrastructure (World Health Organization 2017). At the time, there was no foreseeable cure for the disease—nor has there since been—and neither the

Fig. 5.1 Kenema, Sierra Leone—Volunteers pick up corpses of Ebola virus victims that died overnight due to the contagious virus. (Photo on August 24, 2014)

government response nor the international community's intervention was enough to curb the rising death tolls (Belluz 2014). In July of 2014, I pitched traveling to Sierra Leone to my editor for documenting the Ebola epidemic. The fear of an invisible sickness that can take the life of anyone that comes near it drove many reporters away. I was among the few that were dedicated to sharing the stories of those affected in order to sharing the truth about this region to the world (Belluz 2014).

Being able to live through these terrible times led me to appreciate photography and journalism. Photography was used as a medium to warn people across the Ebola-hit countries to be aware of the symptoms of Ebola. It would be difficult to explain with words how to take precautions or to explain to volunteers how to wear their protective gear. Diseases have hit Africans in the past such as Pneumonia, Malaria and HIV/AIDS that have left millions dead (Answers Africa n.d.). Had there been a lack of photojournalism documenting the case of Ebola, we would have only heard of the death tolls without any visual proof (Fig. 5.1).

Through photojournalism, visual representations of the casualties from the Ebola virus was useful in prompting an international response from aid groups and health organisations to countries in West Africa that were plagued with the disease (Ebola outbreak: the UK sending 750 troops to Sierra Leone 2014).

The Ebola outbreak in West Africa was first reported in March 2014, and rapidly became the deadliest occurrence of the disease since its discovery in 1976. According to the US National Library of Medicine at the National Institutes of Health, "[s]ince the first outbreak 40 years ago, EVD outbreaks have been rare, small and localized," (Kaner and Schaack 2016).

Health workers were at risk, so were photojournalists. "Healthcare workers are especially at risk for exposure to Ebola because they are more likely to come into contact with contaminated bodily fluids" (Kaner and Schaack 2016). Photojournalists such as myself were as close as health workers and were therefore, equally at close risk of infection (Weiss 2014). Correspondents were afraid to risk their lives in order to report this epidemic. At the time, one was lucky not to get infected, and I was one of the lucky ones. However, some journalists lost their lives. Antwi-Boasiako notes that:

> In Guinea, for instance, three journalists who fell prey to the mistrust and conspiracy theories of the people were killed and had their bodies dumped in sewage in a village while covering an Ebola health campaign. The three journalists were; Facely Camara, a journalist with Radio Liberte FM at Nzerekore near Womey and Molou Cherif, and his technician colleague, both of whom worked at community radio station also at Nzerekore. In Sierra Leone, it became apparent that some journalists who chose to be critical of the Sierra Leone government's response to the Ebola outbreak faced some harassment from the government (Antwi-Boasiako 2017).

In another case, a cameraman got infected while covering the virus, which highlights the directness and severity of the risk journalists were exposed to for merely covering a disease outbreak as dangerous as Ebola (NBC News Freelancer in Africa Diagnosed with Ebola 2014).

Reporting at the time accounted for at least 11,315 deaths from the disease in six countries: Liberia, Guinea, Sierra Leone, Nigeria, the US, and Mali (Ebola: Mapping the outbreak 2016). Countries labelled Guinea, Liberia, and Sierra Leone as infected countries. There were health risks and barred entry for citizens passing through them, which permanently banned efforts to alleviate the outbreak and provide assistance. The disease formed an unofficial no-entry zone into the region, with major airlines halting flights in and out despite the World Health Organization (WHO) advising against imposing travel restrictions (Roberts 2014).

Doctors Without Borders, or Médecins Sans Frontières (MSF) and the World Health Organization (WHO) were the leading relief providers for those suffering. Notably, it was through their services as well that I was able to cover burials, quarantine centers, and receive access to their patients (Fig. 5.2).

The WHO warned in October 2014 that cancelling more flights to the affected countries: Guinea, Liberia, and Sierra Leone, would increase the affected countries' isolation (Nuzzo, Cicero, Waldhorn and Inglesby 2014). Although the deadly nature of Ebola scared off most photojournalists. As a young African photographer, I felt a sense of obligation to cover this disease. Upon arriving in a remote village ravaged by Ebola, I learned that some doctors refused to travel to Sierra Leone to care for ailing patients despite offers of an abundant amount of money and compensation. I felt an active ethical obligation to draw attention to the lives of the local health volunteers who risked their lives for little to no pay. I wanted to combat this stigma and honour the life of Doctor Sheikh Umar Khan, one of Africa's prominent doctors and a national hero in Sierra Leone who died from Ebola (Huggler 2014).

> "I am afraid for my life, I must say, because I cherish my life," Dr Khan told reporters in June, before he contracted the disease.

Yet, Dr Khan paid the ultimate price by losing his life, hoping to contain a disease that was destroying his country (Huggler 2014).

Fig. 5.2 Monrovia, Liberia—Liberian Red Cross health worker sanitizes body of Mambodou Aliyu a 35-year-old suspected Ebola victim from West Point slum in Monrovia. (Photo on October 15, 2014)

Covering Ebola was not a usual assingment for me. It was a story I was personally committed to as I pushed to the back of my mind that hundreds of people were losing their lives due to this virus. I reached out to health organizations to find out how to get myself ready for the invisible disease, and I learned that despite not finding a cure for it, the only way was to prepare myself was with the right protective gear and equipment that I received. While covering conflicts in South Sudan and Northern Nigeria, I was aware I needed a flak jacket, but for Ebola, it was entirely unknown how protection looked like and what I should look for. I fastidiously followed the instructions I received from MSF, knowing full well that nothing could wholly guarantee my protection from contracting the disease. I knew this was a risky undertaking, but if I did not cover this, few others would or even could. Access to infected countries was tricky, and the appeal to even try was low.

The travel warnings and return bans placed on transit going through these countries not only isolate those who did not contract the disease, but they also limited tremendously foreign press' free movements and adequate coverage of the outbreak. Without visuals, Ebola could have quickly become a mysterious and unseen virus. The victims would have been faceless numbers as international media has had a track record of not giving proper coverage to crises that occur in our continent. Proper, sophisticated, and transparent media coverage is rare when highlighting the loss of lives in Africa, highlighting even further the need for serious reporting. Photojournalism during the Ebola outbreak proved as the living proof of death, corpses; it showed countries in curfews and the lockdowns of restaurants and schools. In essence, it captured the shutdown of civilian daily life during the Ebola

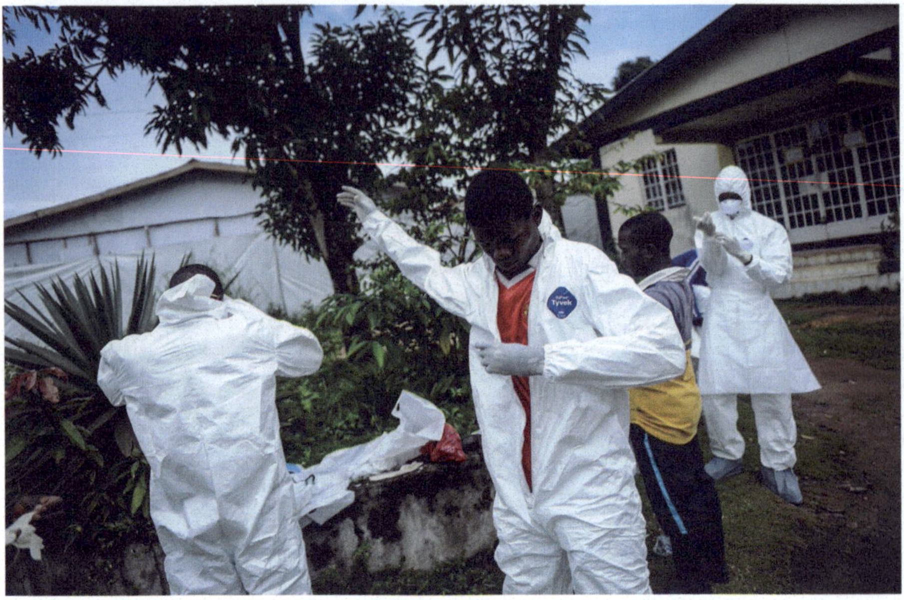

Fig. 5.3 Kenema, Sierra Leone— Amadou Diallou dresses up before heading to bury Ebola victims at Kptema cemetery in Kenema, Sierra Leone. (Photo on August 31, 2014)

outbreak. Without photojournalism, we would have only heard of Ebola as headlines and numbers. But the power of photojournalism and the photos that came out of the Ebola crisis showed the toll of the outbreak, the relatability, and led the international community to act as fast as it could.

Despite the thousands of lives claimed, I believe the response yielded did indeed help curb the disease from spreading across the entire continent. This would have been a total nightmare for the continent which is already hit by civil wars, military coups, malnutrition and poverty.

While much of the world was primarily focused on their borders, shutting down their airports and airlines from nations hit in West Africa, a group of fearless volunteers ventured into their neighborhoods to help cure the infected and bury the dead. Amadou Diallou, a young 20-year-old volunteer and a fanatic football enthusiast, prepared bodies for burials and dug their graves (Fig. 5.3).

Between burials, Mr. Diallou spoke to me at length about our shared passion for football. Despite being surrounded by the shadow of death, he was optimistic about the disease ending and envisioned fulfilling his dream of becoming a professional football player.

These volunteers like Mr. Diallou, who were barely paid anything for their brave work, had their lives and dreams just like any other person—they were not robots nor should they be part of a forgotten narrative. Only serious photojournalism looking to capture multiple, nuanced facets of the outbreak would show that they had families, feelings and should not be neglected. People like him were combating a stigma that caused chaos worldwide. Photojournalism was the medium through which Mr. Diallou was able to tell his story to the world. Photojournalists were not only documenting

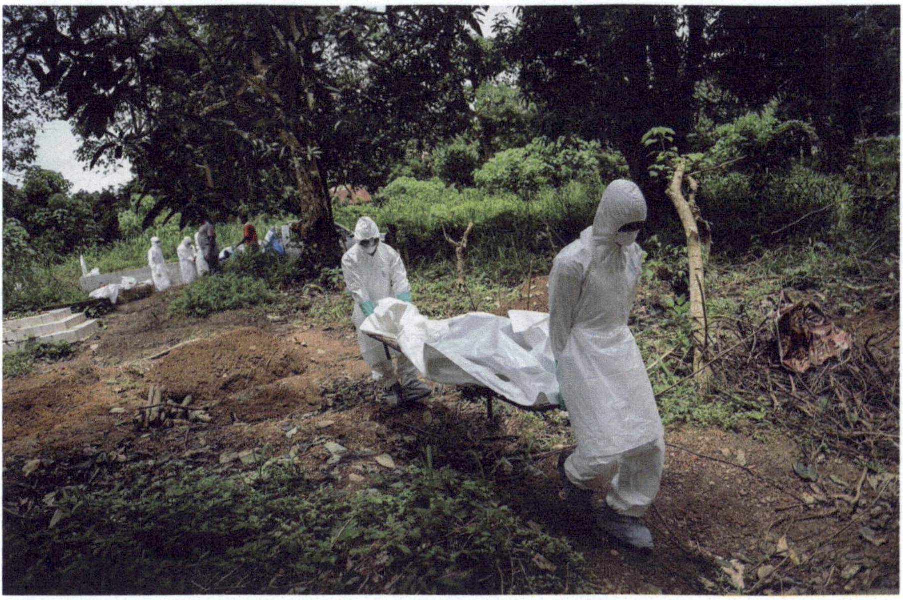

Fig. 5.4 Kenema, Sierra Leone-Health workers carry a corpse of an Ebola victim at Kptema cemetery. (Photo on August 31, 2014)

those who were affected by diseases, but they also documented the lives surrounding the conflict: the volunteers, doctors, journalists, and more than risked their lives to make a change in the world. Behind every victim to the disease was a story left untold.

As some cases were successfully treated, I observed the stigmatisation of survivors due to misinformation. These survivors would experience devastating marginalisation even though they were given certificates indicating they were virus-free. These survivors were starting a new life. To them, surviving death was like being newly born, going from counting days to a new life. Some survivors still faced isolation from their communities and families. However, as some international agencies and photojournalists (seeking to highlight life post-Ebola) interacted with some of these survivors, their immediate families became more accepting and convinced that since the media had interacted with them, then they are safe to be around once again (Fig. 5.4).

People with whom I interacted with were dying daily, and the number of fatalities was rising with no sign of a cure. Daily burials, school closures and the limited health services were being stretched to the brink. These further strained life for citizens of Sierra Leone and Liberia where essential family structures were falling apart in front of my eyes. Donations made to fight the outbreak were solicited wholly on awareness of the severity of the Ebola outbreak. This awareness could have only been gained through international attention, which was aided by photojournalism. A study by Slovic, Västfjäll and Erlandsson underscore the powerful imagery of photojournalism emphasising that "a single photo of a single individual could stir the emotions and arouse public concern more powerfully than statistical reports of body counts" (Slovic, Västfjäll, Erlandsson and Gregory 2017).

Fig. 5.5 Kenama, Sierra Leone—Ebola survivor Rigiatu Kamara poses for a portrait after her release from the hospital in her room. (August 31, 2014)

Fig. 5.6 Cairo, Egypt—A supporter of ousted president Mohammed Morsi wears the Egyptian flag as protection during clashes between pro-Morsi and police forces on the streets of El Zeitun neighborhood near the Qubba presidential palace. (Photo on December 6, 2013)

Fig. 5.7 Bor, South Sudan—People have to leave their homes without enough supplies, due to the ongoing clashes between security forces and opposition groups of Riek Machar. (Photo on February 27, 2014)

I have personally seen how a portrait of a 38-year-old Ebola survivor (Rigiatu Kamara), evoked emotional reactions about where she lived, where she eats, and, visually—the hardships she faced.

Donors respond strongly to photos. Intense photos could result in higher donations to an organization. As my photos of the Ebola crisis were being distributed, many people reached out to me asking for more information on how they can donate. When people donate and get involved, human rights are promoted, and action is taken to alleviate suffering. Photojournalism has the power to start movements of humanitarian assistance. Those who were inspired by Fig. 5.5 to donate to Rigiatu Kamara may not have known her, but that photo was the connection between her and people with resources (Slovic, Västfjäll, Erlandsson and Gregory 2017). The donations sent to Rigiatu Kamara and her family made a difference for her given that she struggled to establish a new life after been discharged from an Ebola ward. Photojournalism can ultimately pave the way towards human rights realisation by the basic notion of bringing human rights issues to light.

3 Conclusion

Photojournalism plays an essential role in the furtherance of human rights. In this chapter, I have emphasised the significance of photojournalism in promoting human rights by presenting visual evidence on vital issues. In this chapter, I highlighted the impact of photojournalism in drawing attention to the Ebola epidemic, which I covered in Sierra Leone and Liberia. Photojournalism helped influence governments in West Africa and further afield to take steps to curb the infection. While photojournalism can assist in promoting human rights by drawing attention to important issues, it can also place journalists at risk, notably in situations where the human rights issues they spotlight are in repressive societies. As such, independent and free press must be guaranteed. I hope in writing this chapter that photojournalism can assist in furthering a better future for Africa, a continent I belong to and to which I dedicate my efforts, for the sake of perfecting its photojournalism industry (Figs. 5.6 and 5.7).

References

Al Jazeera. (2011) Al Jazeera camera equipment seized. https://www.aljazeera.com/news/middleeast/2011/01/2011131123648291703.html. Accessed 4 Sept 2018

Allison S (2013) African journalism is being stifled by a lack of resources. The Guardian. https://www.theguardian.com/world/2013/mar/01/african-journalism-stifled-lack-resources. Accessed 1 Oct 2018

BBC (2018) Somalia's capital Mogadishu hit by huge explosion. BBC. https://www.bbc.com/news/world-africa-45387620. Accessed 4 Oct 2018

Chandler D (2017) All work and no pay: creative industries freelancers are exploited. The Guardian. https://www.theguardian.com/small-business-network/2017/may/18/all-work-andno-pay-creativeindustries-freelancers-are-exploited. Accessed 14 Oct 2018

Clarke H, Duggan B (2018) Kenya TV stations shutdown enters 5th day as government defies court order. CNN. https://edition.cnn.com/2018/02/03/africa/kenya-tv-stationsshutdown/index.html. Accessed 2 Oct 2018

Feinstein A (2017) War photography: the physical and psychological costs. J Human Rehab, Emory University. https://owl.purdue.edu/owl/research_and_citation/using_research/citation_style_chart.html. Accessed 5 Oct 2018

Nunn N (2008) The long term effects of Africa's slave trades. Q J Econ 123(1):139–176. https://inequality.stanford.edu/sites/default/files/media/_media/pdf/Reference%20Media/Nunn_2008_Development%20Economics.pdf. Accessed 5 Oct 2018

Sanschagrin G (2010) 6 real-life stories where photographers were expected to work for free. Photoshelter (blog). https://blog.photoshelter.com/2010/09/6-reallife-stories-where-photographers-were-expect/

Slovic P, Västfjäll D, Erlandsson A, Gregory R (2017) Iconic photographs and the ebb and flow of empathic response to humanitarian disasters. Proc Natl Acad Sci U S A 114(4):640–644; http://www.pnas.org/content/114/4/640.full. Accessed 15 Oct 2018

The Committee to Protect Journalists (2018) 1953 Journalists and Media Workers Killed. The Committee to Protect Journalists. https://cpj.org/data/killed/?status=Killed&start_year=1992&end_year=2020&group_by=year. Accessed 4 Oct 2018

United Nations Human Rights Council Working Group on Arbitrary Detention (2016). Opinion No. 41/2016 concerning Mahmoud Abdel Shakour Abou Zeid Attitallah (Egypt). https://www.ohchr.org/Documents/Issues/Detention/Opinions/Session76/41-2016.pdf. Accessed 29 Sept 2018

Zayed D, Hammond A (2011) Egypt state media run to catch up with revolution. Reuters. https://www.reuters.com/article/idINIndia-54832020110211 Accessed 22 Dec 2018

Chapter 6
Soap Operas and Human Rights in Africa: African Feminist and Human Rights Perspective on the Representation of Black Women in the Media

Reshoketswe Mapokgole

Abstract Negative depictions of women in television shows contribute to the widespread cultural stereotyping of women. This chapter questions how black women are represented in SABC television shows—*Skeem Saam* on SABC 1, *Muvhango* SABC 2 and *Isidingo* on SABC 3. The chapter uses content analysis and the Bechdel test, along with African feminist theory as tools to examine black women's representations. This chapter argues that how black women are showcased fails to meet the obligations set out in the Convention on the Elimination of Discriminataion Against Women (CEDAW) and Protocol to the African Charter on Human and Peoples' Rights on the Rights of Women in Africa (African Women's Protocol). Additionally as African feminist theory illustrates, the raceless and often a historical depiction of black women on these shows renders them invisible. The goal of this chapter is to add to the growing epistemology of African feminism and representations of black women in the media.

Keywords African feminist theory · Bechdel test · Intersectionality · Black women · Television shows · Soap Operas

1 Introduction

> The whole process of watching television has social significance. Television provides us with the pictures of the world, of our world, and the knowledge that most of these pictures are fictional does not immunize us from believing in them. The beliefs we form become part of the context within which we understand who we are. To understand prime-time television, then, is to understand an important part of the way we view the world and ourselves (Jhally and Lewis 1992).

R. Mapokgole (✉)
Faculty of Law, Centre for Human Rights, University of Pretoria, Pretoria, South Africa

R. Adeola et al. (eds.), *The Art of Human Rights*, Arts, Research, Innovation and Society, https://doi.org/10.1007/978-3-030-30102-6_6

For centuries stories have invented new profiles for what the woman is, reproducing new meanings of gender, and sometimes reinforcing old stereotypes. Stories are important for societies, they provide places for audiences, viewers and readers to find themselves and be able to imagine new possibilities for their lives. In the essay, 'Restaging the universal- hegemony and the limits of formalism', Judith Butler contends that there are different spaces and mediums in which power is remade, and that these spaces influence the manner in which the social world is made (Butler 2000). Media is one of the key spaces in which the dominance of particular groups over others is performed and reinforced.

bell hooks in her book from *Reel to Real: race, class and sex at the movies*, observes that audiences often discuss how 'real' a movie or a television show is (hooks 2009). Indicating a failure to understand that films provide audiences with the 'reimagined or reinvented versions of the real' (hooks 2009). This, the assumption that what is portrayed is real, is indicative of the power of film; echoing Njabulo Ndebele's sentiments that often what matters is what is seen; and that 'thinking comes secondary' (Ndebele 1986). It is clear that audiences are deeply affected by what they see on television; as such it is necessary to pay attention to television shows and the realities they present.

The Protocol to the African Charter on Human and Peoples' Rights on the Rights of Women in Africa (the African Women's Protocol 2005) and the United Nations' Convention on the Elimination of All forms of Discrimination Against Women (CEDAW) require states to fairly represent women in the media. Both human rights instruments view representations of women in the media as vital to eradicating discrimination against women. Article 12 (1) (b) of the Protocol to the African Charter on Human and Peoples' Rights on the Rights of Women in Africa (African Women's Protocol 2005) obligates states to eliminate stereotypical portrayals of women in the media. While CEDAW does not explicitly mention the media, the Committee on the Elimination of Discrimination Against Women (the Committee) has over the years, through concluding observations, recommended that states should abstain from using gender stereotypical projections of women in the media (CEDAW Committee 2009).

Almost half of South Africa tunes in everyday to watch some of the popular shows on the South African Broadcasting Corporation (SABC) (McKane 2018). The most watched television shows are *Generations—The Legacy* at nine million viewers, *Muvhango* with five and half million and *Skeem-Saam* with eight million viewers (McKane 2018). This chapter investigates how SABC television shows represent black women and the impact the representations have on gender discrimination in the country. For this chapter, five consecutive episodes from each television program were watched on the digital video streaming service YouTube, in October 2018.

The SABC is a focus of this chapter because it has the highest audiences across all other broadcasting networks in South Africa (McKane 2018). The television shows selected for analysis are the most watched, with the highest ranking in viewers. Moreover, as a public broadcaster under the Broadcasting Act, the SABC has responsibility under the Broadcasting Act to ensure the material showcased on their channels promote gender equality (South African Broadcasting Act 1999).

The violent lived experiences of black women in South Africa make it urgent that analysis is made on how they are represented in the media. The lives of many black women are characterised by violence and poverty, consequences of apartheid which can still be seen today. (Armstrong 1994). Black women are among one of the most disadvantaged groups in the country and, as a result of their gender and race, are even more vulnerable to economic and social violence.

The intersecting forms of identities—gender, class, and race—that black women hold, shape their experiences of the world. African feminist scholar, Ogundipe Leslie characterises the African women 'as those who carry six mountain on their backs' (Gqola 2001). The six mountains metaphorically refer to the different oppressions black women live under. Thus, an African feminist lens, which considers class, race and gender, is fit to analyse the portrayals of women on these shows.

Examination of the black female characters is conducted through content analysis methodology, using the Bechdel Test and African feminist theory as analytical tools. The Bechdel Test analyses the dialogues of the female characters, while African feminist theory assesses women's representation on agency, and the intersection of gender and race. It is resolved through the Bechdel test and African feminist, that the representations of black women are stereotypical, and therefore, reinforce gender stereotypes and gender discrimination in South Africa.

2 Understanding African Feminist Theory

Black women in South Africa are often referred to as the group that bears the 'triple yoke' of oppression, with their race, class and gender (Nolde 1991). This belonging to different social categories has shaped and continues to shape the way black women experience the world. Often, it is this belonging that makes severe their slow progression to realizing their human rights. Therefore, when considering how black women are represented in the media, the theory one uses should acknowledge the intersecting identities black women in South Africa hold.

One of the leading questions for the African feminist is on who the African woman is, and how she is produced in visual and literary texts, both in academic and popular culture (Mekgwe 2006). African feminism is shaped by both anticolonial and feminist discourse, a merge of ideas which address the two leading systems—colonialism and patriarchy—that have defined, and continue to define African women's experiences (Mekgwe 2006). Patriarchy is a socio-political and economic system that bestows men to be dominant against the weaker sex, females and also allows men to use violence to uphold the dominance (hooks 2004). Thus, central to African feminism is in addressing colonially reinforced patriarchy and the manner in which it has affected and continues to affect African women's lives, particularly black women.

As a movement and discourse that rises out of struggle, African feminism seeks to counter systems that not only oppressed African women but also all Africans. This is so because colonialism, which reinforced racism, was a system that affected not only African men, but also African women (Moloswanke 1996). Hence, African feminism, firstly, as an anti-colonial movement, is one that seeks liberation of all African people. Nigerian scholar and feminist, Chieolozona Eze is of the belief that African feminists should not concern themselves with anti-colonial discourse (Eze 2006). She asks 'why should African women claim to wage war against imperialism while the African man never see her as his equal?' (Eze 2006). However, what she fails to account for is that imperialism is not a system that only affects men. In Africa, colonial violence reinforced patriarchal norms, rendered women children, and ripped them of their freedom (Moloswanke 1996). Thus, African feminism's concern with eradicating the legacy of colonialism is not an effort to help only men as Eze contends, but rather to also help women and all groups affected by it.

In the 1970s African women's writing was born out of the need to dispel and respond to misrepresentations of African women in African literature (Boswell 2010). Due to the image of Africa as the 'dark continent', African writers—predominantly male writers—engaged in literature that curated images of Africa where men and women lived harmoniously together (Petersen 1999). Understandably, these writers wanted to showcase African communities which opposed notions of barbarism and one of the consequences was failing to critique the violences women lived under. According to Petersen, this depiction of women living harmoniously was not truthful and can also be seen in one of the revered African books, *Things Fall Apart* (Petersen 1999). For her, Achebe makes light of violence against women because when Okwonkwo, the protagonist, beats his wife, he is punished not because of the crime he has committed against the woman but rather because it was during the week of peace (Petersen 1999). The women in *Things Fall Apart*, like in many African literary texts of the 1960s and 1970s, never complain yet they live under harsh conditions (Petersen 1999). This representation of women, who are simply happy with oppression, is one of the false ideas African women's writing sought to address.

The question that drives African feminist theory, on how African women are produced is an essential part of this study. By addressing the representations of black women on SABC, this chapter seeks to analyse how black women are produced in South African visual texts.

Lugones argues that black women are rendered invisible when they are not seen as both gendered and racialised people. Crenshaw first identified the issue of intersectionality when African American women who brought cases to USA courts on discrimination based on both gender and race were dismissed (Crenshaw 1989). In the cases of *DeGranffeireid v General Motors* and *Moore v Hughes Helicopter*, black women's discrimination complains on the basis of their gender and race were dismissed. In the *DeGranffeireid v General Motors* black women complained that the layoffs that took place in the company after 1970 were only targeted at black women (Crenshaw 1989). In the *Moore v Hughes Helicopter*, Hughes Helicopter practised gender and race discrimination when they only promoted white women, white men and black men (Crenshaw 1989). For both cases, the courts refused to view the issues as matters of discrimination, asserting that it would mean creating a new class focused solely on the discrimination of black women (Crenshaw 1989).

In the courts' view, because both companies had not discriminated towards white women, it meant there was no gender discrimination, and because there was no discrimination on black men, it meant there was no race discrimination (Crenshaw 1989). Crenshaw contends then, that without the acknowledgement of intersectionality, black women's issues are only considered if they are either connected to those of black men, or white women (Crenshaw 1989). The requirement for black women to present as either only black or female is the erasure that takes place when the intersectionality of gender and race are not acknowledged.

Black women in South Africa experience oppression that is both gendered and racialised. Even the gender stereotypes associated with black women are often racialised, for example, the hyper-sexuality of black women. The caricatures of the black South African woman with exaggerated buttocks also are rooted in both sexualisation of the body and racism (Mail & Guardian 2014).

3 Bechdel Test

The Bechdel test is a quantitative formula that measures women's dialogue in films, television shows, video games and plays (O'Meara 2016). It originated from Alison Bechdel's comic *Dykes to watch out for* with a conversation between two characters on how to choose a film to watch (Bechdel 1986). A film can either pass or fail the Bechdel test. For the film to pass the test, it must include three things: at least two women whose names are known, who have at least one conversation, which is about something other than a man (O'Meara 2016). The test emerges out of the need to address the silencing of women in cinema, and the common media trope in which female characters in television programs only exist to push the male characters' stories. It has since been used by websites, bloggers and as popularly known, by Swedish cinema. In 2013, the Swedish cinema academy pledged to place a pass or fail of the Bechdel test next to a film's ratings (Selisker 2015).

While the test is useful for assessing agency and the roles women play in cinema, it is quite simplistic (O'Meara 2016). For instance, for a film to pass the test, even one conversation that is not about a man between two female characters is enough. This fails to consider how complex women's conversations can be, even those that involve men. As Ellis indicates, women can have conversations about other men that assert their agency (Ellis 2016). For example, when women talk to each other about men seeking guidance from one another it does not mean the women lack agency. Additionally, the test fails to acknowledge that there are different ways to communicate, even in film, such as through music and even silence (O'Meara 2016). Motsemme notes in 'The meanings in silence', that silence does not always constitute the absence of voice (Motsemme 2004). For Motsemme, 'in circumstances of violence, silence can assume presence and speak volumes' (Motsemme 2004). Thus, analysis of characters should involve more than simply addressing what they say to each other.

Given some of the limits of the Bechdel test, for this chapter, it is used alongside other content analysis methods, such as assessing what female characters discuss and discerning the patterns that emerge from the discussions (Wilkinson and Birmingham 2003). Together, these analyses enable a full and complex assessment of the female characters.

4 Content Analysis and Bechdel Test

4.1 Skeem Saam

Skeem Saam is a SABC 1 educational television program. Of the three shows assessed, it is the only one that is sponsored by the South African department of education. The show, created by Winnie Serite is centred on young South Africans—in and out of school—and the different challenges they face. The show airs every weekday for 30 min on SABC 1 from 18:30–19:00. It has since its inception remained one of the most watched shows across the SABC channels. For September 2018 it was one of the top three most watched television programs in South Africa, with just over seven million viewers.

The analysis provided is on the episodes that aired between 4 October 2018 and 10 October 2018, episode 64 to episode 68. The black female characters that featured in the episodes were Rachel, Mantuli, Meiki, Botshelo, Mokgadi, Mapitsi, Pretty and Katlego's grandmother. During this period, the only themes covered in the show by the women were on romance and parenting; with Rachel seeking to reunite with her boyfriend, and Mantuli and Mokgadi being concerned about their children. Generally, the younger women were preoccupied with romantic issues while the older women focused on their children. Only in two instances do the characters, Rachel and Mapitsi mention their work, and the audience learn that one is a blogger, and the other an events coordinator.

In all the five episodes, only episode 64 which aired on the October 4, 2018 can pass the Bechdel test. And even thene pisode 64 passes because of only one conversation that takes place between Mokgadi and her legal aid Ms. Baloyi. It is shocking that in all the five episodes watched, only one conversation between two female characters is not about a man or the duties in their roles as mothers.

4.2 Muvhango

Muvhango is one of the oldest television dramas that has been playing on SABC since 1997. The show's main focus was on the royal family, the Vhakwevhos, and their rivals who are continuously challenging their rule. In its fifteenth season the show is still concerned with the royal throne, however now it's between two families, the Mojalefas and the Vhakwevhos. The show airs every day on SABC 2 from 21:00 to 21:30. And, similar to Skeem Saam it is one of the most popularly watched television show in the country, with the most watched episode in September 2018 receiving five million viewers (TV SA Team).

The research analysed *Muvhango* episodes that aired from 4 October 2018 to 10 October 2018, from episode 192 to episode 196. The female characters that made up the five episodes were Molieli, Mishumo, Rendani, Livhuwani, Imani, Thobile. Little is revealed about the female characters and what they do in the episodes watched. What is known about the characters is how they relate to the male characters on the show.

In all five episodes the female characters' main conversation revolved around romance, with Molieli, Livhuwani and Mishumo's storylines centred on how to fix their marriages. Only Imani and Hulisani Ravele—a South African radio broadcaster who appeared on the show as herself—stories were centred on their work. It is no surprise then that all the episodes fail the Bechdel test. While there are many scenes of two women talking to each other, often mothers and daughters, the discussions are about men and in particular romance.

4.3 Isidingo

Isidingo airs on SABC 3 and has been on television since 1998 (SABC/Isidingo 2018). It is one of the few multi-racial shows on the SABC. The show is based on a fictional mining town, and so the story is centred on the miners and different businesses that exist as a result of the mines. From the five episodes watched, there was only one constant black female character- Kgothalo, who runs one of the businesses in the town. Thus the content analysis will be focused on only Kgothalo.

In the episodes assessed, which aired between 4 October 2018 and 10 October 2018. Kgothalo mainly talks about her work, and often it is with other male characters. In the only conversation she has with another women she discusses romance instead, and not her business ventures. While Kgothalo often discusses her work, she only does so with the male characters. And, since the Bechdel test looks at conversations between women, and the content of these conversations, all of the Isidingo episodes watched fail the test.

5 African Feminist Analysis

5.1 Agency

The African feminist movement arises as a result of black women's agency (Boswell 2010). Black women in South Africa have time and time again dared and confronted the patriarchal and colonial structures that oppress them. It is black women's agency that is at the core of the African feminist movement. It is therefore a significant part of being a black woman in South Africa.

One of the uses of the Bechdel test is to assess the agency of female characters in film, and because the test only works when there are two or more women, it assesses an agency that requires networks or group consciousness (Selisker 2015). This is not to say that one alone cannot have agency, but rather to indicate the importance of working with other women to ensure one's felt agency leads to change. The idea of agency reinforced in networks is also seen in Virginia Woolf, whose work, Alison Bechdel says she developed the idea from (Selisker 2015). African feminists have also noted the importance of groups and networks between women as a tool to respond to the oppression they face (Collins 2000). For African women, developing strong relationships with one another was always an important tool not only for eradicating oppressive systems, but also for their own survival as individual women (Lorde 1984, Collins 2000). Thus, for this part of the paper, the analyses on agency also involve exploring relationships between the female characters.

5.2 Female Networks

From the most popularly watched television shows in South Africa—*Skeem Saam*, *Muvhango* and *Isidingo*—the female characters do not exist as independent people. They are concerned mainly with romance and their roles as mothers. To have female characters that are only concerned with others suggests that the women only exist in relation to others. In media scholarship this is known as females serving as intermediaries between male characters (Selisker 2015). Intermediaries are considered 'passive vehicles', characters that do not have actions of their own (Selisker 2015). As intermediaries, the black female characters are therefore presented to have no agency, they function only to enable men to channel their desires, and never as characters with their own goals and desires. Such representations are problematic because, while they are fictitious, they strengthen the idea that women only exist to serve the needs of men and their children, never themselves.

The programs also push forward another gender stereotypes, that women cannot be friends with each other. In all the shows analysed, zero female friendships exist, instead the women are portrayed to always be in a feud. A few examples are *Skeem Saam's* Mapitsi and Botshelo, *Muvhango's* Molieli and Imani, and again *Skeem Saam's* Mokgadi and Meiki. Julia Pozner in *Reality Bites* notes that women finding other women as untrustworthy is one of the popularly used gender stereotype in both literary and visual fiction (Pozner 2010). In A room of one's own, Virginia Woolf makes the same observation. She writes:

> And I tried to remember any case in the course of my reading where two women are presented as friends. …There are now and then mothers and daughters. But almost without exception they are shown in relation to men (Woolf 1929).

More often, black women are the one group that is mostly portrayed to be untrusting of one another. Yet as literature indicates, friendship and bonding between black women is highly valued (Gqola 2001). In South Africa it was the feeling of 'sisterhood' among women that enabled them to form ties and work together to confront the apartheid regime (Mekgwe 2006). It is also this feeling that guides black women today in their grouping to protest against their oppressions. Thus in black women's literature the focus on female friendships has remained important to portray (Mekgwe 2006).

Female friendships in a story give women agency. Yet if the gender stereotype of female feuds is untrue, why is it popularly used in the media? What does it serve society to portray women as unsupportive of each other? In *A room of one's own,* Woolf suggests that if women are portrayed to have relationships that are not concerned only with men, it can transform not only their role in stories but also the story itself (Woolf 1929). She writes:

> Chloe liked Olivia, and it struck me how, immense change was there. Chloe liked Olivia perhaps for the first time in literature. Cleopatra did not like Octavia. And how completely Antony and Cleopatra would have been altered had she done so. ... Cleopatra's only feeling about Olivia is one of jealousy (Woolf 1929).

Woolf is making an argument about the power of female friendships. She is arguing, similar to African feminists that the relationships women have can be and often are transformative, revolutionary.

Pozner analyses the use of the female feuds stereotype further. She contends that through this stereotype popular culture suggests that it is women who prevent other women from achieving their goals (Pozner 2010). For example, in South Africa, the notion of women preventing other women from succeeding is a popular topic of discussion in the media, even named as the 'pull her down syndrome' (Real Talk With Anele 2015). In this regard the stereotype also serves to prevent women from focusing on the root causes of gender discriminating. Instead television tells women that it is other women who are the problem. Thus, instead of showcasing the agency women have had in forming relationships and networks with one another, women are portrayed to simply be enemies of one another.

Again, instead of showing women and how they relate to each other, the shows rather focus only on the women in their roles as mothers and wives. This is an overused gender trope in the media (Pozner 2010). *Skeem Saam's* Meiki, and Mantuli and with Molieli in *Muvhango* are clear indications of this. The argument here is not to suggest that family should not be focused on in women's lives, given its importance. However, it is concerning that the only thing the women are portrayed to be concerned with are domestic issues.

The repetitive representation of women being only concerned with the domestic and romantic plays into the gender stereotype that there is such a thing as the 'woman's place'. A 2016 study on gender equality in South Africa indicated that 40% of adults in South Africa believe that a 'woman's place' is in the kitchen (Chiloane 2016). It is not farfetched to contend that the repetitive representation of women in the media as mainly concerned with domestic issues contributes to this belief.

Black women are represented as characters without agency, and also often as unsupportive of each other. Pozner warns that repetitive depiction of women as enemies in the media reinforces the idea that women are each other's problem (Pozner 2010). Even though, as indicated in black feminist theory, black feminist literature and history, black women have relied on each other to survive and to challenge oppressive systems (Lorde 1984), the stereotype that women are other women's problems creates situations in which gender discrimination and systems that benefit men at the expense of women are not addressed. And how can they be addressed, when the story that is continuously told is that it is other women who prevent women from succeeding (Pozner 2010).

Already South Africa is a country a steeped in gender stereotypes that are discriminatory towards women, which affect black women more severely than other groups (Booysen and Nkomo 2010). For example, research shows that the advancement of black women to managerial positions is made more difficult by the both their gender and race (Booysen and Nkomo 2010). Additionally, it is black women who are more vulnerable to violence and poverty in South Africa. Davis' research on the attitudes audiences hold regarding mothers as a result of television indicates that representations of women mainly concerned about domestic issues can influence potential employers on their capability to do work (Davis 2013). With this context, gender stereotypes in the media about black women exacerbate the negative experiences of black women. The continuous use of gender stereotypes in the media to represent black women only serves to reinforce the discrimination they encounter.

5.3 Intersectionality: Gender and Race

African feminist theory discourse makes it clear that black women's experiences are shaped by gender and race. In particular, South African feminists have highlighted the 'triple yoke' of oppression—as it has been referred to—and the way it shapes the experiences of black women in South Africa (Nolde 1991; Moloswanke 1996). This is an examination on how the intersection of race, class and gender shape the lives of the black women in *Muvhango*, *Isidingo* and *Skeem Saam*.

Surprisingly, race and racism are not at all addressed in the television programs. While it is clear the women are black, their racial identity is presented as having no effect on their lived experiences. As noted with the content analysis and Bechdel test, the problems the women encounter are often regarding their children and romantic lives. Sara Ives makes a similar observation in her research on the television show *Generations* during its 2005 run. In her research she states that on *Generations*, the 'idea of race remains untroubled', it is something that is made to seem non-existent (Ives 2008). Equally, for American television shows that cast black women, Petersen found that their race was rarely given any attention, rendering the black women invisible (Petermon 2014). Recently, South African, black female filmmaker Zamo Muhwanazi spoke openly about the lack of representation of black women in the media (Vourlias 2018). Saying 'we are black and we are women at the same time, unless we are speaking about these things together, you're not speaking to me' (Vourlias 2018). Mkhwanazi echoes the sentiments of African feminist scholars. For her, to depict black women as raceless, is to fail to speak to the real experiences of black women in South Africa.

Failure to acknowledge the complex experiences that black female characters experience as a result of their racial identity minimises who they are. In several reviews regarding the American television show *The Bold Type*, media commentators noted the program's failure to address the leading black characters' race, contending it reduced her to a one-dimensional character (Griffiths 2017, Brown 2018, Bennett 2018).

The representations of black female characters in *Muvhango Isidingo* and *Skeem Saam* render them raceless. They promote the idea that race issues are no longer a problem in South Africa, and that the 'rainbow nation has been achieved' (Ives 2008). In a *Mail and Guardian* review of *Generations* in 2005, an observation was made that the show flattened and silenced memories of apartheid (Ives 2009). Adding to Anderson's observation, the television shows refusal to acknowledge race flattens and silences the experiences of black women in South Africa.

The national discourse that was adopted to build the new South Africa was based on non-racialism and stories of men who fought against the apartheid regime (Boswell 2010). In this discourse, the narratives of women were considered secondary to those of men. There was a 'masculinist undertaking of nation building' (Baiada 2008). Hence, Motsemme's observations that during South Africa's Truth and Reconciliation Commission, women were not empowered to bring forward stories of trauma and violations they experienced under the apartheid era (Motsemme 2004). Therefore, under the context of South Africa's rainbow, non-racial nation, it is not surprising that the intersecting social categories of race, class and gender are not represented in television. While they have black women in their programs, the depictions of these women fail to connect with the lived realities of black women in South Africa. The shows, in the same manner as South Africa's national discourse render women to be 'both of and not of the nation' (Boswell 2010). Black women are present in the shows but they do not actually acknowledge the real experiences of black women in South Africa.

To present black women as either exclusively black, or exclusively women, without acknowledging the intersection of the two, is to render them invisible (Lugones 2008). While *Muvhango*, *Skeem Saam* and *Isidngo* use visuals to present the black women as diverse, in their clothes and hair, they fail to recognise their racialised selves. As South African filmmaker Zamo Mkhwanazi noted, 'South Africa's film industry still fails to address the challenges facing black women' (Vourlias 2018).

The imagined realities that many people consume about black women from the media suggest that race, class and gender do not have meaning in the way black women's lives are shaped. This repetitive portrayal of women affects what people believe about the experiences of black women in South Africa. If gender discrimination is to be addressed, and black women stand a chance to attain justice, then gender and race have to be recognised as intersecting categories. However, television programs suggest that black women do not suffer on the basis of their intersecting identities. When popular television programs propagate images of black women that fail to address their lived realities in South Africa, they help maintain the gender discrimination black women face.

5.4 Human Rights Analysis

Gender stereotypical representations of women in the media constitute a violation of South Africa's obligations to CEDAW and the African Women's Protocol. Pursuant to article 5(a) of CEDAW, television programs reproduction of gender stereotypes serve to reinforce social and cultural practices based on stereotypes. Notably, the African Women's Protocol requires state parties to eliminate gender stereotypes in the media because they can lead to practices of gender discrimination (Article 12 of the African Women's Protocol). Research on the influence of television on audiences indicates that there is correlation between the amount of television watched and the sexist gender ideologies men hold (Davis 2013). Additionally, the research found that television serves as a reinforcement of people's stereotypical gender roles (Davis 2013). Both the African Women's Protocol and CEDAW view gender stereotypes as the root causes for gender discrimination, thus the continued perpetuation of gender stereotypes in the media is a reinforcement of gender discrimination practices.

The gender stereotypical representations of black women in *Muvhango*, *Skeem Saam* and *Isidingo* are a violation of South Africa's obligations to the African Women's Protocol and CEDAW. The repetitive depiction of women as enemies, wives and mothers is a failure on the state and the SABC to eradicate gender stereotypes that inform harmful cultural and social practices. As part of creating an environment that promotes gender equality, gender stereotypes in the media have to be eliminated. The SABC, and as such South Africa are enabling systems and practices that reinforce gender discrimination. The repetitive use of stereotypes to portray black women reinforces the gender discrimination they already struggle within society.

The Committee on the Elimination of Discrimination Against Women in their 2011 report to South Africa encouraged the state to address its stereotypical representations of women in the media (CEDAW Committee 2011); contending that the country remains plagued by harmful practices and stereotypes and that the media's stereotypical depictions of women 'encourage discrimination and undermines the equality of women and men' (CEDAW Committee 2011). The African Women's Protocol's article 12 (1) (b) explicitly requires states to eliminate gender stereotypes in the media to address gender discrimination.

Still, it should be noted that section 16 (1) (a) of the South African Constitution also guarantees freedom of expression for the press and other media. However, media houses such as the SABC also have the obligation in accordance with the Broadcasting Act, to ensure their productions promote gender equality (South African Broadcasting Act no 4 of 1999). In the *Tshabalala-Msimang v Makhanya* case, the High Court of South Africa contended that while freedom of press is celebrated, it does not mean that the press is 'free to pollute the cause of justice' (Tshabalala-Msimang and Another v Makhanya and Others 2008). Reading the court's stance together with the Broadcasting Act on gender equality, one can understand that the media should not disseminate work that plays a part in reinforcing gender discrimination in the country. Because to do so, is to 'pollute the cause of justice' (Tshabalala-Msimang and Another v Makhanya and Others 2008).

Freedom of expression for the media is essential for a democratic country. However, as seen with the *Tshabalala-Msimang v Makhanya* case, and South Africa being a state party to both CEDAW and the African Women's Protocol, the media is not free to propagate gender stereotypical representations of women. But currently the state is failing to meet its obligations of promoting gender equality as required in CEDAW and the African Women's Protocol.

6 Conclusion

Negative depictions of women in television shows contribute to the widespread cultural stereotyping of women (Ibinga 2007). Yet, because these are imaginative works, it means institutions like the SABC who produce them can do better in promoting different images. And work towards eradicating gender discrimination. Liberating narratives about women can create new forms of power and paths to fight against past and present discrimination against women (Ibinga 2007). Research indicates that diverse representations of women in the media can also influence viewers to be accepting of a variety of gender roles. If the 'function of art is to do more than tell it like it is but rather to imagine what is possible' then storytellers have a responsibility to imagine a better gendered worlds (hooks 2012). Not only is this a moral responsibility, it is, according to CEDAW and the African Women's Protocol also a legal responsibility.

SABC television shows depict black women in stereotypical ways. In addition, through the concept of intersectionality, the study also found that black women were represented as raceless and without agency. The SABC's failure to represent women as independent characters with ambitions and desires of their own propagates the notion that women are important only in their roles as mothers and wives. Moreover, the intersection of race and gender and the manner in which they shape black women's lives is not at all addressed; and therefore, the shows do not speak to the lived experiences of black women in South Africa today.

Yet it does not have to be this way. Globally, research indicates that films that are more diverse and offer new outlooks on the role of women make more money (Guibourg 2018). The same trend runs true for South Africa, films and television shows with complex female characters earn more viewers and profit. There is an interest for on screen diverse representations of women. Gender stereotypes are not the only route media houses and filmmakers can use as moneymaking tools. If diverse and complex representations of women can create profit, what does this mean for the future of storytelling in the SABC?

References

Armstrong S (1994) Rape in South Africa: an invisible part of apartheid's legacy. Focus Gend 2(2):35–39

Baiada C (2008) On women, bodies, and nation: feminist critique and revision in Zoe Wicomb's David story. Afr Stud 67(1):33–47

Bechdel A (1986) Dykes to watch out for. Firebrand Books, Ithaca, NY

Bennett A (2018) How the bold type finally started to address Kat's blackness, one step at a time. Buzzfeed.News. Accessed 12 June 2018

Booysen LA, Nkomo SM (2010) Gender stereotypes and requisite management characteristic. The case of South Africa. Gender Manag Int J 25:285–300

Boswell B (2010) Black South African women writers, narrating the self, narrating the nation. Unpublished PhD thesis, University of Maryland, College Park

Brown K (2018) Where's the happily ever after for black women. Bazaar. https://www.harpersbazaar.com/culture/film-tv/a12022020/how-women-of-color-portrayed-tv-film/. Accessed 9 Mar 2018

Butler J (2000) In: Butler J, Laclau E, Zizek S (eds) Contingency, hegemony, universality - contemporary dialogues on the left. Verso, London

CEDAW Committee (2009) United Nations Committee on the Elimination of All forms of Discrimination against Women 'Concluding observation of the committee on the elimination of discrimination against women. Germany' 43rd session (19 January – 6 February 2009), CEDAW/C/DEU/C0/6, para 27 – para 28

CEDAW Committee (2011) United Nations Convention on the Elimination of All forms of Discrimination against Women 'Concluding observation of the committee on the elimination of discrimination against women. South Africa' 48th session (17 January – 4 February 2011) CEDAW/C/ZAF/C0/4, para 20

Chiloane M (2016) Gender stereotyping in SA deepening- Study EWN. https://ewn.co.za/2016/08/09/Ipsos-study-Some-in-SA-believe-women-still-belong-in-the-kitchen Accessed 10 October 2018

Collins PH (2000) Black feminist thought: knowledge, consciousness and the politics of empowerment. Routledge, New York

Crenshaw K (1989) Demarginalising the intersection of race and sex. A black feminist critique of antidiscrimination doctrine, feminist theory and antiracist politics. Univ Chicago Legal Forum 140:139–167

Davis SN (2013) Gender differences in the influence of television on gender ideology. TV hours and attitudes towards mothers. Int Rev Modern Sociol 39:205–223

Ellis S (2016) Why the Bechdel test doesn't always work. The Guardian. https://www.theguardian.com/lifeandstyle/womens-blog/2016/aug/20/why-the-bechdel-test-doesnt-always-work. Accessed 20 Aug 2016

Eze C (2006) African feminism. Resistance and resentment. Quest Afr J Philos 20:97–117

Gqola P (2001) Blackwomen, feminisms and postcoloniality in Africa. Agenda 16(50):11–22

Griffiths K (2017) The bold type won't talk about Kat's race and that's unacceptable. Bustle. https://www.bustle.com/p/the-bold-type-wont-talk-about-kats-race-thats-unacceptable-78048. Accessed 22 Aug 2017

Guibourg C (2018) Oscars 2018: Female led Oscar films more profitable. BBC. https://www.bbc.com/news/entertainment-arts-43146026. Accessed 1 Mar 2018

hooks b (2004) Understanding patriarchy. Imagine no boarders 2

hooks b (2009) Reel to real: race, sex and class at the movies. Routledge Classics, New York

hooks b (2012) Outlaw culture: resisting representation. Routledge, New York

Ibinga SS (2007) The representations of women in the works of three South African novelist of the transition. Unpublished PhD

Ives S (2008) Visual methodologies through a feminist lens - South Africa's soap operas and the post apartheid nation. GeoJ 74:245–255

Ives SF (2009) Visual methodologies through a feminist lens: South African soap operas and the post-apartheid nation. GeoJournal 74(3):245–255
Jhally S, Lewis JM (1992) Enlightened racism: the Cosby show, audiences and the myth of the American dream. Westview Press, Boulder, CO
Lorde A (1984) Sister outsider: essays and speeches. Crown Publishing, New York
Lugones M (2008) The coloniality of gender. Worlds Knowledges Otherwise 2:1–17
Mail & Guardian (2014) Blackface students suspended from residences. https://mg.co.za/article/2014-08-09-blackface-students-suspended-from-residences. Accessed 9 Aug 2018
McKane J (2018) The most-watched TV shows in South Africa. My Broadband. https://mybroadband.co.za/news/broadcasting/251461-the-most-watched-tv-shows-in-south-africa-5.html. Accessed 19 May 2018
Mdoda, A Real talk with Anele (2015) Pull her down syndrome SABC 3 25 April 2015 https://www.youtube.com/watch?v=TJ6Q4mdSW9U&t=959s Accessed 13 October 2018
Mekgwe P (2006) The colonial question. In: Osha S (ed) The African Philosophy Journal: Special Issue on African Feminisms 16 Vol 20
Moloswanke S (1996) Black women's participation in politics in South Africa: a study of perceptions of a group of decision makers in the government of the North West province. Unpublished PhD thesis, Brandeis University, p 66
Motsemme N (2004) The meanings in silence. Rhodes Journalism Rev 24:4–5
Ndebele N (1986) Rediscovery of the ordinary: some new writings in Southern Africa. J South Afr Stud 12:143–157
Nolde J (1991) South African women under apartheid: Employment rights with particular focus on domestic service and forms of resistance to promote change. Third World Legal Stud 10:208
O'Meara J (2016) What "The Bechdel Test" doesn't tell us: examining women's verbal and vocal (dis)empowerment in cinema. Fem. Media Stud. 16(6):1120–1123
Petermon JD (2014) Hyper(in)visibility: reading race and representation in the neoliberal era. Unpublished PhD thesis, University of California
Petersen KH (1999) First things first. Problems of a feminist approach to African literature. In: Ashcroft B et al (eds) The post-colonial reader. Routledge, London
Pozner JL (2010) Reality bites back. Seal Press, Berkeley, CA
Protocol to the African Charter on Human and Peoples' Rights on the Rights of Women in Africa (2005) Adopted by the 2nd ordinary session of the Assembly of the African Union, Maputo, CAB/LEG/66.6
SABC (2018) Isidingo. http://www.sabc3.co.za/sabc/home/sabc3/multimedia/details?id=d2d2fadb-aa1b-4945-8b0a-b3d139945c96&title=Isidingo%20Episodes
Selisker S (2015) The Bechdel Test and the Social Form of Character Networks. New Literary History 46(3):505–523
Tshabalala-Msimang and Another v Makhanya and Others (2008) 6 SA 102 (W) para 35
Vourlias C (2018) For black women in South African film biz, equality is still a struggle. Variety. https://variety.com/2018/film/news/black-women-in-south-african-film-biz-equality-a-struggle-1202880315/. Accessed 21 July 2018
Wilkinson D, Birmingham P (2003) Using research instruments. A guide for researchers. Routledge Falmer, London
Woolf V (1929) A room of one's own. Hogarth Press

Chapter 7
Commemoration and Human Rights in Africa: Revisiting the Politics of Memory Through Visual Arts in Kenya

Josephat M. Kilonzo

Abstract When societies experience widespread patterns of injustice, exploitation and gross human rights violations, normative international human rights standards require accountability and generally the establishment of measures to address them. By and large, societies subjected to the scourge of blatant human rights violations, repression and widespread patterns of injustice, have to find ways to mourn the dead, remember the painful past, preserve the memory and work towards reconstruction. Some of the measures established to address the past include truth commissions, reparations, memorials and reconstruction of institutions. However, these measures have their own limitations in terms of time, money and dependence on political will of the individuals in power. To counter the limitations of these mechanisms, visual arts may be employed as their unofficial counterpart. Visual arts create a platform for victims of gross human rights violations to voice their views and concerns. This chapter seeks to shed light on the complexity of memory, highlight state of amnesia and denial of gross human rights by the Kenyan government and to discuss ways that visual art be a means to commemorate and liberate memory and promote respect for human rights.

Keywords Commemoration · Visual art · Memory · Remembrance · Amnesia · Forgetting · Reconciliation · Human rights · Kenya

1 Introduction

At the stroke of midnight on 12 December 1963, Kisoi Munyao lowered the union jack and hoisted the Kenyan flag in honour of the new Kenya that the founding fathers and mothers had brought forth (Standard Media 2013). The new nation was conceived in hope and optimism for a democratic future. The fight against poverty,

J. M. Kilonzo (✉)
Faculty of Law, Centre for Human Rights, University of Pretoria, Pretoria, South Africa

R. Adeola et al. (eds.), *The Art of Human Rights*, Arts, Research, Innovation and Society, https://doi.org/10.1007/978-3-030-30102-6_7

disease and ignorance was seemingly going to be a success. For many, this was a watershed in the history of the nation and a triumph over the evil of colonialism which had caused a deleterious wound on native sovereignties, ways of being and indigenous knowledges.

The ontological edifice of the colonial state had been established on patronage, appropriation, and the repression of natives whose ways of being for ages had orbited on non-western epistemologies, cosmologies and legalities (Ghai 2010). In Kenya, the colonial government armed with this ideological justification established oppressive, exploitative and autocratic structures by subjugating the natives, alienating natives' fertile lands for the whites and confining the natives in reserves or rural areas (Burnell et al. 2008).

The edifice of the colonial state was to be shed off at independence, when the post-colonial Kenya was born. Independence indicated an end to practices that had been sanctioned by the colonial state; the closure of detention camps, tortures, massacres and other vile inclinations that had been institutionalized under British rule (Truth, Justice and Reconciliation Commission 2013a, b). The post-colonial state inherited and sedimented the political, social and economic structures of the colonial state (Onyango 2015). The African elites did not focus on dismantling the oppressive colonial government structures that were inimical to democratic progress of Kenya. The bright sun of hope and aspirations at independence was soon eclipsed by gross human rights violations, socio-economic exclusion, deeply-rooted ethnicity and intolerance for political dissent.

Although the post-colonial state was burdened by structures of the colonial state, the politics of memory at independence depicted that the Kenyan people had triumphed over colonialism (Pan-African Magazine 1963). The same narrative is constantly refueled on public holidays and continues to dominate Kenya's collective memory. This politics of memory created a false chronicle of rupture and newness which presented decolonisation merely as an act of politics and the transformation of Kenya into a geographically independent state.

As a result, the false rupture propagated by the dominant politics of memory in Kenya undermined the judicious memorialisation of colonialism as subjugation, of not only the Kenyan geographical space, but also psychic, institutional and cultural spaces. As the politics of memory on triumph over colonialism continued to attend public and private spaces, the inherited legacy of the colonial state gradually spread its tentacles over decades, increasingly siring a fatal blend of historical injustices, impunity, institutional decay, structural violence and tribal politics, eventually resulting in the pernicious 2007/2008 post-election violence (PEV) which left Kenya starring into the abyss of a failed state. As stated by the Truth Justice and Reconciliation Commission (TJRC):

> The violence, bloodshed and destruction of the PEV shocked Kenyans into the realisation that their nation, long considered an island of peace and tranquility, remained deeply divided since independence from British colonial rule in December 1963 (TJRC 2013a, b).

Essentially, when societies, like Kenya experience widespread patterns of injustice, repression, exclusion, exploitation, disappearances, kidnappings and atrocious acts of brutality, normative international human rights standards call for accountability and generally the establishment of mechanisms to address them (Aguilar and Isa 2011). Importantly, societies in such circumstances have to find ways to mourn the dead, remember the event(s), preserve the memory, and work towards rebuilding (Golebiewski 2014). In order to mourn, to come to terms with the painful past and to chart a new path for the future of the society, truth commissions, reparations, memorials and rebuilding of institutions are established as remedy mechanisms (Golebiewski 2014).

The wanton violation of human rights, destruction of property, brutality and exclusion of communities in Kenya led to the establishment of a taskforce on the establishment of the Truth Justice and Reconciliation Commission, the Truth Justice and Reconciliation Commission (TJRC), the enactment of the Constitution of Kenya 2010, the trial of the key suspects in perpetrating the 2007/2008 post-election at the International Criminal Court (ICC) and trial of other suspects under domestic courts. These mechanisms focused on addressing the root causes of largescale human rights violations, discrimination, ethnic clashes etc.

However, most of these mechanisms are dependent and continue to depend, on either time or money (Golebiewski 2014), and the political will of those in control of the levers of power. Therefore, in certain circumstances where resources are limited or where political will is lacking, the success of these mechanisms may be limited. For instance, truth and reconciliation commissions, which are established to help discover and reveal facts of past human rights violations by government or non-state actors and the root causes and the consequences of such violations, as a result of time constraints and resources, may only select a limited number of victims to appear and testify before them (Golebiewski 2014). As such, the findings and truths revealed and redress provided by these mechanisms may be limited.

Secondly, the effectiveness of truth and reconciliation commissions may be limited by lack of political will. For instance, in Kenya most of the findings of the TJRC and the recommendations such as compensation, rehabilitation, memorialization for victims as well as a raft of reforms to ensure that human rights violations witnessed in the past do not recur, have not been implemented. Although the TJRC Report was presented to Parliament, it has not been debated as at the time of writing this chapter (The Star 2017).

Also, mechanisms such as trial of the perpetrators of wanton human rights violations can only deal with a limited number of perpetrators, witnesses, and victims (Bahun 2015). For instance, only six suspects were indicted in the ICC in respect to the 2007/2008 post-election violence.

Following the limitations of these mechanism, arts such as theater, music, film and storytelling may be employed as useful 'unofficial counterparts for truth-finding, reconciliation, civic repair and psychological reparation, lustration, public apology, and other mechanisms of transitional justice, often enabling empowerment of underrepresented groups (Bahun 2015), and promoting the culture of justification of use of force and respect for human rights.

Importantly, arts generally and in particular, visual arts (photographs, films etc.), create a platform on which victims of human rights violations and their families can express their views and concerns, 'tell their stories, and even evaluate the transitional justice mechanisms in their societies' (Golebiewski 2014). Essentially, visual arts make victims visible, and in certain circumstances, offer them an avenue to share their stories for the first time (GSDRC 2016). Interventions through visual art have the potential to amplify the efforts of other transitional mechanisms (Golebiewski 2014). For example, visual art may be useful in publicizing the findings of truth and reconciliation commissions in ways that are both accessible and powerful (Golebiewski 2014).

In light of this, this chapter seeks to highlight the complexity of memory, underscore the state of amnesia and denial of brutality and human rights violations by the Kenyan government (politics of memory) and how visual art can be a means to liberate memory and promote respect for human rights.

2 The Complex Puzzle of Memory: Can Visual Art Escape It?

Santayana reminds us that 'those who forget the past are condemned to repeat it (Santayana 1905). This underscores the importance of addressing memories of the past and acknowledging the impossibility of freedom without memory (Thesnaar 2011). Remembrance is central to liberation from the past in order to 'live in the present with a new identity and to hope for a new future' (Thesnaar 2011).

In addition to other mechanisms such as truth and reconciliation commissions and memorials, visual art is a powerful medium that can be instrumental in reminding us not to forget the past (Khan Academy 2019). The utility of visual art in addressing the past, helping us to remember and liberating us from the past cannot be underestimated. Visual art can help us to create a new identity and to hope for a different society were a painful past will not be repeated; a society characterised by respect for human rights, rule of law and democratic ideals.

According to Thesnaar 'the more we remember the past, listen to it and interpret it, the more freedom we will experience' (Thesnaar 2011). The complex question is how we should deal with this: how do we remember? (Thesnaar 2011). How do we use visual art to remember? Moreover, Soyinka asks 'how far should memory reach? How deeply into the recess of the past?' (Soyinka 2000). What should be the reach of visual art in respect to our past? Soyinka's response is that memory is not subject to the statute of limitations (Soyinka 2000). As such, the reach of visual art in reminding us of our moments of pain, happiness and struggles in the past should not be limited in terms of time.

The question that follows is what strategies should be employed through visual art to remind us of our past? How should we use visual art to construct narratives about the past? Essentially, all the strategies of remembrance have the inclination to sabotage their purposes because forgetting is at the heart of and is a companion of every effort of remembrance (Du Toit 2016). Thus, whichever strategy employed to remember through visual art may not escape forgetting or limiting the remembrance of 'other' narratives since remembrance and forgetting go hand in hand. Also in certain instances, artists 'deliberately frame the past in different or unexpected ways to change the way we think about history' (Khan Academy 2019). Because of this, art is caught up in the politics of memory.

As Du Toit points out, every memory allows us to remember certain things while at the same time, ironically, prompts us to forget others (Du Toit 2016). Therefore, devices of remembrance are inclined to work against themselves in the sense that forgetting, exclusion and repression lie at the heart of the enterprise of remembering (Du Toit 2016). For this reason, memory is best appreciated as a site ongoing struggle or an arena of conflict; an arena of conflict 'between forgetting as an action directed against the past and the return of the forgotten' (De Certeau 1997).

Generally, art, in the attempt to preserve memory, depicts memory as a site of ongoing struggle because of the existence of the inevitable tension between a subjective mind and the objective fact or event it seeks to present (Khan Academy 2019). Understanding this, many artists employ art to present narratives about personal and cultural memory in a manner that is open to interpretation and 'reframe the past not as a fixed narrative but a multiplicity of voices from diverse points of view' (Khan Academy 2019). This enables societies to think about their history, interpret it and appreciate how it has been shaped and how they may document things to come.

Notably, Snyman points out that the struggle to present and interpret the past lies at the core of any politics of memory (Snyman 1998). In other words, history is more about the present as the past and it depicts 'the choices of who and what must be included and who and what is excluded' (De Vos 2001). This makes man's struggle against power, the struggle against forgetting which reduces man's fight to take charge of the future to the fight to change the past (Du Toit 2016). Thus there is wisdom in Orwell's assertion that 'who controls the past controls the future. Who controls the present controls the past' (Orwell 1949).

History is therefore politics and a field of force (Khobe 2017), in which events of the past are organised for particular purposes in a manner that excludes and includes (Jenkins 2003). The narratives of the past which detract from the history as presented by those who control it are suppressed or marginalised. In such a context then, the narratives of the oppressed or the marginalised are subjected to selective amnesia or denied. Based on this understanding, it behooves us to ask who has been excluded. How many people and narratives have been excluded from history, the reason for their exclusion and the effect of their exclusion?

Visual art can be an important means to raise the question of who has been excluded. A means to tell the narratives of the suppressed, marginalised voices and human rights violations that are subjected to amnesia and denial by those who wield positions of power. This is essentially a struggle against forgetting of suppressed narratives. A struggle to help the marginalized to take charge of changing their past and future.

This points to the fact that there is no single way of telling a story. There is always a counter-narrative to the grand narrative that can be presented through visual art. Visual art can be used to tell individual stories; stories of individual struggles, pain and their past generally; and stories that may not be reflected in the grand narrative. This is instrumental because every individual in a society has their own view and story about the past because largely 'memory exists in the mental space where cognitive understanding and emotional intelligence intersect' (Greenwald 2014). However, if one views the past in this manner, one has to reach the conclusion that history or the past is problematic.

The way in which history is collected, recorded, stored and remembered has a bearing on who retains power and who is oppressed. Thus inevitably, in looking at the past we have to take a position thus selecting a certain version of the past and appropriating it for particular material effects or outcomes (Khobe 2017). In presenting the past through visual art, we have to weigh the effects and outcomes of such presentation. We have to consider the side we are taking, the side of the oppressed who have been subjected to brutality and violation of their human rights or the side of the oppressor.

In the Kenyan context, based on the expectations of constructing a democratic future founded on egalitarian principles and respect for human rights, a re-look into history and politics of memory should be made. We should however, remain alive to the fact that any particular reading of the past or remembering is a choice that involves forgetting thus including and excluding certain narratives. Visual art presents an opportunity to interpret Kenya's past, an opportunity to make the choice to remember the narratives that have been marginalised or deliberately suppressed. Narratives that have been subjected to denial and amnesia.

3 State Terror and Amnesia: Can Visual Art Provide a Counter-Narrative?

It is common knowledge that Kenya is an invented state through systems of western epistemology, conquest and colonisation. To govern and exploit the geographical space known as Kenya, the colonialists brought together indigenous tribes who had settled within the space. As stated by Onyango (2015), these groups were distinct in relation to the manner in which they exercised their sovereignties and had peculiar ways to pursue their means of livelihood as farmers, fishermen, ironmen or pastoralists.

Ghai notes that the colonialism brought together these different communities without due consideration to their peculiar cultures and ways of being generally. This is more or less a reflection of Soyinka's assertion that 'much of the division of Africa owed more to a case of brandy and a box of cigars than to the intrinsic claim about what the boundaries enclose' (Soyinka 2000). Therefore, the growth of the colonial state was not organic or gradual as European states.

Essentially, the capitalist colonial state was resistant to democracy and relied on coercion as well as destruction of the rhythm and sovereignty of local social systems (Ghai 2010). As the TJRC concluded, in order to establish colonial authority in

Kenya, between 1895 and 1963, the colonial government committed 'unspeakable and horrific gross human rights violations' by meting violence of unprecedented scale on native Kenyans (TJRC Report IV 2013a, b).

Worth noting is the fact that, as Ghai states, despite the oppressive character of the colonial government, at independence the colonial state was not transformed in its essence (TJRC Report IV 2013a, b). Ironically, on the eve of independence, the Duke of Edinburgh speaking to the Kenyans who were soon to be 'free' people stated (TJRC Report Volume IIA 2013a, b):

> Tomorrow a new volume will be opened and an independent Kenya will start to write a new story. The pages of this volume are still blank and empty; the story that is to be written on them is still in the hands and minds of all the people of Kenya.

Without much effort, critical intelligence would tell that the politics of memory propagated by this statement was the denial of the indelible imprint of savage and repressive colonialism on the collective psyche, cultures, sense of identity and modes of governance of the colonised peoples. In addition, as noted by Onyango, the British trained President Jomo Kenyatta who stood for continuity of the colonialist values and system of administration (Onyango 2015).

The TJRC states that Jomo Kenyatta's 'government used many of the laws and institutions of the institutions of the colonial government to minimize and even suppress dissent' (TJRC Report IIA).

Further, Onyango asserts that the African elites at independence who had understood and inherited colonial state structures and culture continued to suppress fellow Africans (Onyango 2015). He notes that the three successive post-independence governments led by Presidents Kenyatta, Moi and Kibaki employed colonial, political, economic exclusionary strategies to rule Kenya (Onyango 2015). Pursuant to the repressive character of the state, the Task Force on the Establishment of a Truth, Justice and Reconciliation Commission led by Mutua stated (Government of Kenya 2003):

> Since its creation by the British in 1895, the Kenyan state has largely been a predatory and illiberal instrumentality, an ogre defined by its proclivity for the commission of gross and massive human rights violations. Little need be said of the colonial state, which was specifically organized for the purposes of political repression to facilitate economic exploitation.

In addition, the TJRC upon investigating the tragic episodes of wanton human rights violations in Kenya's history concluded that the violence generated under colonialism was perpetuated in the post-colonial Kenya through 'unaltered colonial structures, institutions and mentalities' (TJRC Report IIA 2013a, b). The TJRC made the finding that the long history of human rights violations in Kenya was attributable to factors such as: the failure of the first government under Jomo Kenyatta to dismantle the repressive colonial government structures; 'the use and subsequent enhancement' of oppressive laws by Jomo Kenyatta's and Moi's governments; establishment of *de jure* one party state by President Moi's administration which provided room for human rights to take place with little public scrutiny and accountability; erosion of judicial and legislative independence; and cover-up as well as lack of the genuine commitment to punish of human rights violations (TJRC Report IV 2013a, b). This has continued to sire more human rights violations to date.

Besides, the TJRC noted that most of the atrocities such as massacres, political assassinations, extrajudicial killings, detention, torture and ill-treatment were committed between 1963 and 2002 during the authoritarian, corrupt and oppressive Jomo Kenyatta's and Moi's regimes (TJRC Report IIA 2013a, b). This resulted in a traumatised nation of thousands of citizens living with both physical and psychological wounds in a state that had 'no time or space for their experience and stories' (TJRC Report IIA 2013a, b).

Though the various tragic episodes of gross human rights violations in Kenya are attended by politics of memory that seek to suppress the narratives of pain and subjugation of the victims, below is a brief highlight of particular massacres and incidents of sexual violence which demonstrate amnesia, denial, impunity and cover-ups by the post-colonial state. The capacity of visual art in countering the amnesia, denial, impunity and cover-ups by the state is discussed.

3.1 Massacres

The TJRC established that massacres took place throughout the history of Kenya and in particular during the colonial period. The massacres that took place include: Kedong massacre; massacres during the Giriama Rebellion; Kollowa massacre and massacres during the Mau Mau war including Hola and Lari massacres (TJRC IV 2013a, b).

Visual art has been useful in documenting some of the atrocities committed by the colonial government and those who were fighting against the colonial government. For example, in the Lari Peace Museum, there is a collection of photos with the names of the victims of the Lari Massacre. This has been followed by the establishment of peace clubs in schools and colleges to rebuild inter-ethnic trust in the area.

In the post-independence Kenya, most of the massacres committed by state security apparatus took place in Upper Eastern, Nothern Kenya and in the North Rift regions (TJRC IV 2013a, b). The massacres committed by state agencies according to the TJRC include: the massacres during the Shifta war, Bulla Karatasi massacre, Wagalla massacre, Lotirir massacre and Malka Mari massacre (TJRC IV 2013a, b). This period also witnessed massacres committed by civilians which often occurred in the context of cattle rustling or inter-ethnic conflicts, sometimes with complicity of state officials or politicians (TJRC IV 2013a, b).

Notably, the TJRC regrets and laments that most of the massacres presented to it 'were undocumented which made investigating such incidents difficult if not impossible' (TJRC IV 2013a, b). Unfortunately, most of the perpetrators responsible for the commission of the massacres have not been held to account (TJRC IV 2013a, b). Without documentation of the massacres, visual art can provide an avenue for the communities to tell their stories about the atrocities committed during the massacres.

3.1.1 Wagalla Massacre

The Wagalla massacre which took place in 1984 as pointed out by the TJRC is 'the most spoken about massacre in Kenya and represents a tragic story of how government can turn against and massacre its own citizens' (TJRC Report IIA). The massacre which was as a result of excesses of a security operation took place over a duration of 4 days starting on the morning of 10 February and culminating on the morning of 14 February 1984 'with a stampede and a shootout' (The Star 2016). All the boys over the age of 12 and men of the Degodia sub-clan of Northern Kenya had been rounded up and detained at the newly built Wagalla airstrip in Wajir (The Star 2016). During the period they were subjected to cruel, degrading and inhumane conditions: starvation, heat of scotching sun, shootings and slicing with machetes (TJRC Report IIA 2013a, b).

In the meantime, women and girls who had been left in the village were subjected to sexual violence and torching of houses (TJRC Report IIA 2013a, b). As stated by Sheikh, the 'Wagalla massacre destroyed a community, changed its social cohesion and placed a burden of generating the dead society on the shoulders of widows' (The Star 2016). However, the most contentious issue remains the number of people who died during the carnage. The government for decades stuck with 57 as the number of those who died without providing names (TJRC Report IIA 2013a, b). Some sources claim that 1000 people died while certain community groups state the number was close to 5000 (TJRC Report IIA 2013a, b).

Worse still, all the five reports on inquiries carried out during the Moi regime did not evaluate the effects of the security operation on the human rights of the victims (TJRC Report IIA 2013a, b). The devastating effect of the carnage on the rights of the victims was first considered by the military board of inquiry that was established in 2009 and later the TJRC (TJRC Report IIA 2013a, b). Be that as it may, as aptly stated by Professor Nyong'o in 2000 on the floor of parliament the 'incident is very difficult to wipe out of the memory of the society as well as the conscience of the government' (TJRC Report IIA 2013a, b).

Despite the cloud surrounding the Wagalla Massacre through visual art, films in particular, the survivors of Wagalla Massacre have had a chance to tell their side of the story. A chance to express a fraction of their feelings in respect to pain and agony that they went through individually and as a community during the massacre. Several documentaries have captured the painful memories of the massacre. For example the series run by Citizen TV under the title 'Wagalla Massacre Death in the Dessert' (Citizen TV 2011).

The chance availed by visual art to the survivors of the massacre to narrate the human rights violations that took place during the massacre and the trauma experienced by the community is complementary to the TJRC Report. It also serves as an opportunity to counter some of the official narratives by the state that seek to deny or cloud some of the details of the massacre.

3.1.2 Malka Mari Massacre

The Malka Mari massacre is a classic demonstration of complexity of memory, denial and official amnesia. The TJRC pointed out that the nature of the security operation that resulted in the massacre is undocumented and therefore TJRC was uncertain on when the operation took place (TJRC Report IIA 2013a, b). The TJRC stated that from its investigation the 'best guess is that the operation took place in 1981, but research and testimony have unearthed an array of dates from 1980 onwards' (TJRC Report IIA 2013a, b). The situation is worsened by the fact that witnesses could not offer any clarity or consistency (TJRC Report IIA 2013a, b). Some of the witnesses seemingly conflated the Malka Mari massacre and Bulla Karatasi massacre (TJRC Report IIA 2013a, b).

The TJRC had to settle on 1981 because this was that was the year around which most popular narratives of the operation clustered (TJRC Report IIA 2013a, b). Therefore, it was not possible for the TJRC to specify the particular month, much less the particular day (TJRC Report IIA 2013a, b). The TJRC had to finally arrive at the conclusion that because the details of the Malka Mari massacre are depended on the fuzzy recollections and failing memories 'it may never be possible to arrive at a more accurate understanding of when the operation actually took place' (TJRC Report IIA 2013a, b).

The TJRC notes the accounts of the massacre allude to the fact that that security forces had set upon the civilians 'with a brutal determination as they sought information on bandits' in the Malka Mari area (TJRC Report IIA 2013a, b). The security forces were ruthless on those who failed to comply as skulls of men were allegedly crushed with boulders and others hung from trees (TJRC Report IIA 2013a, b). Women also bore the brunt of the operation. Cruel incidents of rape were said to have occurred (TJRC Report IIA 2013a, b). It was recounted that mothers pleaded with security officers to rape them in place of their daughters (TJRC Report IIA 2013a, b). According to the TJRC, the biggest challenge surrounding the Malka Mari massacre is estimating the number of dead and those who disappeared (TJRC Report IIA 2013a, b). The TJRC estimated the numbers as between 60 to 70 on the lower end and 200 on the upper end of the scale (TJRC Report IIA 2013a, b).

The most glaring and shocking aspect of Malka Mari massacre is the loud sound of silence. As the TJRC stated, officially the Malka Mari operation is non-existent (TJRC Report IIA 2013a, b). The TJRC found no reports, no minutes, no documents or briefing papers and no retired government officers in the position to shed light on the massacre (TJRC Report IIA 2013a, b). Searches of documents from the Kenya National Archives yielded no fruit (TJRC Report IIA 2013a, b). The last lifeline for the TJRC to unearth some details about the massacre was a Mandera district file that had monthly intelligence reports from independence to 1992 (TJRC Report IIA 2013a, b). It was later discovered that the monthly intelligence reports were destroyed routinely after every 3 months. That was the last straw that broke the camel's back.

The TJRC was then caught up in a dilemma. How could it state that a massacre had taken place with no date, no single documents and no known number of dead?

How could it be called a massacre? Be that as it may, there were victims who had survived the massacre and their testimonies did not waver on the fact that the operation and massacre had taken place in Malka Mari (TJRC Report IIA 2013a, b). The TJRC concluded that the collective memories of the victims could not be dismissed on the account of lack of some details necessary to ascertain the occurrence of the killings (TJRC Report IIA 2013a, b). Though for decades the amnesia from the state was loud, the TJRC finally provided a platform for the victims of Malka Mari massacre to tell their stories about the traumatic event.

To counter the state's amnesia and denial about the massacre visual art, films/documentaries in particular, can be used to record the recollections of the victims about the violation of their rights. The films can also serve a complementary mechanism to the TJRC Report in respect to telling the story of the victims of the massacre. This can immortalize the horrific event despite its non-existence in government's records. It can also provide a room for the victims to remember, relive the event, mourn and to walk the path of healing and forgiveness.

However, considering that most of the victims who are alive today only have a fuzzy recollection of the massacre through visual art cannot unearth the complete details or narratives about it. Visual arts, just like the TJRC, can only document/reflect the limited details that the witnesses/victims can remember. Therefore, it would be impossible to have a complete narrative about the horrific happenings during the massacre. As such visual art cannot succeed in completely countering the amnesia and denial by the state in respect to certain aspects of the massacre like dates etc. This is also a classic illustration of the limitations of visual art as a means to democratize or liberate memory.

Moreover, the streaming of documentaries about the massacre can also be used to invite discussions on amnesia and denial of human rights violation by the state in other spaces. Such discussions can help victims of hushed state oppression to reflect on their pain, to have dialogues on restoration of their dignity and to call for accountability. It can also be an opportunity to call for respect for human rights by both the state and non-state actors.

3.2 Sexual Violence

Despite the fact that discrimination based on gender is embedded in culture, the state has played a major role in oppression of women (Kamau 2010). Kamau (2010), observes that the failure to dismantle the colonial structures in the post-colonial Kenya propagated forms of class as well as gender discrimination that existed in the colonial era. The colonial state had been founded on Victorian worldview which clearly defined gender roles with the effect that the political or public space was man's sphere and domestic domain the place of the woman (TJRC Report IIC 2013a, b). Moreover, Kamau (2010) notes that apart from failure to dismantle the colonial structures which promoted direct and structural violence against women, on attainment of independence the state was further masculanised and ethnicised.

The TJRC states that the state acquiesced to or sanctioned most harmful practices against women (TJRC Report IIC 2013a, b). The outcome was that systematic and structural discrimination was propagated by the state itself (TJRC Report IIC 2013a, b). Although the independence Constitution under Section 82 proscribed discrimination on among other grounds sex, under Section 82(4) it did not prohibit discrimination on matters of adoption, marriage, divorce, burial and inheritance of property on death.

Contrary to popular assumptions, women were subjected to deliberate violence during both the colonial period and post-colonial period. Women were not only victims of sexual violence perpetuated by colonial government's soldiers and home guards but also by Mau Mau fighters (TJRC Report IIC 2013a, b). In the new constitutional dispensation, this memory should be a constant reminder that even those who fight for freedom are not beyond fallibility. They can visit harm on others.

Essentially, during the various massacres in the post-colonial era as already illustrated women and girls were also victims of atrocious incidents of sexual violence in the hands of security forces. One chilling account is told by a female victim of the Wagalla Massacre (TJRC Report IIA 2013a, b):

> We do not have houses because they were burnt down and we have been poor from the day of Wagalla up to now. We have not had any assistance from the government. We were stigmatized and we were told that we were "the rape women". We did not get married and even the daughters we bore before are also stigmatized. They are suffering because of that.

As the TJRC concluded, sexual violence was commonplace during the colonial period and regrettably 'continued unabated through independence to the present day' (TJRC Report IIA 2013a, b). Indeed, Kenyan women have been subjected to terrible and unspeakable atrocities. The TJRC states that documenting atrocities committed against women is not only for historical purposes but a bold statement that attaining a just and fair Kenya depends on the initiatives taken to 'heal the soul of the Kenyan woman' (TJRC Report IIC 2013a, b).

Presently, there are several initiatives that are employing visual arts (documentaries/photos) to fight against sexual violence through to advocating for accountability for sexual violence and calling for respect for women rights in Kenya. For example, the Young Women's Leadership Institute (Kenya) with the support from Women's Initiatives for Gender Justice in collaboration with WITNESS produced a documentary titled '*Bridging the Gap: Reinforcing Gender Desks in Nairobi*' which entails interviews with victims/survivors of rape, medical practitioners, lawyers and police officers speaking on the response by the law enforcement to sexual and gender-based violence within Nairobi County (Women's Initiatives for Gender Justice 2013).

The documentary captures the challenges faced by women with respect to reporting sexual violence to the police. Some of the challenges highlighted by the women include perceived corruption of the police and their reluctance to seriously and effectively conduct investigations into alleged sexual violence against women (Women's Initiatives for Gender Justice 2013). The documentary also underscores challenges faced by victims/survivors in regard to accessing 'timely medical care due to the limited referral by the police' (Women's Initiatives for Gender Justice 2013).

The film underscores the fact that although the Kenya police has, since 2004, established Gender desks within police units and stations to facilitate reporting of domestic and sexual violence, more needs to be done. The films points out that there is need for specialized training for police officers assigned to Gender Desks, location of the Desks in secure and private setting, effectiveness in conducting investigations of sexual and gender-based violence and the 'establishment of a comprehensive referral mechanism by the Gender Desks (Women's Initiatives for Gender Justice 2013).

The use of visual art to highlight and fight sexual and gender-based violence in Kenya is also demonstrated by the documentary titled *'I will not be silenced'* directed by Judy Rymer. The documentary is based on the court case of the unfortunate rape of Charlotte Campbell-Stephen's, an Australian Aid worker in Kenya (Vimeo 2015). She left Australia in 2006 to work for African Leaf, a Kenyan aid organization which deals with support for abused children. She was gang raped 2 months into her stay in Kenya, at a home that she had rented on the edge of the Rift Valley, South of Nairobi (The Guardian 2015).

In addition to capturing her story, the documentary highlights the 'stories of Kenyan women who gained strength in the fight against their perpetrators by watching Campbell-Stephen's case unfold' (The Guardian 2015). The documentary captures the protracted 7-year legal battle which exposes and challenges the systems which keep women powerless in Kenya (The Guardian 2015).

The documentary was launched in 2015 in Melbourne, Australia during the Human Rights and Film Festival (The Guardian 2015). Notably, the documentary team was granted access to all Kenyan's courts and permission to film by the Chief Justice (as he then was) Willy Mutunga (The Guardian 2015). The Chief Justice screened the documentary before 400 magistrates and judges during a legal seminar in Nairobi (The Guardian 2015). The Chief Justice intimated to Campbell-Stephen' that: 'This is all I need to change the system (The Guardian 2015). Perhaps to emphasize the power of visual art in the enforcement of the rights of victims/survivors of sexual and gender-based violence.

Essentially, the challenges underscored by the two documentaries *Bridging the Gap: Reinforcing Gender Desks in Nairobi*' and *'I will not be Silenced'* are corroborated by the Human Rights Watch Report of 2017 titled 'They Were Men in Uniform.' The Report documents incidences of sexual violence in Nairobi's informal settlements, Kisumu and Bungoma during the 2017 elections in Kenya. In the Report which is based on interviews with 65 women, 3 girls and 3 men who allegedly experienced sexual violence shows 'lack of confidence in the police, largely because of their history of human rights abuses.' Only a handful of the women interviewed had reported their experiences with the police (Human Rights Watch 2017).

The Report also points out that Kenyan authorities has not taken action against those who perpetrated widespread sexual violence during the 2007–2008 election. The Report underscores that failure to investigate incidences of sexual violence and to hold those accountable for the heinous act to account beget further sexual violence. Lack of effective investigations and accountability has led to continued violation of rights of women rights.

As demonstrated above, visual art can be an important means to call for effective investigations and accountability by the government. Documentaries can provide an avenue for the victims of sexual violence to tell their side of the story, especially the victims whose violations are ignored by the state. Films can be used to remember these unfortunate incidences and to enhance/facilitate dialogue on how to tackle the culture of rape in Kenya.

4 Select Initiatives Zeroing on Visual Arts, Memory and Human Rights

This part seeks to highlight three initiatives that have zeroed in on the use of visual arts to foster dialogue on the Kenyan past and the state of human rights in Kenya. The first initiative is an exhibition organized by human rights activists Boniface Mwangi, Ory Okollah and Chief Justice (as he then was) Willy Mutunga in October 2015. The second is a project on extrajudicial killings and forced disappearances in Kenya which was undertaken by Amnesty International in partnership with Karen Village Art and Cultural Centre and African Uncensored, an independent media house. The third is an initiative by the Museum of British Colonialism which seeks to creatively communicate 'a more truthful account of British colonialism,' through various mechanisms including visual art (Museum of British Colonialism 2019).

In 2015, Boniface Mwangi, Ory Okollah and Chief Justice (as he then was) Willy Mutunga organised a photo exhibition along the Tom Mboya Avenue in Nairobi detailing Kenya's struggle from independence until 2015 (Kenyan Monitor 2015). Among the questions raised by the exhibition is who is a true hero in light of the Kenyan struggles for a democratic society, respect for human rights, rule of law and good governance. The exhibition also featured some of the heroes from pre-independence Kenya, some of whom were raped, tortured and killed as they fought to free the country from colonialism (Kenyan Monitor 2015). Further, the exhibition gave a chance to Kenyans from all walks of life to share their sentiments about Kenya's peaceful co-existence and growth.

In 2016, due to increased cases of extrajudicial executions and forced disappearances without accountability, Amnesty International in partnership with Karen Village Art and Cultural Centre and African Uncensored, an independent media house, worked with artists to document their 'experiences of watching the documentaries of victims of extrajudicial executions and enforced disappearances from different parts of the country' (Amnesty International 2016). The artists came up with pieces of art that reflected their 'coming to terms with this exposure' (Amnesty International 2016). A film maker also came up with a documentary capturing how behaviour as well as the attitudes of the artists changed in the course of the process (Amnesty International 2016).

The project was particularly important because the state had not formally documented the number of individuals who had lost their lives through extrajudicial execution and forced disappearances yet there was an indication that extrajudicial executions had become a systemic problem in the country (Amnesty International 2016). The exhibition was based on the fact that, through art, it was possible to influence people to take the injustice personally, 'to demand not only truth and justice for victims, but a complete end to enforced disappearances and extrajudicial executions' (Amnesty International 2016).

In respect to the brutality and atrocities committed by the British in Kenya during the colonial era, the Museum of British Colonialism is establishing an initiative on the Mau Mau Uprising (1952–1960) which 'was one of the most brutal episodes of British colonial episodes history, but remains one of the least well known and understood, both in the UK and in Kenya (Museum of British Colonialism 2019). The colonial government had established more than 100 detention camps, works camps and emergency villages during the period when hundreds of thousands of Kenyans were tortured with the objective to extra confessions of allegiance to the Mau Mau movement (Museum of British Colonialism 2019).

The initiative will utilise archival and current day documents, photographs and footage to envision how the detention camps looked and subsequently develop '3D digital reconstructions showing the physical structures and outlines' (Museum of British Colonialism 2019). The exhibition under the project will be developed collaboratively in both Kenya and the UK and to publicise it as widely as possible (Museum of British Colonialism 2019). The project aims to 'bear witness to the events that passed and the legacy of colonialism; bring communities together to share and document experiences because there has been little opportunity to speak of openly; broaden awareness of and engagement with these aspects of our shared history; address contemporary and abiding issues such as the restitution of archival records and access to historical documents; develop significant and powerful ways of working across countries to build fuller, more honest collective memory' (Museum of British Colonialism 2019).

These initiatives demonstrate how visual art can be used as a powerful medium to advocate for human rights, shed light on human atrocities, call for accountability for past human rights issues and to demand respect for human rights. Visual art can influence and inspire change in the society in regard to culture and values as well as entrenchment of democracy.

5 Conclusion

As demonstrated in this chapter, visual art is a useful means of reclaiming Kenya's history, liberating memory and promoting human rights in Kenya. As stated by Stevens et al. (2013), reclamation of history entails the inclusion of silenced voices and experiences of the marginalised. In addition, the process seeks to reflect a 'different socio-political light on the past by understanding its substance, rethinking the substance historically, in present, and imagining its impact on the future (Stevens et al. 2013).

Essentially, from independence, successive governments 'employed silence, denial and selective amnesia whenever individuals and agencies raised the concern to address historical injustices (TJRC Report 2013a, b). Visual art had shed light on some of the silenced voices and incidences of selective amnesia with regard to human rights violations by different regimes of government. Visual art has also allowed ordinary citizens to re-occupy, interact and contest narratives that have been propagated or silenced by the repressive Kenyan governments.

Ordinary Kenyans are able to question the institutionalisation and normalisation of horrid human rights violations, structural violence and abuse of power through visual art. Also, visual art has been an avenue to extricate the past from people who have been controlling the narratives of the past to serve their interests. Importantly, visual art has been employed to call for social justice, inclusivity, empowerment, respect for diversity and democratisation of memory.

References

Aguilar GO, Isa FG (eds) (2011) Rethinking transitions: equality and social justice in societies emerging from conflict. Intersentia Ltd, Cambridge

Amnesty International (2016) Kenya: behind the brush strokes, art meets human rights. https://www.amnesty.org/en/latest/campaigns/2016/12/kenya-behind-the-brush-stokes-art-meets-human-rights/

Bahun S (2015) Transitional justice and the arts: reflections on the field. In: Eisikovits N et al (eds) Theorizing transitional justice. Ashgate, Farnham, pp 153–166

Burnell PJ, Randall V, Ranker L (2008) Politics in the developing world. Oxford Press, New York

Citizen TV (2011) Wagalla massacre death in the dessert. https://www.youtube.com/watch?v=cZj6-rzV6kg

De Certeau M (1997) The capture of speech and other political writings (trans Conley T). University of Minnesota Press, Minneapolis/London

De Vos P (2001) A bridge too far? History as context in the interpretation of the South African constitution. S Afr J Hum Rights 17(1):1–31

Du Toit L (2016) The south African constitution as memory and promise: an exploration of its implications for sexual violence. Politikon 43(1):31–51

Ghai YP (2010) Chimera of constitutionalism: state, economy, and society in Africa. In: Deva S (ed) Law and (in)equalities: contemporary perspectives. Lucknow, Eastern Book Company, pp 327–342

Golebiewski D (2014) The arts as healing power in transitional justice (December 1, 2013). E-International Relations, 2014. https://papers.ssrn.com/sol3/papers.cfm?abstract_id=2399850

Government of Kenya (2003) Report of the task force on the establishment of a Truth, Justice and Reconciliation Commission

Greenwald A (2014) Politics of memory in global context: remembering the past in public – a conversation. https://www.youtube.com/watch?v=RWC9VTtV6AU

GSDRC (2016) Transitional justice topic guide. http://www.gsdrc.org/wp-content/uploads/2016/08/TransitionalJustice_GSDRC.pdf

Human Rights Watch (2017) World report 2017. https://www.hrw.org/world-report/2017/country-chapters/kenya

Jenkins K (2003) Rethinking history. Routledge, London/New York

Kamau N (2010) Women and political leadership in Kenya: ten case studies. Heinrich Böll Stiftung, Nairobi

Kenya Monitor (2015) Chief Justice Willy Mutunga, Boniface Mwangi and Ory Okolloh team up to recognise Kenya's heroes. http://www.monitor.co.ke/2015/10/24/chief-justice-willy-mutunga-boniface-mwangi-ory-okolloh-team-recognise-kenyas-heroes/

Khan Academy (2019) What role does memory play in art?. https://www.khanacademy.org/partner-content/tate/archives-memory/art-and-memory/a/what-role-does-memory-play-in-art

Khobe W (2017) The Supreme Court versus Royal Media Services: history as 'Super Context' in constitutional interpretation. The Platform Magazine. https://www.theplatform.co.ke/the-supreme-court-versus-royal-media-services-history-as-super-context-in-constitutional-interpretation/. Accessed 16 July 2019

Museum of British Colonialism (2019) An exploration of British colonialism. https://www.museumofbritishcolonialism.org

Onyango M (2015) Postcolonial politics in Kenya. In: Omeje K (ed) The crises of postcoloniality in Africa. Council for the Development of Social Science Research in Africa, Dakar, pp 183–195

Orwell G (1949) 1984. Secker and Warburg, London

Standard Media (2013) Kenya at 50: Late Kisoi hoisted flag on Mt. Kenya. https://www.standardmedia.co.ke/ktnhome/video/watch/2000067261/kenya-at-50-late-kisoi-hoisted-flag-on-mt-kenya. Accessed 5 September 2017

Santayana G (1905) Reason in common sense. Dover Publications, New York

Snyman J (1998) Interpretation and the politics of memory. Acta Juridica. pp 312–337

Soyinka W (2000) Politics of memory: memory, truth and social healing. In: Amadiume I, An-na'im A (eds) Politics of memory. Zed Books, London, pp 21–37

Stevens G, Duncan N, Sonn CC (2013) Memory, narrative and voice as liberatory praxis in the apartheid archive. In: Stevens G, Duncan N, Hook D (eds) Race, memory and the apartheid archive: towards a psychosocial praxis. Wits University Press, Johannesburg, pp 25–44

The Guardian (2015) I will not be silenced: fight for justice that gave Kenyan rape victims a voice. https://www.theguardian.com/film/2015/may/12/i-will-not-be-silenced-fight-for-justice-that-gave-kenyan-victims-a-voice

The Guardian (n.d.) Uncovering the Brutal Truth About the British Empire. https://www.theguardian.com/news/2016/aug/18/uncovering-truth-british-empire-caroline-elkins-mau-mau. Accessed 18 August 2016

The Pan-African Magazine Special Issue (1963) Jomo Kenyatta's speech at independence. https://soapboxie.com/world-politics/Message-from-Jomo-Kenyatta-Prime-Minister-at-Kenyas-independece-in-1963

The Star (2016) Chronicles of Wagalla Massacre. https://www.the-star.co.ke/siasa/2016-02-13-chronicles-of-the-wagalla-massacre/. Accessed 13 February 2016

The Star (2017) Ruto wrong, TJRC report is the key to peace not chaos. https://sgbvjusticekenya.net/2017/07/25/ruto-wrong-tjrc-report-is-the-key-to-peace-not-chaos-by-christine-alai/. Accessed 16 July 2019

Thesnaar CH (2011) Memories liberate the past. Dutch Reform Theol J 52(3&4):531–541

Truth, Justice and Reconciliation Commission (2013a) "TJRC Report (Abridged Version)": The final report of the Truth Justice and Reconciliation Commission of Kenya

Truth, Justice and Reconciliation Commission (2013b) The final report of the Truth Justice and Reconciliation Commission of Kenya (TJRC report)

Vimeo (2015) I will not be silenced. https://vimeo.com/ondemand/iwillnotbesilenced

Women's Initiatives for Gender Justice (2013) Bridging the gap: reinforcing gender desks in Nairobi. https://4genderjustice.org/home/documentaries/bridging-the-gap-women-in-kenya-call-for-strengthening-police-response-to-sexual-and-gender-based-violence/

Chapter 8
Sculpting and Human Rights: An Exploration of Fasasi Abeedeen Tunde's Works in Italy

Elizabeth Lisot-Nelson

Abstract This chapter engages the use of sculptures in spotlighting human rights focusing on the issue of migration and specifically the plight of migrants at sea. It explores the significant work of Fasasi Abeedeen Tunde—a Nigerian migrant—who crossed the Mediterranean sea into Europe. Through sculpting, Fasasi has been able to share powerful visuals depicting both the horrors and kindness he witnessed during his voyage. His artwork has been exhibited in Italy and garnered notable attention. His artworks accomplish what philosopher Emmanual Levinas called meeting the "Other" face to face, bringing about a moral imperative, based upon intrasubjective experience, which calls the viewer to action. This chapter examines this intersection through the work of Fasasi Abeedeen Tunde and the possibility for art to create changes in society in order to improve the application of human rights.

Keywords Refugees · Sculpture · African Migrants · Italy · Fasasi · Empathy

1 Introduction

The recognition of human rights of all people regardless of race, gender, class, religion, and whether citizen or migrant, has been articulated at the level of the United Nations, the African Commission on Human and Peoples' Rights and the European Union (United Nations Declaration of Human Rights 2015), (Anon n.d. - 1 African Banjul Charter of Human and Peoples' Rights 1981, 1986), (Charter of Fundamental Rights of the European Union 2016). Though there are common agreements about rights including liberty of movement, non-discrimination, human dignity, freedom from torture or enslavement, and the right to life, the implementation of these rights vary from country to country, and depend upon the political will of governments to

E. Lisot-Nelson (✉)
University of Texas at Tyler, Tyler, TX, USA
e-mail: elisot@uttyler.edu

R. Adeola et al. (eds.), *The Art of Human Rights*, Arts, Research, Innovation and Society, https://doi.org/10.1007/978-3-030-30102-6_8

implement them. Because of the large number of refugees and migrants moving within Africa and out of Africa to Europe, these discrepancies have become apparent as tens of thousands of human beings suffer discrimination, mistreatment, enslavement and death during their transit and within host countries.

In a world in which most people are busy with their lives and concerns it is difficult to draw attention to the mistreatment of others. According to Abdullahi A. An-Na'im and Jeffrey Hammond writing in *Cultural Transformation and Human Rights in Africa*, "cultural factors are crucial for the development of the political will to… sustain… the protection of human rights" (An-Na'im and Hammond 2002, pp. 18–19). The question becomes "how to promote political will that is consistently supportive of the systematic protection of human rights" (An-Na'im and Hammond 2002, p. 19). This chapter argues that art is capable of affecting political will because it can reach the hearts and minds of individuals who constitute a society. Art has an extraordinary ability to evoke empathy in a viewer who may be touched by its power to convey human emotion and create connections with the experiences of others. Vivienne Wang in her chapter, "Art, Research and Society: New Ecology: The Affective Power," in *Arts, Research, Innovation and Society*, shares a quote from OAM: "Art can sometimes change the way we look at the world; which [is] beyond aesthetic pleasure" (Wang 2015, p. 88). The Jewish Lithuanian philosopher Emmanuel Levinas (1906–1995), while held as a prisoner of war in a Nazi camp during WWII, developed an ethical theory that humans achieve an intersubjective experience when meeting the face of the "Other" (Levinas 1989, pp. 37–58, 75–87). It is the compassion found in human relationships—recognizing the humanity of the other—which propels a person beyond the temporality of ego into a present that includes a shared future (Levinas 1989, p. 45). The sculptures of Fasasi Abeedeen Tunde, a Nigerian artist forced to flee his country because of political violence, are examples of artworks capable of changing minds by bringing the viewer face-to-face with the trauma of displacement and the horror of witnessing women, children and men drown while crossing the Mediterranean. His art gives voice to the suffering of refugees while also depicting moments of human kindness such as when resources are shared or when rescue workers help those in need. Fasasi Abeedeen Tunde, a refugee himself, is able to express through art the universal call for human rights and the dignity of each individual person. This chapter recounts his story as an example; it explores his evocative creations while examining the state of human rights protection for refugees and migrants traveling through Africa and seeking asylum in Italy.

Most of African migration (about 80%) takes place within the continent, from one country to another, there are large numbers of people who travel to other continents, many of them legally with passports and visas (Flahaux and De Haas 2016). However, the irregular movement of people, those attempting to flee to Europe without legal transit papers, often travel through the Sahara Desert. This journey involves great risk and is becoming more dangerous as pressure mounts from European countries to stem the flow of migrants to the north.

2 Fasasi Departs Nigeria

Fasasi Abeedeen Tunde was born on 5 March 1985 in the city of Saki, Oyo State in the Southwest of Nigeria (Fig. 8.1).

Fasasi did not begin life with an intention to become a great artist or leave his country, his family, and everything he knew to make a perilous voyage to a foreign land; however, his life would unfold in ways he never imagined. Fasasi's drawings and sculptures come from his heart, his pain, his sorrow and his love of story-telling through art. Fasasi personally experienced great hardship while witnessing firsthand the suffering and death of many and the kindness of a few. His art is a testament to the need for human rights to be recognised and practiced in both Africa and Europe, as well as the world. Fasasi's journey began through the northern region of Nigeria and continued north through the Sahara (Lisot-Nelson E 2018a). Fasasi was taken by an open truck (anon n.d. - b Africans through the Desert). The bed of the truck was packed with a large number of people, so many that they were squished together and could not move. The people in the truck came from many countries, from Niger, Gambia and Senegal among others. They went through the Sahara Desert. Fasasi was not prepared for this type of journey, nor were the other travelers. He says it was a horrible ordeal, torturously hot, burning hot. Hotter than he had ever experienced in Nigeria. It took days to travel through the desert. They were given just a small amount

Fig. 8.1 *Fasasi with sculpture of man rescuing woman from drowning*, 2017, terracotta fired and painted, Casa Benvento, Rome (image credit: E. Lisot-Nelson, 2018)

of food and drink to survive, but for some it made no difference. The heat was too much; Fasasi said he saw people die right before his eyes (Lisot-Nelson E 2018a).[1]

3 Fasasi Arrives in Libya and Is Detained

When Fasasi arrived in Libya, he said "it was like going from the frying pan into the fire." (Lisot-Nelson E 2018a).[2] He has faith that God protected him because he does not know how he endured what came next. The truck stopped and the driver told them to get out, this was as far as their money covered. They would have to find their own way to the coast. He walked with five people with whom he had traveled in the truck. They were thirsty; they were hungry. Some Arab men stopped and asked them what they were doing. They could not fully understand what was said as the locals were speaking in Arabic, but the boss man named Muhammad conveyed to the travelers that because they were Africans they were in great danger. They should not be walking about in Libya. He warned them they would be taken and sold into slavery. He offered to help them and told them to come with him. The Arabs took the group to a compound behind a fence. They were put in a box and later went to a building and were able to shower. The group was given mere scraps of food to eat and very little juice to drink. During the night they could hear AK-47s being fired. All of them were utterly afraid. They did not know what would happen, but they were even more terrified to leave because of the warning given to them that they would be captured and enslaved if they left the area (Lisot-Nelson E 2018a).[3]

After the fall of Muammar Gaddafi in 2011 Libya essentially became a failed state (Rahman A A S 2017). Based upon estimates from embassies, the International Organization for Migration believes that there are between 700,000 and 1,000,000 migrants residing in Libya (International Organization for Migration n.d.-a, b). According to the International Labor Organization 2017 report, "Global Estimates of Modern Slavery," though migrants often begin their journey by voluntarily placing themselves with human smugglers, they run the risk of exploitation by human traffickers (International Labor Organization 2017, p. 30). Many migrants in Libya come from Sub-Saharan Africa (de Aguílar Hidalgo 2018). Arrest, detention, forced labor, rape, torture, enslavement and even death are common. Armed militias detain, buy and sell black Africans, sometimes demanding they contact their families to pay ransom for their release (Naib 2018). In an interview for *Time Magazine*, Hanan Salah, senior Libyan researcher for Human Rights Watch, explains that in Libya "dark skinned people in general face discrimination" (Vick 2016). Racism against black Africans is widespread in Libya (Searcey and Barry 2017). Many African

[1] Interview of Fasasi Abeedeen Tunde conducted by the author in Rome, Italy, on 19 October, 2018.

[2] Interview of Fasasi Abeedeen Tunde conducted by Elizabeth Lisot-Nelson in Rome, Italy, on 19 October, 2018.

[3] Interview of Fasasi Abeedeen Tunde conducted by Elizabeth Lisot-Nelson in Rome, Italy, on 19 October, 2018.

migrants are bought in open air markets; some only to be resold several times (Elbagir et al. 2017). Though much of the trade is conducted by non-state militias, according to a 2017 report by Peter Tinti for *Foreign Policy*, the Libyan government through militias—who now call themselves "Coast Guard Units"—run detentions centres operating with EU funding. They are intended to curb the flow of migration to Europe. According to Tinti, this makes the Libyan government and the EU complicit in the confinement and mistreatment of migrants (Tinti 2017). The human rights abuses are rampant. In *Migrant, Refugee, Smuggler, Savior* written by Peter Tinti and Tuesday Reitano, published by Oxford University Press in 2017, the documentation of violations are detailed. Tinti and Reitano describe that in both militia and de-facto government detention centres migrants are tortured sometimes being hung upside-down, whipped with metal wires and electrocuted; women are forced into prostitution, many become pregnant; thousands live in subhuman conditions where they may be beaten while their families are put on the phone listening in order to extort money from them. If the relatives do not pay, the migrant will suffer indefinite detention or be sold into slavery (Tinti and Reitano 2017, p. 125).

4 Fasasi Travels Across the Mediterranean Sea

Though Fasasi's detention was frightening and a month long, he was fortunate not to have been enslaved or beaten. He and others worked for about 2 weeks to construct a building inside the compound. Their labor would pay for their passage to Italy. After about a month, the boss man told Fasasi and his companions that he would transport them to ships to go to Italy. This was 26 August, 2015. Fasasi was excited. He imagined that on the ship he would finally be able to relax, to get some food and drink and sleep without the sound of gunfire. He was gravely disappointed. When the group arrived at the seaside there were rubber boats being pumped full of air. This was not what he had imagined. He could not fathom that those were the means they were going to use to journey across the Mediterranean. There were many people waiting to depart. When the boats were ready they began to load people into them: children, women, pregnant women and men. The people supervising the embarkation told them to take off and leave their shoes and belts, any sharp object that might puncture the rubber. They began to fill the boats with people, more and more, beyond what Fasasi thought could fit. He estimated that there were about 130 people on each boat. Once more he was packed in and unable to move, but now all he had was his t-shirt and trousers, nothing else: no jacket, no hat, no money, no food, no water and no idea what would happen to him. He prayed (Lisot-Nelson E 2018a).[4]

[4] Interview of Fasasi Abeedeen Tunde conducted by Elizabeth Lisot-Nelson in Rome, Italy, on 19 October, 2018.

Fig. 8.2 Fasasi, *Man and Boy Drowning*, 2017, pencil on paper (image credit: E. Lisot-Nelson)

Fig. 8.3 Fasasi, *Family Drowning*, 2017, pencil on paper (image credit: E. Lisot-Nelson)

Four rubber boats traveled together and after they were out to sea away from land, about 3 pm, one boat started to lose air. The people on it began to shout. As evening came and it grew dark the boat continued to leak, then it began to sink. The other three boats were already completely packed with people but they tried to help those who they could, women with babies, children, but there was very little room. People screamed and cried for help as they drowned: women, children, babies, men. Their voices went silent as they sank beneath the water. More than a hundred died before his eyes (Figs. 8.2, 8.3, and 8.4).

Fig. 8.4 Fasasi, *Women Drowning*, 2017, terracotta fired, painted (image credit: Yossuf Amini)

As Fasasi shares this experience he is shaking and rocking back and forth. His eyes water, his breathing becomes short. He continues to be horrified more than 2 years later. He feels guilt that so many drowned and only a few were saved. He recalls their voices. The experience is still very raw for him, this is why he makes sculptures about it. He wants the rest of the world to know what happened, what is still happening out on the Mediterranean Sea as the migrants cross the sea. But there was more tragedy to come. The three remaining boats continued through the night and the water began to get rough, very rough. A large wave came and one of the boats capsized. The people all fell into the sea. Once again, the sound of terrified screaming rang out, crying, desperate thrashing, begging for help. There was no room left on the two boats. The sea was churning as another hundred plus souls died, sinking into the depths (Figs. 8.5 and 8.6). Fasasi did not know if he would make it; he feared that the last two boats would also sink.

Finally, at about 9 pm, a ship appeared. It was a German NGO. It came close to the two remaining rubber rafts and helped the survivors up on deck. They were safe at last. Later they were transferred to an Italian Coast Guard ship (Lisot-Nelson E 2018a)[5] (Figs. 8.7 and 8.8).

Fasasi was among the fortunate who survived at sea. The European Political Strategy Centre, which is the European Commission's in-house think-tank, published a report in 2017 stating that between 2011 and 2016 about 630,000 refugees and migrants reached Italy by way of the central Mediterranean Sea, but during that time more than 13,000 died while crossing, and even more perished during travel through the Sahara Desert (European Political Strategy Centre 2017, p. 1). In 2015,

[5] Interview of Fasasi Abeedeen Tunde conducted by Elizabeth Lisot-Nelson in Rome, Italy, on 19 October, 2018.

Fig. 8.5 Fasasi, *Mother and Child Drowning*, 2017, pencil on paper (image credit: E. Lisot-Nelson)

Fig. 8.6 Fasasi, *Man Drowning*, 2017, terracotta fired and painted (image credit: Yossuf Amini)

the year Fasasi journeyed across the Mediterranean, he was one of 153,842 who made safe passage, while a total of 2869 died during the crossing. The year with the most deaths was 2016: with 181,436 making it safely to Italy but 4579 losing their lives on the water (European Political Strategy Centre 2017, p. 2). The figures from

Fig. 8.7 Fasasi, *Mother and Child Rescued*, 2017, terracotta, painted (image credit: Yossuf Amini)

Fig. 8.8 Fasasi, *Life from Water*, 2017, terracotta, painted (image credit: Yossuf Amini)

2017 show a decrease in deaths, but still the numbers are high: 2383 migrants died at sea with 100,308 making a safe voyage to Italy (Tondo and McVeigh 2018). In mid-2018, the governments in Italy and Malta decided to refuse NGO ships to dock and unload migrants at their shores, which frustrated the efforts to prevent drownings. The ratio of deaths to successful crossings appears to be rising (Tondo and

McVeigh 2018). The reason given for turning away of NGO ships is that they are working with human traffickers and facilitating irregular migration into Europe where there is currently a lack of political will to accept and integrate large numbers of foreigners (The Local DE 2018). This was not always the case.

In 2014 Italy ran a rescue operation called "Mare Nostrum" at a cost of $12 million a month, it probably saved the lives of around 130,000 people, but by late 2014 it was shut down. Instead, the European Union border agency, Frontex, launched a program named "Triton." It only had a budget of $3.6 million and was therefore not as effective as the Italian emergency operation (Taylor 2015). In April of 2015, over 800 people died in a single incident when a ship traveling from Tripoli carrying migrants to Italy sank. Only 27 persons survived (Bonomolo and Kirchgaessner 2015). After this disaster the EU decided to increase search-and-rescue operations (Faiola and Murphy 2015). In addition to official efforts, non-government organizations (NGO) became involved with ships of their own at the end of 2015.

5 Fasasi Arrives in Italy and Is Sent to Borgo Mezzanone

Fasasi and the other survivors who were rescued were brought to Messina, Sicily, where they were processed. The date was 28 August, 2015 and Fasasi says he was able to call his parents to tell them he was alive; however, he lost track of the other people he had traveled with through the desert. From Sicily he was sent to Foggia in the Southeast of Italy and transferred to a place called Borgo Mezzanone (Lisot-Nelson E 2018a).[6]

Originally built by Italy's former fascist government in 1934, Borgo Mezzanone has functioned at various times as a military air base or as a refugee camp after the Kosovo War. In 2005 it was converted into an asylum reception centre, categorized as a CARA (*Centri di Accoglienza per Richiedenti Asilo*, Centres for the Accommodation of Asylum Seekers); it is the third largest such accommodation in Italy (Goffredo and Meret 2017). Overcrowding and poor living conditions have been reported since 2014, and the wait time for those requesting asylum has continued to increase causing tensions and rioting (Observatorio Detenione Accoglienza Migranti Puglia 2017).[7] Next to the official reception centre, on the old airfield runway, a ghetto called Pista-Borgo Mezzanone has formed with between 500 and 700 people living without sanitation and healthcare services; however electricity, hot water and even amenities like Wi-Fi are taken from the adjacent asylum facility. Holes in the fence separating the two areas allow for a free flow of persons and supplies (Goffredo and Meret 2017). The inhabitance of the ghetto are, for the most

[6] Interview of Fasasi Abeedeen Tunde conducted by the author in Rome, Italy, on 19 October, 2018.

[7] In a report dated 29 November 2017 by the *Observatorio Detenzione Accoglienza Migranti Puglia*, online publication by Universita Degli Studio di Bari Aldo Moro, it is stated that the accommodations that were intended to house 636 people, were filled with 1071 persons. http://www.osservatoriomigranti.org/?scheda-centro&centro=cara-foggia-mezzanone.

part, failed asylum seekers. Some have set up small businesses with services such as barber shops, bicycle repair and ethnic restaurants, additionally the population increases during the tomato harvesting season when many of the inhabitants work in the fields (Manara 2016). The migrants who are employed as day laborers face exploitation. They are hired, not directly by the farmers, but by middlemen called "*caporali*"—gangmasters. According to a March 2018 CNN report, the gangmasters charge the workers to transport them to the fields and for food and water, while taking a large portion of the pay given by the farmers (D'Agostino 2018). Not only are the migrants abused as day laborers, but prostitution, drugs sales and use proliferate. These illicit activities are mostly run by a powerful Nigerian mafia operating in both the asylum centre and the ghetto (Zancan 2017). In September 2016, Fabrizio Gatti, an Italian investigative journalist who goes undercover to live, travel and work with migrants, published an article, "Sette giorni all'inferno: diario di un finto rifugiato nel ghetto di Stato" ("Seven days in hell: diary of a fake refugee in the state ghetto") in *L'Espresso* detailing his experience in Borgo Mezzanone (Gatti 2016). Gatti describes a world that resembles Purgatory or even Hades in which gangsters force girls into prostitution and people live as animals, all while awaiting the results of their asylum application (Gatti 2016). The journalist claims that the consortiums running the reception centre are making a lot of money from the Italian government as they are paid 22 euros a day per person, which adds up to more than 5 million euros a year; not much of that money is actually spent on the asylum seekers (Gatti 2016).

Fasasi applied for asylum in Italy; but he says he was at first denied (Lisot-Nelson E 2018a).[8] He did not know what he would do next until a man name Emmanuel at the refugee centre introduced him to a lawyer, Gerard. He told the attorney that he was an artist, but Gerard did not believe him and asked him to prove it. Gerard googled a picture of *Justice* and challenged Fasasi to sculpt it. The artist said he could, but needed some materials: cement and wire. It took Fasasi 3 weeks to finish the sculpture of *Lady Justice* (Fig. 8.9). When he was done Gerard was convinced that he was indeed an artist. He helped get Fasasi's college transcripts to document that he had a degree, and photos of the artworks he had done. Gerard wrote down what had happened to Fasasi in Nigeria and how he had to flee for his life. Gerard appealed the asylum decision. It took 6 months but finally after a year at Borgo Mezzanone Fasasi was granted a humanitarian protection permit in Italy, which lasts for 2 years (Associazione per gli Studi Giuridici sull'Immigrazione (ASGI) n.d.-a, b).[9] His permit expired October 2018 and he had to reapply to stay legally in Italy.

[8] Interview of Fasasi Abeedeen Tunde conducted by Elizabeth Lisot-Nelson in Rome, Italy, on 19 October, 2018.

[9] Interview of Fasasi Abeedeen Tunde conducted by Elizabeth Lisot-Nelson in Rome, Italy, on 19 October, 2018.

Fig. 8.9 Fasasi, *Lady Justice*, 2016, cement, wire, paint (image credit: Fasasi)

6 Fasasi Goes to Rome and Makes Art About His Voyage

Fasasi was transferred to Rome to live in a dorm-like house, Casa Benvento, with other migrants. The organization runs Benvento is *In Migrazione*, which is a social cooperative society created by a group of professionals who welcome and support foreigners. They bring in people who have received asylum to help them transition to their new host country (Migrazione n.d.). At Casa Benvento, refugees are given a place to live, food, phones, Italian language and history classes. They are allowed to stay a year in order to adjust to Italian society and figure out what they can do to earn a living. Fasasi was at the house for about 2–3 weeks when the president of *In Migrazione*, Simone Andreotti, asked him what he wanted to do. Fasasi responded that he desired to "express what happened during my journey." (Lisot-Nelson E 2018a)[10] He needed to share what was in his heart as an artist. Simone got the materials that Fasasi required: a pencil, a pad of paper, clay, paint and access to a

[10] Interview of Fasasi Abeedeen Tunde conducted by Elizabeth Lisot-Nelson in Rome, Italy, on 19 October, 2018.

Figs. 8.10 and 8.11 Fasasi, *Homeless Family Drinking*, 2017, raw terracotta, terracotta fired and painted (image credit: Fasasi and E. Lisot-Nelson)

kiln. Fasasi was given a small studio space to work. Simone invited two Italian artists to visit Fasasi. One was Lu Tiberi, the other Lena Salvatori. They advised Fasasi to develop his own style, a combination of African and European aesthetic traditions. They suggested that he not model too smoothly but keep the surface rough. Lu and Lena helped him discover that he had his own particular treatment of the materials and did not need to copy others. Fasasi's process is to draw from memory or life and then form his subjects in clay or with chicken wire if he is going to create a large cement sculpture. When working in clay, after the first firing, he paints the works because of limited resources he cannot use glaze and finish with a second firing (Figs. 8.10 and 8.11).

It took Fasasi 2–3 months to create 15 terracotta sculptures about his experience crossing the Mediterranean Sea. His first piece (Fig. 8.12) depicts an Italian man in uniform helping refugees out of the water. He explains that the coast guard rescue ship had security workers who aided the pregnant women and women with babies first. Now with a solid body of work, Fasasi was ready to show his sculptures to the public. (Lisot-Nelson E 2018a)[11]

In Migrazione arranged for Fasasi's first exhibition in Rome in 2017. They advertised in the newspaper and on television. They invited Gabriel, the head of the local police to come. The name of the art show was "L'approdo, dopo tanti pericoli l'arrivo in un porto sicuro" (The Landing: After So Many Dangers the Arrival in a Safe Harbor) (Fig. 8.13).

Fasasi gave the police chief Gabriel one of his sculptures. *In Migrazione* scheduled two more exhibitions: one in Riete and another in Orvieto. They knew that

[11] Interview of Fasasi Abeedeen Tunde conducted by Elizabeth Lisot-Nelson in Rome, Italy, on 19 October, 2018.

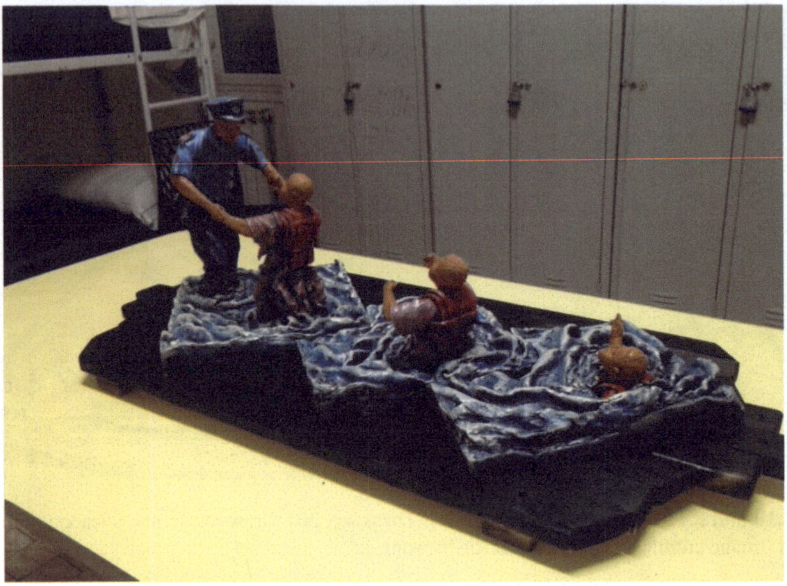

Fig. 8.12 Fasasi, *The Rescue*, 2017, terracotta painted (image credit: E. Lisot-Nelson)

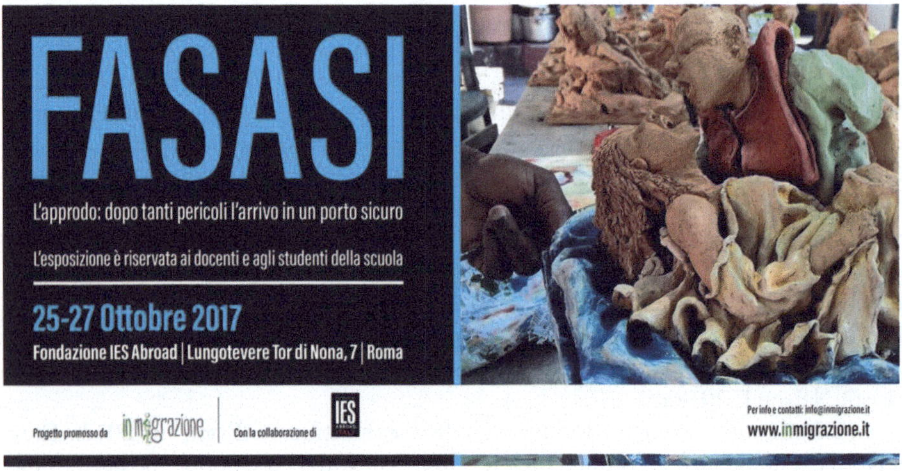

Fig. 8.13 Fasasi's first exhibition in Rome, *L'approdo*, 2017 (image credit: Yossuf Amini)

when people saw Fasasi's work it would help them understand the plight of the refugee, and possibly change the minds of those who were against helping foreign migrants in Italy. *In Migrazione* also arranged for Fasasi to meet and give one of his sculptures to Pope Francis, who has been a strong advocate for hospitality to immigrants (Fig. 8.14).

Fig. 8.14 *Fasasi giving one of his sculptures to Pope Francis*, 2017 (image credit: Yossuf Amini)

Simone Andreotti, the president of *In Migrazione*, is concerned about the bill approved by the cabinet of the Italian Prime Minister, Giuseppe Conte's cabinet in 2018 (Lisot-Nelson E 2018b),[12] popularly called "the Salvini Decree" after Matteo Salvini, the interior minister who drafted it (Gostoli 2018). It will likely be passed into law with some revision. Changes to Italy's immigration policy will directly affect Fasasi and tens of thousands of asylum seekers in Italy and those attempting to come. Over the last few years most migrants arriving in Italy, like Fasasi, received humanitarian protection permits, which allowed them residency and work permits for 2 years (Giuffrida 2018). Humanitarian protection was given to those fleeing violence like Fasasi, but also to victims who are persecuted because of their sexual orientation or religion, and women avoiding FGM or forced marriage. The new bill reserves refugee status for those fleeing war and the humanitarian permits only for people suffering from domestic violence, trafficking, labor exploitation, natural disasters or those needing special medical care (Scherer 2018a, b). Simone Andreotti says that Fasasi has to apply for a work permit to stay in the country as he will not qualify to reapply for humanitarian protection status under the new rules. Andreotti has no idea if this will be possible or how this will affect the many other migrants his organization helps (Lisot-Nelson E 2018b).[13] What is likely to happen is that more people in Italy will lose legitimate status, without residency or work permits,

[12] Personal interview conducted by Elizabeth Lisot-Nelson on 19 October, 2018, with Simone Andreotti, Presidente of In Migrazione Scs, Via del Fosso di Centrocelle 62/b, Roma. www.inmigrazione.it.

[13] Personal interview conducted by Elizabeth Lisot-Nelson on 19 October, 2018, with Simone Andreotti, Presidente of In Migrazione Scs, Via del Fosso di Centrocelle 62/b, Roma. www.inmigrazione.it.

creating more homelessness and poverty. There has already been a reduction in the amount of humanitarian protection permits issued. In 2017, out of 81,000 applications, only one in four were granted humanitarian protection. Half of asylum applications were rejected (Gostoli 2018). If the bill passes as-is, asylum seekers can be detained for 180 days rather than the current 90, in order to give the government more time to review their application and deport them, and migrants can be repatriated if they are accused of a crime, without due process. These measures appear to run contrary to the 1951 Refugee Convention and EU asylum law (Sunderland 2018a, b; UN Refugee Convention 1951; Council of Europe 2013). The "Salvini Decree" also plans to reduce funding for SPAR, which are the small municipal reception centres that house migrants and helps them integrate, get jobs and become autonomous. This is the type of accommodation where Fasasi was living during the interview for this chapter.

7 Fasasi Moves to Casa Scalabrini and Makes Art About the Homeless in Rome

After a year at Casa Benvento Fasasi's time was up and Fasasi had to leave. Fortunately, there was another place that offered him accommodations. The Scalabrini (ASCS) are a non-profit religious congregation who have a number of humanitarian missions in many countries (Scalabrini n.d.).[14] One of their projects is to support a house in Rome, Casa Scalabrini—run mostly by volunteers—where about 30 refugees, single men and families with men, women and children, stay for 6 months to a year after they leave a large refugee reception center or other municipal housing, such as Casa Benvento. At Casa Scalabrini there are private bedrooms, a shared kitchen and a common space with a television. The refugees are aided in becoming autonomous. They take Italian and English language classes, find contract part-time jobs, study for the *patente* (Italian driver's license) and are integrated into Italian society (Lisot-Nelson E 2018a).[15]

Rita Urbano is a social worker who helps the refugees at Casa Scalabrini. She explains that she sees room for improvement with the Italian immigration system, which focuses more on large emergency refugee camps but not as much on integrating migrants into society by supporting small community houses like Casa Scalabrini (Lisot-Nelson E 2018c).[16] Urbano explains that there are two types of government supported accommodations for refugees: (1) CARA (Centres for the Accommodation of Asylum Seekers), these are the large camps, such as Borgo Mezzanone, where people seeking asylum stay and await the government's decision about their status,

[14] *The Scalabrini*: http://www.scalabrini.net/it/ascs1.html.

[15] Interview of Fasasi Abeedeen Tunde conducted by Elizabeth Lisot-Nelson in Rome, Italy, on 19 October, 2018.

[16] Personal interview conducted by Elizabeth Lisot-Nelson on 19 October, 2018, with Rita Urbano, Area Socio-Legale, Casa Scalabrini 643, Sede Operativa ASCA Onlus, Via Casilina, 634–00177, Roma.

either positive or negative, and (2) SPRAR (System for the Protection of Asylum Seekers and Refugees), which are small municipal reception houses (like Casa Benvento and Casa Scalabrini) where people who have been given asylum can stay and begin to learn to integrate into society (Associazione per gli Studi Giuridici sull'Immigrazione (ASGI) n.d.-a, b). While these latter facilities hope to make the refugees autonomous helping them get vocational training or internships, immigrants are not always able to live on their own and get a job sufficient to support themselves after only 1 year at a SPRAR facility (Scherer 2018a, b). The government tends to focus their financial resources on the CARA and less on the SPRAR where the refugees can only stay 1 year before being forced to find their own place to live; there are a lot of people waiting to get into a small number of SPRAR facilities. After leaving the SPRAR some migrants find themselves homeless, though there are also homeless refugees who never make it to either the large refugee centres or the municipal houses (Busby and Dotto 2018). This is often the case if migrants do not want to seek asylum in the first country they enter. There are a variety of reasons for this, some may have relatives in other countries, or have language skills better suited to countries other than the first one they enter; however because of the Dublin Convention rules (Dublin IV Agreement 2016), refugees are required to seek asylum in the first country they enter. According to Rita Urbano, the Dublin Agreement is part of the problem that causes issues with accommodating, processing and helping refugees (Lisot-Nelson E 2018c).[17]

Fasasi moved into Casa Scalabrini in fall 2017. While living in this location, he commutes by bus to teach art classes to migrants at Casa Benvento, where he also has a small space to use as an art studio. Additionally, he goes to local schools with a member of the Scalabrini to talk about his experience as a refugee and show the children his artworks; however his stay at Casa Scalabrini is almost done. His 1 year time limit at Casa Scalabrini is finishing at the end of October, 2018, and his 2 year Humanitarian Asylum Permit expired 26 October, 2018. He needs to find an apartment where he can live. He earns some money teaching art classes but it is not enough to live on his own. It is not possible for him to get a job teaching in an Italian school as he does not have the required certification, which would take several years and funding beyond his means. The people at *In Migrazione* and at Casa Scalabrini will try to help him find a place to live, but financial resources are scarce. Fasasi is nervous. His latest art projects have focused on homeless migrants and he could soon become one himself. He has gone to sketch the many displaced people who stay near the Tiburtina train station, living under a bridge (Fig. 8.15).

Fasasi was shocked to see not only single people, but women with children, and families who are homeless. He says their situation is desperate. Some have jobs but still do not earn enough for a place to live. *In Migrazione* helped Fasasi promote another exhibition to display his recent works, called "In Viaggio" (Fig. 8.16). They are now identifying his style as "Refugee Art." Fasasi hopes his sculptures will bring attention to the grave situation of the homeless migrants in Rome and also the

[17] Personal interview conducted by Elizabeth Lisot-Nelson on 19 October, 2018, with Rita Urbano, Area Socio-Legale, Casa Scalabrini 643, Sede Operativa ASCA Onlus, Via Casilina, 634–00177, Roma.

Fig. 8.15 Fasasi, *Homeless Mother and Two Children*, 2018, pencil on paper (image credit: E. Lisot-Nelson)

perilous voyage they made to get to Italy (Lisot-Nelson E 2018a)[18] (Figs. 8.17, 8.18, and 8.19).

According to the Catholic journal *Crux* there are close to 15,000 homeless people in Rome with only about 300 shelter beds available (Giangravè 2018). Some migrants have taken up residence in abandoned buildings, but the government has cracked down and evicted them. On 19 August, 2017, Italian police violently scattered migrants with a water canon after they had begun sleeping in Piazza Indipendenza, just outside the abandoned building where they had resided for about 3 years (Kington 2017). Around 800 people, mostly from Eritrea and Ethiopia, were evicted from the building but had nowhere to go thus they moved into the piazza. Some had received asylum permits, but were not given accommodations after they left the CARA, others were transit migrants hoping to make it north to other countries, but were now stuck in Rome (Paynter 2018). The authorities have justified this harsh treatment of foreigners as necessary for national security from terrorism, but the physical and psychological harm to the innocent migrants is severe. These are victims of a broken immigration bureaucracy that does not have an effective system

[18] Interview of Fasasi Abeedeen Tunde conducted by Elizabeth Lisot-Nelson in Rome, Italy, on 19 October, 2018.

Fig. 8.16 Fasasi's exhibition, "In Viaggio" 2018 (image credit: Yossuf Amini)

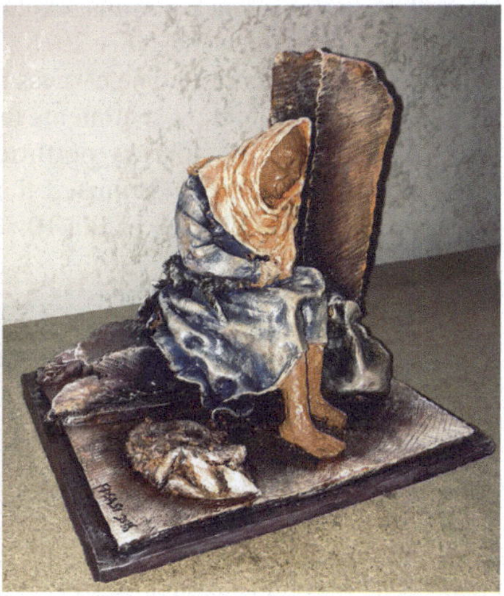

Figs. 8.17 and 8.18 Fasasi, *Homeless Series*, 2018, pencil on paper, terracotta painted (image credits: E. Lisot-Nelson)

to deal with the people needing asylum. Fortunately, because of pressure from the Baobab Experience, a non-profit association dedicated to helping migrants, the city of Rome has budgeted 300,000 euros to open an information centre in 2019 for the homeless migrants of Tiburtina; it will give them information about how to apply

Fig. 8.19 Fasasi, *Homeless Men*, detail, 2018, pencil on paper, terracotta painted (image credits: E. Lisot-Nelson)

for asylum and residency permits, explain where they might find accommodations and also hand out meals (ANSA 2018). Still, the new anti-immigration legislation is sure to produce further homelessness and severe tactics dealing with migrants. In spite of rising anti-migrant sentiments in Europe, millions of Africans are expected to make the dangerous journey north to the continent. The European Parliament president, Antonio Tajani, estimated that as many as 30 million immigrants may come to Europe from Africa within 10 years' time (Reuscher and Tauber 2017).

8 Why Are So Many People Leaving Africa to Come to Europe?

Some people leave their home countries in Africa to escape violence, like Fasasi, but many others are encouraged to go because of utopian dreams told to them by recruiters for smugglers and human traffickers. Migrant smuggling is a billion dollar business in North Africa (Tinti and Reitano 2017, p. 163). One victim of an unscrupulous recruiter is Esther, a young Nigerian woman from Lagos. Her story is told in Peter Tinti and Tuesday Reitano's book, *Migrant, Refugee, Smuggler, Savior* (Tinti and Reitano 2017, pp. 103–105). Esther had a job in a bank after earning a degree in accounting. She was earning decent money and was able to save it. A woman she met said she knew a grocer who would hire Esther to work for him in Spain. Esther left with the woman and ended up on the same route through the desert taken by

Fasasi. She was beaten on the journey. Things got worse in Libya when she was imprisoned by human traffickers and forced to work as a prostitute to purchase back her freedom (Tinti and Reitano 2017). Sadly, this is not an isolated story.

When asked why he thinks so many African's are leaving their countries and coming to Europe, Fasasi said that the governments in Africa do not appreciate their people. He sees this as a big problem in Africa as there are so many talented athletes, doctors, and people with exceptional skills who are not given the opportunity to be employed or contribute to their society. Fasasi says that he is more appreciated in Italy as an artist than he was in Nigeria, even though he does not have all the equipment he would like to produce better artworks. With the limited materials and facilities he has had available to him he has created some very impressive artworks.

9 Fasasi's Life Size Sculpture of Msgr. Scalabrini

Fasasi wanted to make a statue to show his gratitude to Casa Scalabrini and give them something to remember him after he moves out (Lisot-Nelson E 2018a).[19] He asked for an image of the Scalabrini founder, Msgr. Giovanni Battista Scalabrini (1839–1905), Bishop of Piacenza, who was concerned with the care of immigrants. In 1997 John Paul II beatified him as the "Father of Migrants" (Borrelli 2002). Fasasi also requested cement, wire and rebar to construct the armature for the sculpture. It took him several months to create a life size sculpture of Msgr. Scalabrini holding the hands of two immigrant children. Fasasi was careful to model the face to resemble the founder of the Scalabrini Congregation (Scalabrini Congregation n.d.)[20] (Figs. 8.20 and 8.21). The work currently rests where Fasasi made it, in a shed on the property of Casa Scalabrini. It will be moved to the front of the house for refugees when remodeling is finished. This work is the perfect testament to Fasasi's interest in African and European aesthetics as it combines both. The features of the children appear African; they hold the hands of Msgr. Scalabrini and gaze up at him. The figure of Scalabrini looks down at the female child and the viewer notices that he also holds a sandal in his hand, which the girl has lost as she is walking with only one shoe. Both children carry packs and a bundle of their belongings; they are being taken to shelter. This is a scene of hope and comfort, something positive as a response to the suffering that Fasasi has experienced and witnessed. Another sign of hope is that in April 2019, Fasasi received his *permesso di soggiorno* from the Italian government giving him legal status to work in the country until March 2021.

---

[19] Interview of Fasasi Abeedeen Tunde conducted by Elizabeth Lisot-Nelson in Rome, Italy, on 19 October, 2018.

[20] *Scalabrini Congregation*: http://simn-global.org/history/.

Fig. 8.20 Fasasi stands with his sculpture of *Msgr. Scalabrini and Two Migrant Children*, 2018, cement, Casa Scalabrini, Rome (image credit: E. Lisot-Nelson, 2018)

Fig. 8.21 Fasasi holding image he was given of Msgr. Scalabrini to create a likeness of the founder of the Scalabrini Congregation (image credit: E. Lisot-Nelson, 2018)

10 Fasasi's Artist Vision and How Sculpture Can Evoke Empathetic Response in the Viewer

Fasasi says that artists see differently than others and that their special vision can be shared to help others see differently too. He believes he gets his inspiration for art from God. Fasasi is a Muslim, but he does not think there is any problem with depicting images of people or animals, which are not idols (Lisot-Nelson E 2018a).[21] Depictions of humans and animals is not *haram* (forbidden) in the Qur'an; however there are warnings against it in some Hadiths (Najim 2018). Fasasi believes that God has given him the gift to make art and he should use his hands to express what is in his heart in order to communicate to others what he has seen. Fasasi's theory of art is reiterated by many studies. Jill Bennett, in *Empathetic Vision*, explains how imagery of traumatic memory does not simply convey a personal recollection, but rather represents a present experience of memory to trigger an understanding that is not simply empathy but rather a transmission of meaning that can transform perception. In this way the aesthetic experience is able to "open up trauma to the audience" (Bennett 2005, pp. 10–11). The artwork may not be able to fully communicate a personal subjective memory, but it may be able to "mimic the sudden impact of trauma" (Bennett 2005, p. 11). However, Susan Sontag warns in *Regarding the Pain of Others* that too many photographs of different migrants suffering can make the issue too global and can actually create less compassion as the viewer is overwhelmed and feels helpless, just as non-stop images of war will make people less responsive to "horrors" (Sontag 2003, pp. 79, 101). She suggests that "less polished pictures" embody a "special kind of authenticity" (Sontag 2003, p. 27).

In a study conducted by Zoé Cavnar-Lewandowski and Kelsey Gavin, and documented in there thesis presented in partial fulfillment of their Master's Degree at Loyola Marymount University in Marital and Family Therapy, 2017, their research showed increased empathy towards refugees in those who viewed the artwork of children fleeing war in Iraq, Afghanistan and Syria (Cavnar-Lewandowski and Gavin 2017, p. 54). The authors hope that their study will inspire other similar explorations involving art and art therapy as a means "to reduce discrimination based on fear of the 'other,' such as xenophobia and Islamophobia" (Cavnar-Lewandowski and Gavin 2017, p. 4). Cavnar-Lewandowski and Gavin suggest that the greatest empathy may be evoked by artworks made by the artist who experienced the traumatic events (Cavnar-Lewandowski and Gavin 2017, p. 38).

Part of what makes Fasasi's drawings and sculptures so effective at stimulating empathy in the viewer is that they are a personal, raw expressions of direct emotion. The images of women, men and children in the midst of drowning, screaming for help, appear to cry out from beyond the grave. Fasasi infuses his own horror and feelings of helplessness into the forms. The emotive significance of each piece quietly invites the viewer into a dialogue with their own conscience: what would YOU

[21] Interview of Fasasi Abeedeen Tunde conducted by Elizabeth Lisot-Nelson in Rome, Italy, on 19 October, 2018.

do in these circumstances? Would you survive or surrender to the waves? How would you process the guilt, sorrow and powerlessness of being unable to stop so many deaths? And, how do you respond to the sight of so many homeless women, children and young men starving on the street, knowing that they have already experienced such severe human rights violations as rape, detention, forced labor, forced prostitution and enslavement?

11 Conclusion

Fasasi's artworks are representational, not abstract, and therefore literally bring the viewer face-to-face with the "other" as described by Emmanuel Levinas (Levinas 1989, pp. 37–58, 75–87). The Nigerian artist's creations confront the observer with the human emotions of fear, alienation, and pain, but also kindness, tenderness and altruism. Fasasi's sculptures are concrete depictions demonstrating the importance of human rights laws and the need to garner the political will to enforce them. This can be done by supporting organizations that promote the rights of migrants, such as *In Migrazione*, the Scalabrini, and the Baobab Experience (Baobab Experience n.d.). Larger organizations, such as the United Nations and the European Union, can promote adherence to human rights agreements concerning migrant populations, such as the OAU Convention articles making them a priority (United Nations 1974). The 1951 Refugee Convention and its 1967 Protocol, signed by Italy, explains that because "by definition, refugees are not protected by their own governments, the international community steps in to insure they are safe and protected" (UN Refugee Convention 1951, and 1967 Protocol). The 1967 Protocol extended the time and geographic location from which refugees could come and be protected by the original agreement. In Article 32 refugees are given protections including not being evicted from their host country without due cause or process (UN Refugee Convention 1951, art 32). This is something that Matteo Salvini has threatened to do (Sunderland 2018a, b). The Italian government has even begun to dismantle some migrant camps and evict the refugees and migrants living there (de Fazio 2019). The UN Global Migration Pact, which was signed by representatives from one hundred and sixty-four governments on 10 December 2018 (United Nations Intergovernmental Conference on the Global Compact for Migrations 2018), extends protections for migrants along with refugees. Some European counties either refused to sign or abstained from ratifying the agreement when it was brought before the United Nations General Assembly 19 December, 2018, Italy abstained (Gotev 2018). Though of utmost importance in creating a common goal, a system and laws for the protection of the human rights of migrants, none of these organizations, institutions or pacts will be able to make the changes needed within the heart of each human. It is at the personal level that each of us makes the decision about respect of the "other" and how we treat one another. Fasasi's sculptures have the power to change minds and soften hearts through empathy. The more exposure his art receives the more people, especially in Italy, may experience empathy and will no longer fear the refugee, but rather see them as fellow humans who have suffered and are in need of protection as well as freedom from persecution. As Nelson Mandela wrote in his autobiography *Long Walk to Freedom*, when he was a young man he desired freedom only for himself, but as time went on he realized that he would not be free until everyone who looked like him had the same freedoms: "For to be free is not merely to cast off one's chains but to live in a way that respects and enhances the freedom of others" (Mandela 1994, pp. 624–625).

Fasasi's story is the journey of one man who exemplifies the power of art to communicate the plight of migrants and evoke empathy in the viewer, advocate for human rights and recognize the dignity of each individual. He brings us face-to-face with our own humanity and reveals the compassion of the African heart. Possibly his art can help grow the political will in Europe and beyond to accomplish the formidable task of enforcing human rights laws and prevent the suffering of so many of our fellow brothers and sisters.

References

An-Na'im AA, Hammond J (2002) In: An-Na'im AA (ed) Cultural transformation and human rights in Africa. Zen Books Ltd, London

Anon (n.d.-a) African (Banjul) Charter of Human and Peoples' Rights, adopted 27 June 1981, entered into force 21 October 1986. http://www.achpr.org/files/instruments/achpr/banjul_charter.pdf

Anon (n.d.-b) Africans through the desert. Youtube. https://www.youtube.com/watch?v=cvVRPqTy0Rg&t=137s

ANSA (2018) Info-point in Rome for migrants on housing, meals. 13 August. http://www.infomigrants.net/en/post/11242/info-point-in-rome-for-migrants-on-housing-meals

Associazione per gli Studi Giuridici sull'Immigrazione (ASGI) (n.d.-a) Short overview of the Italian reception system. http://www.asylumineurope.org/reports/country/italy/reception-conditions/short-overview-italian-reception-system

Associazione per gli Studi Giuridici sull'Immigrazione (ASGI) (n.d.-b) Residence permit. http://www.asylumineurope.org/reports/country/italy/content-international-protection/status-and-residence/residence-permit

Baobab Experience (n.d.)https://baobabexperience.org/

Bennett J (2005) Empathetic vision: affect, trauma, and contemporary art. Stanford University Press, Stanford

Bonomolo A, Kirchgaessner S (2015) UN says 800 migrants dead in boat disaster as Italy launces rescue of two more vessels. The Guardian. https://www.theguardian.com/world/2015/apr/20/italy-pm-matteo-renzi-migrant-shipwreck-crisis-srebrenica-massacre. Accessed 20 Apr 2015

Borrelli A (2002) Giovanni Battista Scalabrini. SantiBeati. http://www.santiebeati.it/dettaglio/55525. Accessed 1 Aug 2002

Busby M, Dotto C (2018) "I love Rome, but Rome doesn't love us": the city's new migrant crisis. The Guardian. https://www.theguardian.com/cities/2018/feb/19/rome-italy-migrant-crisis-squatting-emergency-shelters-asylum-seekers. Accessed 19 Feb 2018

Cavnar-Lewandowski Z, Gavin K (2017) The potential of refugee art to inspire empathy and social action. LMU/LLS theses and dissertations, p 299. http://digitalcommons.lmu.edu/etd/299

Charter of Fundamental Rights of the European Union (2016). https://eur-lex.europa.eu/legal-content/EN/TXT/HTML/?uri=CELEX:12016P/TXT&from=EN

Council of Europe (2013) Handbook on European law relating to asylum, borders and immigration. https://resourcecentre.savethechildren.net/node/8021/pdf/handbook-law-asylum-migration-borders_en.pdf
D'Agostino L (2018) Ghettos' and gangmasters: how migrants are exploited in Italy's tomato fields. CNN. https://www.cnn.com/2017/12/07/europe/italy-migrant-camp-exploitation/index.html. Accessed 21 Mar 2018
de Aguílar Hidalgo ID (2018) The Niger-Libya migration route. An odyssey shaped by Saharan connections and European fears, 2000–2017. Instituto Español de Estudios Estratégicos. http://www.ieee.es/en/Galerias/fichero/docs_marco/2018/DIEEEM01-2018_Migraciones_Europa_Niger-Libia_IreneDiazdeAguilar_ENGLISH.pdf. Accessed 15 Jan 2018
de Fazio MI (2019) After 'Salvini decree' evictions, refugees in Italy face an uncertain future. PRI's The World, 1 February. https://www.pri.org/stories/2019-02-01/after-salvini-decree-evictions-refugees-italy-face-uncertain-future
Dublin IV Agreement (2016) Explicated in the European Commission. Proposal for a Regulation of the European Parliament and of the Council establishing the criteria and mechanisms for determining the Member States responsible for examining application for internal protection lodged in one of the Member States by a third-country national or stateless person (April 2016). https://ec.europa.eu/home-affairs/sites/homeaffairs/files/what-we-do/policies/european-agenda-migration/proposal-implementation-package/docs/20160504/dublin_reform_proposal_en.pdf
Elbagir N, Razek R, Platt A, Jones B (2017) People for sale: where lives are auctioned from $400. CNN Exclusive Report, 15 November. https://www.cnn.com/2017/11/14/africa/libya-migrant-auctions/index.html
European Political Strategy Centre (2017) Irregular migration via the Central Mediterranean: from emergency responses to systemic solutions. European Political Strategy Centre strategic notes, issue 22, 2 February. https://ec.europa.eu/commission/sites/beta-political/files/irregular-migration-mediterranian-strategic_note_issue_22_0_en.pdf
Faiola A, Murphy B (2015) E.U. vows to boost migrant search-and-rescue efforts. Washington Post, 20 April. https://www.washingtonpost.com/world/mediterranean-disaster-provokes-calls-to-contain-deadly-exodus-to-europe/2015/04/20/7e9b7fda-e73b-11e4-9a6a-c1ab95a0600b_story.html?utm_term=.add264b3a88e
Flahaux M-L, De Haas H (2016) African migration: trends, patterns, drivers. Comp Migration Stud 4:1. https://comparativemigrationstudies.springeropen.com/articles/10.1186/s40878-015-0015-6. Accessed 22 Jan 2016
Gatti F (2016) Sette giorni all'inferno: diario di un finto rifugiato nel ghetto di Stato. L'Espresso, 12 September. http://espresso.repubblica.it/inchieste/2016/09/12/news/sette-giorni-all-inferno-diario-di-un-finto-rifugiato-nel-ghetto-di-stato-1.282517?ref=HEF_RULLO
Giangravè C (2018) Charities scramble to aid Rome's homeless amid scorching heat. Crux: taking the catholic pulse, 3 August. https://cruxnow.com/global-church/2018/08/03/charities-scramble-to-aid-romes-homeless-amid-scorching-heat/
Giuffrida A (2018) Italian government approves Salvini bill targeting migrants. The Guardian, 24 September. https://www.theguardian.com/world/2018/sep/24/italian-government-approves-bill-anti-migrant-measures-matteo-salvini
Goffredo S, Meret S (2017) Dept. of Culture and Global Studies, Aalborg University, Denmark. "Stuck in Place: Confinement and Survival in Borgo Mezzanone," University of Oxford, Border Criminology Blog, 20 June. https://www.law.ox.ac.uk/research-subject-groups/centre-criminology/centreborder-criminologies/blog/2017/06/stuck-place
Gostoli Y (2018) Italian government adopts hardline anti-migrant decree. Al Jazeera, 24 September. https://www.aljazeera.com/news/2018/09/italian-government-adopts-hardline-anti-migrant-decree-180924114249859.html
Gotev G (2018) "Nine EU members stay away from UN migration pact" EURACTIV. https://www.euractiv.com/section/global-europe/news/nine-eu-members-stay-away-from-un-migration-pact/
In Migrazione (n.d.) https://www.inmigrazione.it/it/chi-siamo

International Labor Organization (2017) Global estimates of modern slavery. Geneva. http://www.ilo.org/wcmsp5/groups/public/@dgreports/@dcomm/documents/publication/wcms_575479.pdf

International Organization for Migration (n.d.-a) IOM Libya brief. https://www.iom.int/countries/libya. Accessed 1 November, 2018.

International Organization for Migration (n.d.-b) The global compact for safe, orderly and regular migration. https://www.iom.int/global-compact-migration Accessed 21 June, 2019.

Kington T (2017) Police use water cannon on migrants in Rome, reflecting new, hard-line tactics. Los Angeles Times, 24 August. http://www.latimes.com/world/europe/la-fg-italy-refugees-crackdown-20170824-story.html

Levinas E (1989) In: Hand S (ed) The Levinas reader. Basil Blackwell, Oxford

Lisot-Nelson E (2018a) Interview of Fasasi Abeedeen Tunde, Rome, Italy, 19 October

Lisot-Nelson E (2018b) Interview of Simone Andreotti, Presidente of In Migrazione. Personal interview conducted by Elizabeth Lisot-Nelson on 19 October, 2018, with Scs, Via del Fosso di Centrocelle 62/b, Roma. http://www.inmigrazione.it. Accessed 19 October, 2018

Lisot-Nelson E (2018c) Interview of Rita Urbano, Area Socio-Legale, Casa Scalabrini 6, 19 October. 43, Sede Operativa ASCA Onlus, Via Casilina, 634-00177, Roma

Manara M (2016) Never settled. The informal refugee settlement of Borgo Mezzanone and its effects on asylum seekers in the reception centre. Oxford Monit Forced Migr 6(1):45–48

Mandela N (1994) Long walk to freedom. Back Bay Books, New York

Naib F (2018) Slavery in Libya: life inside a container. Al Jazeera, 26 January. https://www.aljazeera.com/news/2018/01/slavery-libya-life-container-180121084314393.html

Najim J (2018) Painting and sculpture in the Qur'an. Süleymaniye Foundation, 30 April. http://www.islamandquran.org/research/painting-and-sculpture.html

Observatorio Detenzione Accoglienza Migranti Puglia (2017) Universita Degli Studio di Bari Aldo Moro. http://www.osservatoriomigranti.org/?scheda-centro&centro=cara-foggia-mezzanone. Accessed 29 Nov 2017

Paynter, Eleanor (2018) The liminal lives of Europe's migrants. J Am Sociol Assoc, 17(2): 40–45. http://journals.sagepub.com/doi/full/10.1177/1536504218776959. Accessed 2 June 2018

Rahman, Abdur Alfa Shaban (2017) "Post-Gaddafi Libya: How the current chaos was birthed," with Reuters in African News https://www.africanews.com/2017/07/27/post-gaddafi-libya-how-the-current-chaos-was-birthed//

Reuscher C, Tauber A (2017) Dann werden 30 Millionen Einwanderer in die EU kommen. Interview with Antonio Tajani, Welt, 29 March. https://www.welt.de/politik/ausland/article163215714/Dann-werden-30-Millionen-Einwanderer-in-die-EU-kommen.html

Scalabrini Congregation (n.d.) http://simn-global.org/history/

Scherer S (2018a) Italy's homeless, jobless migrants shunned by Politicians Reuters, 24 January. https://www.reuters.com/article/us-italy-election-migrants/italys-homeless-jobless-migrants-shunned-by-politicians-idUSKBN1FD2BD

Scherer S (2018b) Italy to narrow asylum rights in clampdown on immigration. Reuters, 24 September. https://www.reuters.com/article/us-italy-politics-immigration-security/italy-to-narrow-asylum-rights-in-clampdown-on-immigration-idUSKCN1M41R8

Searcey D, Barry JY (2017) Sub-Saharan African migrants face old enemy in Libya: bigotry. New York Times, 12 September 2017. https://www.nytimes.com/2017/09/12/world/africa/migrants-africa-libya.html

Sontag S (2003) Regarding the pain of others. Picador, New York

Sunderland J (2018a) Italy's dangerous direction on immigration. Human Rights Watch, 11 June. https://www.hrw.org/news/2018/06/11/italys-dangerous-direction-migration

Sunderland J (2018b) New low for Italian migration policies: preventing Rescue at sea, punishing survivors on land. Human Rights Watch, 26 September. https://www.hrw.org/news/2018/09/26/new-low-italian-migration-policies

Taylor A (2015) Italy ran an operation that saved thousands of migrants from drowning in the Mediterranean. Why did it stop? Washington Post, 20 April. https://www.washingtonpost.com/news/worldviews/wp/2015/04/20/italy-ran-an-operation-that-save-thousands-of-

migrants-from-drowning-in-the-mediterranean-why-did-it-stop/?noredirect=on&utm_term=.35e3bb8001ba
The Local DE (2018) The German NGO ship lifeline – people smugglers or life savers? 28 June. https://www.thelocal.de/20180628/the-german-ngo-ship-lifeline-people-smugglers-or-life-savers
The Scalabrini (n.d.) http://www.scalabrini.net/it/ascs1.html
Tinti P (2017) Nearly there, but further away. Foreign policy, 5 October. http://europeslamsits-gates.foreignpolicy.com/part-3-nearly-there-but-never-further-away-libya-africa-europe-EU-militias-migration
Tinti P, Reitano T (2017) Migrant, refugee, smuggle, savior. Oxford University Press, Oxford
Tondo L, McVeigh K (2018) No GNO rescue boats currently in central Mediterranean, agencies warn. The Guardian, 12 September. https://www.theguardian.com/world/2018/sep/12/migrant-rescue-ships-mediterranean
United Nations (1974) OAU Convention Governing the Specific Aspects of Refugee Problems in Africa, 20 June. http://www.unhcr.org/en-us/about-us/background/45dc1a682/oau-convention-governing-specific-aspects-refugee-problems-africa-adopted.html
United Nations Declaration of Human Rights (2015) Printed, first adopted in 1948. http://www.un.org/en/udhrbook/pdf/udhr_booklet_en_web.pdf
United Nations Intergovernmental Conference on the Global Compact for Migration (2018). http://www.un.org/en/conf/migration/
United Nations Refugee Convention (1951) The Refugee Convention and its 1967 protocol. https://www.unhcr.org/3b66c2aa10
Vick K (2016) Libya's migrant economy is a modern day slave market. Time Magazine, 21 October. http://time.com/4538445/libyas-migrant-economy-is-a-modern-day-slave%09market/
Wang V (2015) Art, research and society: new ecology: the affective power. In: Bast G, Caravannis EG, Campbell DFJ (eds) Arts, research, innovation and society. Springer, Cham
Zancan N (2017) Foggia rebels against the ghetto. Hostages of the Nigerian mafia. La Stampa – English Edition, 28 September. https://www.lastampa.it/2017/09/28/esteri/foggia-rebels-against-the-ghetto-hostages-of-the-nigerian-mafia-TWJar9ebkUg5OK1D3rRx4M/pagina.html

Chapter 9
Theatre and Human Rights in Africa: Historical and Literary Representations in South Africa

Albert O. Oloruntoba

Abstract Theatre and dramatic literature play an important role in addressing human rights subject both by enhancing its maintenance and by censuring its numerous violations. Scholarly works have significantly explored the importance of theatre towards human empowerment, development and conscientisation. It is also worthy to note that since the turn of the last century, the world has seen in multiple ways, how practical drama has been adopted through dramatic literature and performance theatre to effectively explore human rights issues. The work of Shakespeare, Judith Malina and Julian Beck's *The Living Theatre* (1947), Brazilian theatre practitioner, Augusto Boal—Theatre of the Oppressed (1960), Market and Protest theatres of apartheid South Africa, Pakistani, and Juliano Mer Khamis' Freedom Theatre are some of many examples of the most influential attempts to address human rights concerns through theatre. In this chapter, I explore specific aspects of human rights and theatre in a country whose political history remains unique in different ways: South Africa. Considering the historical past of this country, Hein Marais describes it as one of the miracles of the twenty-first century (South Africa: limits to change: the political economy of transition. University of Cape Town Press, Cape Town, Hein 2001). In terms of literature and arts in general, this history or what Hein terms 'miracle' has made South Africa a lush site for literary exploration. With this in mind, the chapter interrogates the historical engagements of theatre in apartheid and post-apartheid South Africa along with how theatre/drama as a form of art has endured different forms of limitations. Additionally, it engages a specific South African play text *Green Man Flashing* (2006) by dramatist, Mike Van Graan, which explores the scourge of rape in South Africa to further explore the concept of human rights and theatre/drama.

Keywords Theatre · Violence · Rape · Politics of rape · Artivist(m) · Apartheid · Post-apartheid · Post-transitional · Green Man Flashing · South Africa · Theatre of the oppressed

---

A. O. Oloruntoba (✉)
Department of English, Faculty of Humanities, University of Pretoria, Pretoria, South Africa

R. Adeola et al. (eds.), *The Art of Human Rights*, Arts, Research, Innovation and Society, https://doi.org/10.1007/978-3-030-30102-6_9

1 Introduction

American theatre practitioner and historian, Oscar Brockett contend that although much of theatre's appeals lie in entertainment, if it does not offer additional appeals, it may be (and often is) dismissed as insignificant (1998). Brockett agrees to the entertainment purposes of theatre; however, he believes that it needs more than entertainment to be regarded as noteworthy. Looking at theatre from its original ritual purpose, it has always possessed and performed more roles than mere entertainment. For example, the Greek *Dionysia* of the 700 BC were dramatical performances which honoured the god Dionysus. Earlier Roman theatre became an agent through which the Roman people could express their political emotions during the republican and imperial periods of Rome (Slater 1996). Emphasising on the role of theatre, Brockett and Ball, agree that, theatre has perhaps the greatest potential as a humanizing force, because much of it asks us to enter imaginatively into the lives of others so we may understand their aspirations and motivations. Through role-playing, we come to understand who and what we are and see ourselves in relations to others. In a world given increasingly to violence and tension among ethnic and other diverse groups, the value of being able to understand and feel for others as human beings cannot be overemphasized (2004). Since the middle of the twentieth century, through the works of Brazilian theatre maker, German theatre maker, Bertolt Brecht, and South African protest theatre makers, the importance of theatre in engaging human rights and addressing social, political and cultural institutions have been significant. Theatrical performances engaging human rights issues have ranged from race to gender, and to inequalities of different forms have continued to focus on building conscientiousness as opposed to making art.

Referring to theatre as the "greatest … humanizing force", one could deduce that Brockett and Ball suggest that theatre facilitates peaceful human co-existence and facilitates quick and peaceful reconciliation and unity after a period of conflict. By so doing, theatre upholds the tenets of human rights as stated in the African Charter on Human and People's Rights, Article 28 which states that 'every individual shall have the duty to respect and consider his fellow beings without discrimination, and to maintain relations aimed at promoting, safeguarding and reinforcing mutual respect and tolerance' (1987). Ball and Brockett's declaration establishes the unquantifiable role that theatre plays in maintaining human rights. Writing further on the role of theatre, Richard Boon and Jane Plastow in *Theatre and Empowerment* (2004) agree that theatre has the power to bring together divided communities of different kinds … to engage creatively, productively and meaningfully with a wide range of issues from extreme poverty to AIDS, violence, human rights, sexual, racial and political intolerance and the power of the state. Also writing on the role of theatre and its makers, Paul Rae in his book *Theatre and Human Rights* (2009) posits that theatre-makers play an advocacy role as public intellectuals and civil society actors, … [theatre] performances challenge human rights norms, … theatre itself come under threat from human rights abuses; … theatre aesthetics echo the formal, legal and political contexts within which human rights law is enacted and challenged, … theatricality queasily inherent in some of the most iconic and widely publicised human rights violations of recent years—all these phenomenon colour the relationship between theatre and human rights today (Rae 2009).

Rae's comment here is vital because it seems to thrust some of the roles particular to the legal profession on theatre. The explicit usage of phrases such as 'playing advocacy role,' 'challenging human rights norms,' and 'echoing formal and legal subjects within human rights law' re-emphasize the special duties that theatre performs in human society. For Amine and Carlson as cited by Marvin Carlson, theatre is incitement and praxis that leads to changing people's passivity … it is a real site of debate and the circulation of social energy (2015). Writing in a similar vein, this time about human rights violation, Rae observes that when the freedom to make or watch theatre is threatened, especially by states or institutions, human rights are often perceived to be at stake (2009). Because of their 'artivist' (Asante 2008) proclivity: the quality of being able to use artistic talents to fight and struggle against injustice and oppression by merging commitment to freedom and justice with the pen, the lens, the brush, the voice, the body, and the imagination (Asante 2008), theatre itself has been and continues to be threatened by institutions responsible for subjects which theatre addresses, most especially the political subjects which theatre condemns. This was conspicuous during the period of apartheid in South Africa.

2 History and Memory: Apartheid/Post-apartheid Theatre in South Africa

During the period of apartheid in South Africa which lasted for over four decades (Ottaway 1993; Louw 2004), writers and activists were able to understand the two-faced functions of the theatre: to expose various forms through which human rights were denied and to raise awareness and conscientisation towards the emancipation of the oppressed. This dual role was carefully and successfully dispatched by theatrical activities in the South Africa of that era. While apartheid persisted, agitprop theatre such as Protest Theatre, Victory Sonqoba Theatre, and a few more emerged—in rural settlements with known theatre makers—to fight oppression against black majority. From the early 1960s and onwards, the emergence of township theatre as well as a vibrant tradition of protest plays including the works of Athol Fugard, Gibson Kente, Dennis Walder, Percy Mtwa, Mbongeni Ngema, Barney Simon and Zakes Mda were used not only to condemn the apartheid government, but also arouse the consciousness of the masses especially those who lived in townships and had no access to theatre halls which were mainly in the cities. Describing this form of drama as a truly South African theatre tradition (Middeke et al. 2015) perceive that this theatre form was triggered by existing apartheid laws coupled with artists' desire to contribute to the fight against all forms of inequality. Works of playwrights, actors and directors such as Simon Barney, Athol Fugard, John Kani, Yael Farber, and others were frontrunners of this form of theatre. The rise and influence of this theatre necessitated the enactment of The Publication and Entertainment Act of 1963 which was later modified to the Publication Act of 1974. The 1974 Act prohibited works that were labelled harmful to the state, offensive or obscene, a threat to peace and order, or a risk to what was defined as moral decency. For over four decades, playwrights, actors, musicians and other artists found themselves banned, imprisoned tortured and beaten (Middeke et al. 2015) for violating these laws. Plays performed at state-run theatres were constantly submitted to a censorship board which literally cleansed the scripts before they performed such plays in front of an audience, forcing playwrights to compromise their works or suffer the consequences (Fourie 1995). Not only did this policy limit the creative and artistic ingenuity and rights of theatre makers at a time, it also lessened the possibility of building consciousness to human rights violations among the population. However, by early 1990s when Nelson Mandela was released from prison and the constitutional implementation of the country's first democracy began to take effect, apartheid rules such as the Publication Acts of 1974 were abolished.

Post-apartheid narrative on theatre in South Africa allowed for creative expression. However, it did not start smoothly. Although firm attention has been given to human rights in the post-apartheid or what Frenkel and MacKenzie (2010) term 'post-transitional' South Africa, the theatrical scene was initially marked with confusion due to the fact that the major theme of anti-apartheid had to be replaced by other unfamiliar subjects. Keith Bain describes this post-transitional period as a period of creative confusion, relaxation or inhibition [which] has tended to refocus a great deal of energy within an ever-expanding market of theatrical entertainment (2003). The themes of apartheid and protest which dominated South African theatre in the past have slightly been replaced with more current social issues such as gender, violence, rape, economic inequality, environmental injustice and what I term post-1994 politics. Writing more generally about the literature of this post-transitional period, Ronit Frenkel and Craig MacKenzie argue that post-transitional literature is often unfettered to the past in the way that much apartheid writing was, but may still reconsider it in new ways. Equally, it may ignore it altogether. Other features include politically incorrect humour and incisive satire, and the mixing of genres with zest and freedom (2010). This is also the view of American critic, Lena Slachmuijlder who points to the predominance of contemporary social issues, previously politicised historical events, cultural treasures and personal stories (1999). Speaking also of theatre as an important tool during the period after apartheid, Olga Barrios observes that theatre has been chosen as the most suitable vehicle [preferred] by post-apartheid playwrights to expose the sequels left by apartheid on the South African population. Thus, theatre continues to be the favourite genre to be used to raise consciousness among people as it happened through the 1970s and 1980s during the Black Consciousness Movement (2012). These themes of post-apartheid as noted by these scholars have been the preoccupation of writers of the post-apartheid or post-transitional generation. Playwrights and theatre practitioners at the turn of 1994 such as Nadia Davids, Sindiwe Magona, Zöe Wicomb, Zukiswa Wanner, Lara Foot-Newton, Malika Ndolvu deal with concerns such as gender-based violence, economic inequality, nostalgia and what I term 'post-apartheid racism': a different form of racism to what was practised during the apartheid era. It is post-apartheid racism because it is not legally institutionalised as apartheid did, and secondly, racism in this sense could be perpetrated by people of any race against people of any race.

The new democracy boosted the financial viability of the theatre industry. Employment and jobs were created. Financially, there has been significant funding and resources dedicated to the Arts and Culture ministry, under which theatre is classified. There are significant improvements on the fund appropriated yearly to the department. The record indicates that in 2015–2016, it was 3.9 billion Rand; 4.1 billion in 2016–2017, and 4.4 billion Rand in 2017–2018 was budgeted to the ministry/department of Arts and Culture (Vulekamali, n.d). This shows a considerable progression and government's efforts in making arts accessible to everyone. However, accessibility to these funds remains a challenge. Despite financial provisions, records prove that physical infrastructural development has been lacking. Most of the theatre houses that exist in the country today are those that were erected during the period of apartheid. The effect of this is that since these theatre houses are located in urban areas, accessibility still remains a constraint for poor people. Given the problem of accessibility, theatre continues to reflect the structural legacies of the past and will continue to do so unless structural interventions are made to change this (Graan 2018). However, to address this, the government will need to take measures to ensure that theatres are not only in the cities, but also at suburbs where most of the economically impoverished tend to reside. Having briefly explored aspects of theatre during apartheid and post-apartheid South Africa, this chapter turns to exploring how theatre has contributed to spotlighting human rights concerns. The next section of this chapter entails the exegesis of Mike Van Graan's award-winning play—*Green Man Flashing* (2006). Touching on human rights and fundamental freedoms, the chapter highlights and critiques the issue of rape which in post-apartheid South Africa, has become a prominent problem.

3 Politics of Rape and Justice in Mike Van Graan's *Green Man Flashing*

According to Binaifer Nowrojee, South African women are victims of widespread violence that prevents them from enjoying human rights …One in every six South African women is in an abusive relationship (1995). This is indicative of rape—a scourge in the post-apartheid South Africa—which feminist and author, Pumla Gqola describes as "a huge problem" (2015). Pumla Gqola (2007) and Clive Harber (2001) both ague that violence against women are generally among many legacies of apartheid. One could argue that through the constant intra-racial/party violence between political parties in the 1980s, arms were able to find their ways into the possession of many indigenes including those of African National Congress (ANC) and those of the IFP members who were trained and armed by the ruling party, the

National Party (Marlin-Curiel 2005). Through these events and other means, I would argue that not only did firearms find their ways into the arms of black people, the culture of violence and force was consciously and unconsciously enculturated in the society. Also enhancing the culture of violence especially among Black South African male is the culture of patriarchy which African traditions seem to encourage. This point is also articulated by Gqola who laments that something makes it acceptable for millions to get raped on a regular basis in the South African society: this she calls "patriarchy" (2015). This author further posits that rape is a crime of power, and in patriarchal societies, all men can access patriarchal hegemony. Writing about post-transitional theatre or what I prefer to call post-1994 theatre in South Africa, Olga Barrios observes that the main issues that are repeated in contemporary black theatre plays are: male abuse and violence against women, and the discrimination that affects those people of hybrid identities (coloureds) (Barrios 2012). So, as a way of addressing the increasing scourge of rape in South Africa, literary writers have drawn attention to this subject. Texts such as *Disgrace* (1999) by JM Coetzee, *Bitter Fruit* (2001) by Achmat Dangor, *Tshepang: The Third Testament* (2004) by Lara Foot which was inspired by the rape of a nine-month old child in 2001 and, *Relativity: Township Stories* (2006) by Mpumelelo Paul Grootboom and Presley Chweneyagae, explore this concern by giving outright condemnation of such act. Also striking is the attention given to the subject of gender violence and rape in South Africa by non-fiction scholars such as Lucy Valerie Graham (2003), Meg Samuelson (2006) and Pumla Gqola (2015). In this line, Mike Van Graan's play *Green Man Flashing* (2006) examines an identical subject: rape.

The play is published along other plays in an anthology: *New South African Plays* (2006) edited by Charles J. Fourie. Before its publication in the anthology, the play had been performed severally in Cape Town where it is set and in other cities in the country. Adopting a non-linear plot structure where rather than sequential unfolding of events, actions take place with interweaving scenes where event B comes before event A, the play is able to alert the consciousness of the viewers/readers with the theatrical elements of the play. With this method of non-linearity of events, associated with Bertolt Brecht's Alienation Effect which rather than have one scene flow smoothly into another, calls attention to the knots tying the scenes together, the play is able to conscientize its audience of its important motif. Therefore, he used captions (projected on screens), songs, and other devices to emphasize breaks in action" (Brockett and Ball 2004), audience' consciousness are constantly awakened to the fact that what they are watching is an imitation of reality and not reality in itself. In this way, they would be motivated to take positive actions against concerns raised in the play.

So, *Green Man Flashing* begins at the inquest into the death of Inspector Luthando Nyaka who Aaron describes as a "police informer, a thug, a murderer with no conscience" (2006). Ex-couple, Aaron (a black man) and Gabby (a white woman) prove their innocence concerning the murder of this inspector whom Gabby had shot when his aggression towards her becomes unbearable for her. The following two scenes appear in form of analepsis which allows the reader to have a sort of partial uncovering of the incidents that led to Gabby's shooting of Luthando. These brief scenes are shown as they concretise Aaron's testimony as to the events leading to the inspector's death. Subsequent scenes depict post-apartheid South Africa where the 'New South' is not only trying to find its feet, but also attempting to help other African countries such as Angola and Rwanda who have their internal political struggles at the time the play was set: 6 weeks before South African second democratic election. In the midst of this, Aaron, an ANC struggle stalwart seem to prioritize political loyalty over personal relationship with his family. He values fixing of this new nation over his immediate family consisting of his ex-wife Gabby and his son Matthew. His careless handling of his family leads first to the tragic death of his only child in the hands of violent neighbours who attack him with weapon before hijacking his bicycle. Aaron had promised to take Matthew to a football game taking place that day but a sudden call from his comrades, he departed for Angola leaving his family. And secondly, the rape of Aaron's ex-wife, Anna, a white woman by Khumalo, an influential black South African. I understand this form of inter-racial rape one that challenges the form of inter-racial rape which are depicted in text such as *Bitter Fruit* (2001) by Achmat Dangor where perpetrator of rape is white, and victim is non-white. This chapter's concern is not on racialised rape but on rape as an extreme form of human right abuse which I focus on from now. The theme of rape which this chapter considers is carefully handled by Graan in a manner that does not only question the perpetrators but questions how the problem can be politicised in a post-apartheid South Africa. The dialogues and counter-dialogues that ensue among characters like Anna, Gabby's friend and lawyer, Aaron, Gabby's ex-husband and anti-apartheid stalwart, Inspector Luthando and Gabby, the victim herself becomes the bedrock of my analysis. Aaron comes home after almost 10 months since his son's death and finds himself negotiating Gabby's rape case with Anna. Rather than seek justice for the rape of his ex-wife, Aaron is seen asking the lawyer to bury the case, so it does not affect the status of a politician as influential as Comrade Khumalo and stir up violence in the young and volatile nation:

Aaron: You're aware of the damage to the country if this goes public ... the point is, there would be a major political repercussion.

Anna: No, Aaron! The point is that a woman has been raped. The point is that this woman is ... your ex-wife. Gabby has a right to justice.

Aaron: I agree. A hundred per cent! But life is a little more complex than that. Sometimes ... sometimes ***justice has to be sacrificed for the greater political good***.

Anna: I don't believe I'm hearing this.

Aaron: Anna, you're a lawyer. You represented victims at the TRC. Did you throw your hands then?

Anna: That was different.

Aaron: Was it? How many perpetrators of human rights abuses were brought to book?

How many victims whom you represented got justice? None. Not a single one. Justice had to be sacrificed for the greater political good. The TRC was a deal, Anna. It wasn't about justice. You know that (201 *emphasis added*).

This excerpt encapsulates what I refer to as twin injustice: a situation where an act of injustice is sought to be concealed by another. For Gabby, after being raped by Khumalo, Aaron seeks to constrict her right to equal protection before the law. Rape in the context of the play is politicised. This is similar to what Gqola notes in her book *Rape: A South African Nightmare* (2015) where she examines the Zuma case. To her, it was a difficult moment in South Africa's post-transition period and one that questioned many assumptions about the place of power, gender and sexuality in South Africa (Gqola 2015). There seems to be some sort of synchrony in what is depicted in this play and Gqola argues. Rape is a performance of power and when public figures are involved, politics offsets justice.

Continuing in this vein, the play adopts a metaphoric illustration of the safety of silence over the quest for justice. In the dialogue below, Aaron explains this illustration to a perplexed Anna:

Aaron: Anna, if you were standing at the traffic lights, and the green man's flashing in your direction, whose right of way is it?
Anna: It's hers. So?
Aaron: But there is a taxi coming down the road at eighty kilometres an hour and it's not going to stop, despite the traffic lights being red and green man flashing in your favour. Would you still cross the street?
Anna: Of course not.
Aaron: Why not? It's your right to cross the street!
Anna: And your point is? That Gabby can give up her right to justice and live. Or she can exercise her right, and risk getting wiped out in the process. That's what your metaphor implies.
Aaron: What I'm trying to say is that sometimes exercising your right is not in your best personal interests.
Anna: This is exactly why rapists get away with … murder. It has to stop (207).

The conversation here does not only validate the idea of politicisation of rape and injustice, it simultaneously depicts something more disturbing, a threat to the life of the victim. Despite having the right to cross the road at the time the green man is flashing in Aaron's synecdoche, the uncomfortable stare of death at a victim automatically makes justice a secondary or needless proposition in her life. With this illustration, Gabby's right to equality, right to liberty and equality, right to equal protection by the law are denied with threat to her life. Having created the feeling of terror and the dire necessity for safety in Gabby's life, the men in power also propose solution to the problem they created. They offer to sponsor her disappearance from the country to any country of her choice where she would work in the nation's embassy. She must go into exile not only for her safety, but also to protect the mythical volatile political state of the nation. Seeing truly that her life and those of her family members might be in danger if she stays around, Gabby accepts to the proposal which comes as a shock to Anna, her fried and lawyer who is ready to join her in the battle against the national scourge. Anna problematises Gabby's acceptance to leave and abandon the high-profile rape case as the reason why rape perpetrators escape and why rape has not been able to be curbed: Anna: (*with a hint of bitterness*) So you're just going to let them get away with it. Khumalo will get off scot free, and when he rapes someone else again, how will you live with the guilt then? … you're not betraying me [by abandoning the case]. We had a chance … a chance in a million to put rape on a national agenda. To once and for all strike a blow for all those women, teenagers, girls … babies that are raped every day in this country. A high-profile case like this will not come around every day! (206).

By introducing the motif of rape and patriarchy, the play touches on what scholars such as Charlotte Hooper (1999), Terry Kupers (2005) describe as toxic masculinity. According to Kupers, toxic masculinity is the constellation of socially regressive male traits that serve to foster domination (2005). Exerting this masculine hegemony on the vulnerable Gabby, owing to her gender and the 'gate-keepers' status that men have elevated themselves to, and even more the influential ones among them, Comrade Khumalo violates Gabby's right to protection and adequate security. While the experience of Gabby is a synecdoche for other rape victims especially in South Africa, the play uses the agent of masculinity through violence and emotional blackmail to enhance the denial of these rights. By doing so, the play criticises gender inequality on the one hand, and government's unresponsiveness to the plight of rape victims especially when it involves influential figure such as Khumalo on the other hand.

This means that the play acknowledges and criticises the various ways in which people of the 'other' (De Beauvior 1949) gender are often the victims of human rights abuse than men, whom the society according to Simone de Beauvoir, citing Frazer James' exalts to the position of gods whom women worship (De Beauvoir 1949). The play critiques the abuse of women as born free and equal in dignity and rights, it addresses their right to life, liberty and security, their right not to be subjected to torture or to cruel, inhuman or degrading treatment or punishment, the denial of their right to equality before the law and entitlement without any discrimination to equal protection of the law, all listed in the UDHR. It is also a significant part of the Protocol to the African Charter on Human and Peoples' Rights on the Rights of Women in Africa where Article 3 (1-2) stipulates that 'every woman shall have the right to dignity inherent in a human being and to the recognition and protection of her human and legal rights; every woman shall have the right to respect as a person and to the free development of her personality' (ACHPR 2003, art 3(1-2). By doing so, we once again experience theatre speaking to a socio-political concern which Pumla Gqola calls a 'nightmare' in the title of her book, *Rape: A South African Nightmare* (2015). Although the focus of this chapter is on South Africa, rape is however a transnational nightmare.

4 Conclusion

Having briefly reviewed the journey of South African agitprop theatre or what I term 'theatre of conscientisation' through the period of the late 1950s through till late 1980s and how this theatre represents a form of activism and 'artivism' against racial inequality, this chapter argues that at different stages in human societies, theatre is significant as it depicts or mirrors the position of the society at such a time. A famous speech in William Shakespeare's (1855) play *Hamlet* describes the objective of drama/theatre as being able to hold … the mirror up to nature; to show virtue her own feature, scorn her own image, and the very age and body of time his form and pressure (1599–1602). In fulfilling these responsibilities, what this chapter has been able to observe is that theatre is a robust vehicle used to conscientize its audience. The chapter also lays bare the scourge of rape and emphasizes ... the maintenance of human rights and equally criticising their abusers. South African plays such as *Sizwe Bansi is Dead, The Islands* (1973), *How Long* (1974) and *Too Late* (1974) and many others have proven Shakespeare's assertion right. In the light of the works of Athol Fugard, John Kani, Winston Ntshona, Zakes Mda and Mbogeni Ngema, Graan's play can be placed along this line, albeit, with themes that speak more to post-apartheid Africa. In the second part of the chapter, I analyse a post-millennial South African play which I study in relation to human rights subjects such as right to life, right to equality, right to liberty and equality, right to equal protection by the law, right against torture and inhuman treatment, and many more. In so doing, the chapter concludes that African theatre and most narrowly, contemporary South African theatre have not only fostered global human rights through anti-racist themes, themes of economic, gender, religious, cultural and social concerns, they have themselves been victims of oppression through institutional set-ups as recorded in apartheid-South Africa yet have continue to perform its duties relentlessly.

References

African Union (2003) Protocol to the African Charter on Human and Peoples' Rights on the rights of women in Africa. African Union, Maputo, Mozambique, pp 1– 32. http://www.achpr.org/files/instruments/women-protocol/achpr_instr_proto_women_eng.pdf

Asante MK (2008) It's bigger than hip hop: the rise of the hip hop generation. St. Martin's Griffin, New York

Barrios O (2012) Male violence against women and hybrid identities in post-apartheid South African Black Theatre. Int J Arts 2(5):39–48. https://doi.org/10.5923/j.arts.20120205.02

Boon R, Plastow J (2004) Introduction. In: Boon R, Plastow J (eds) Theatre and empowerment: community drama on the world stage. Cambridge University Press, Cambridge, pp 1–12

Brockett O (1998) History of the theatre. Allyn & Bacon Incorporated, Boston

Brockett O, Ball R (2004) The essential theatre. Wadsworth/Thompson Learning, California

Carlson M (2015) Jalila Baccar and Tunisian theatre: we will not be silent. In: Luckhurst M, Morin E (eds) Theatre and human rights after 1945: things unspeakable. Palgrave Macmillan, pp 190–206

De Beauvoir D (1949) The second sex. Parshley HM (trans and ed). Pan Books, New York

Fourie C (1995) Introduction to New South African Plays. 2006. Aurora Metro Publications Ltd., Hampshire

Frenkel R and MacKenzie C (2010) Conceptualizing 'Post-Transitional' South African Literature in English. *English Studies in Africa*. 53(1):1–10 pp

Graham LV (2003) Reading the Unspeakable: Rape in J. M. Coetzee's Disgrace. *Journal of Southern African Studies* 29(2): 433-444

Gqola DP (2007) How the 'cult of femininity' and violent masculinities support endemic gender based violence in contemporary South Africa. Afr Identities 5(1):111–124. https://doi.org/10.1080/14725840701253894

Gqola DP (2015) Rape: a South African nightmare. MF Books Joburg, Johannesburg

Graan MV (2006) Green man flashing. In: Fourie CJ, Abrahams R (eds) New South African plays. Aurora Metro Press, London, pp 172–221

Graan MV (2018) A vision for the theatre. *Lecture delivered at the Musker Theatre, University of Pretoria*. Date: 24 April 2018

Harber C (2001) Schooling and violence in South Africa: creating a safer school. Intercult Educ 12(3):261–271. https://doi.org/10.1080/14675980120087471

Hein M (2001) South Africa: limits to change: the political economy of transition. University of Cape Town Press, Cape Town

Hooper C (1999) Masculinities, IR and the 'gender variable': a cost-benefit analysis for (sympathetic) gender sceptics. Rev Int Stud 25(3):475–480. https://doi.org/10.1017/S0260210599004751

Kupers T (2005) Toxic masculinity as a barrier to mental health treatment in prison. J Clin Psychol 61(6):713–724

Louw PE (2004) The rise, fall, and legacy of apartheid. Praeger, Cape Town

Marlin-Curiel S (2005) Wielding the cultural weapon after apartheid: Bongani Linda's Victory Sonqoba Theatre Company, South Africa. In: Boon R, Plastow J (eds) Theatre and empowerment, community drama on the world stage. Cambridge University Press, Cambridge, pp 94–124

Middeke M, Schnierer PP and Homann G (eds) (2015) Introduction: *The Methuen Drama Guide to Contemporary South African Theatre*. London:, Bloomsbury Publishing. 9–25

Ottaway M (1993) South Africa: the struggle for a new order. Brookings Institution Press, Washington

Rae P (2009) Theatre and human rights. Palgrave Macmillan, Hampshire

Samuelson M (2006) Fictional representations of rape in South African Fiction of the Transition. In: Arndt, Susan and von Brisinski, Marek Spitczok (eds). *Africa, Europe, and post-Colonialism: Racism, Migration and Disapora in African Literatures*. Bayreuth: Bayreuth African Studies. 183–193 pp

Slachmuijlder L (1999) Culture: redefining relevance: the new South African theatre. South Africa Rep 14(2):18–21

Slater JW (1996) Roman theater and society. The University of Michigan Press, Ann Arbor

Vulekamali (n.d.). Department Budgets https://vulekamali.gov.za/2017-18/national/departments/arts-and-culture?? Accessed 15 Jan 2019

Chapter 10
Music and Human Rights in Africa: The Role of Music in the Promotion of Human Rights in Uganda

Ronald Kakungulu-Mayambala

Abstract At the global level, the use of art in the form of music has become significant in the realisation of human rights. Music has been used to highlight human rights abuses, raise awareness and shape the human rights scholarship. This chapter deals with music and human rights in Uganda. The chapter provides a useful overview in the way music and artistic expression can be used to promote human rights in Uganda. This article begins with a general introduction in music and human rights, while the second part examines the relevance of music as a tool for human rights advocacy in Uganda. Overall, this chapter critically examines the intersection between music as an art and human rights law in Uganda as an innovative pattern of thinking about human rights gives concluding remarks and recommendations on the furtherance of this objective.

Keywords Music · Human rights · Bobi Wine · Uganda · Artistic expression · Indigenous languages

1 Introduction

Artistic expression often contributes to social, political and economic change. The playwright Bertolt Brecht asserted that 'art is not a mirror held up to reality, but a hammer with which to shape it' (Schumann 2008). This is done challenging cultural shibboleths compelling the audience to revisit culturally inherited ideas and concepts. Artists contribute to social debates, often bringing counter-discourses and potential counterweights to existing power centres (Shaheed 2013). The artist is considered 'the bad conscience of a society who calls ideology into question by representing all the ways in which it poisons our lives' (Davis 2007). Art 'represents

R. Kakungulu-Mayambala (✉)
Human Rights and Peace Centre (HURIPEC), Makerere University School of Law, Kampala, Uganda
e-mail: rkakungulu@law.mak.ac.ug

R. Adeola et al. (eds.), *The Art of Human Rights*, Arts, Research, Innovation and Society, https://doi.org/10.1007/978-3-030-30102-6_10

the disorders of its time…to make it impossible for us to ignore them any longer' (Davis 2007). Chinua Achebe, the Nigerian novelist, observed that:

> …9an African creative writer who tries to avoid the big social and political issues of contemporary Africa will end up being completely irrelevant like that absurd man in the proverb who leaves his house burning to pursue a rat fleeing from the flames (Achebe 1975).

As a vehicle of social change, arts must of necessity engage with topics that make us uncomfortable. Philly Lutaaya, an enormously popular Ugandan singer and songwriter in the 1980s, was the first prominent African to acknowledge that he was infected with HIV. He toured churches and schools performing songs he had written about his battle with the infection and spreading a powerful message of prevention and hope (World Bank 1997). His most famous song *Alone and Frightened* is to this day considered the anthem for the struggle against discrimination on the basis of HIV/AIDS victims (Isabirye 2008). Many musicians have since contributed to educating people about the danger of HIV/AIDS, how to prevent, how to live with it and the need to end discrimination against victims as is documented by Gregory Barz in his book *Singing for Life* (2006). It is in this context that the potency of music as a tool for the promotion of human rights resounds. Music serves to provoke change especially pro-human rights change. The use of music in the fight against both slavery and apartheid attest to this phenomenon (Danaher 2010). Social justice and equity are major corner stones in any human rights dispensation and there is no doubt as to the ability of music to transmit the two (Abrahams et al. 2012). Even during the fight against slave trade, one of the worst human rights violations to have been faced by mankind, music was key (Knepper 2009). Indeed, common wisdom holds that there is no music where there is silence or noise (Carvalho 2013). Music can be used to create a sense of hope even to seemingly hopeless societies or communities. In South Africa, for instance, 'music, together with cultural forms such as poetry, theatre and dance, was used to garner international support for the struggle against apartheid' (Shirli 2007). Indeed, music plays a very crucial role in story-telling and helps to promote political ideology (Tiefenburn 2005). Music remains helpful in restorative justice and reconciliation in most Ugandan societies. Music inspires a sense of belonging for most people and Uganda is no exception (Rajan 2001–2002). This is the case because the connection between music and emotion is very strong (Curtis and Bharucha 2009). Music creates a culture of activism. Social movements are galvanized through music (Reed 2005). Music also helps to build revolutionary consciousness. This is best underscored in the emergence of the so-called "freedom songs" during the civil rights movement in the United States as consciousness raising techniques (Reed 2005). The power of music in resisting human rights violations is best captured in the aftermath of the September 11, 2001 terrorist attacks on the United States of America.

As Randall notes:

> Immediately following the events of September 11, 2001, the song "God Bless America" was everywhere. Everyone, it seemed, was singing it— from senators on the capitol steps to traders at the New York Stock Exchange to ordinary citizens who kept candlelight vigils outside the White House. Other patriotic standards dominated the airwaves; we heard

nonstop over radio, television, and the Internet "Amber Waves of Grain," "America," and of course, "The Star Spangled Banner." For a televised memorial moderated by Oprah Winfrey at Yankee Stadium days after September 11, "Battle Hymn of the Republic" was also performed. The promise of "Battle Hymn's" avenging Christ figure, to loose "the fateful lightning of his terrible swift sword" and to "crush the serpent with his heel," seemed particularly suited to the moment (Randall 2011).

2 Music and Human Rights in Uganda

Notably, music is used to air human rights violations or to discourage such violations (Osofisan 1998). In Uganda, music appeals to a big section of the population since much of it is sung in the local languages which helps promote human rights. The use of music to discuss topical issues has become prominent. For example, Ronald Mayinja, a prominent Ugandan artist, uses music to discuss corruption. Some of his most popular hits are *tuli kubunkenke* (we are on tenterhooks) sang in 2005 and *tuwalana nguzi naye tetuwalana gavumenti* (we despise corruption, we do not despise the government) sang in 2013 (New Vision 2018). In 2018 he released a popular hit titled *Bizzeemu* (repeat) in which he bemoaned the fact that President Museveni is repeating the very mistakes of his predecessors that he so frequently condemned including arbitrary arrests and corruption (Chimp Reports 2018).

However, attempts to use music to support human rights activism have faced challenges (Saud 2007). Whereas it is clear and of no doubt that music can and indeed plays a leading role in the promotion of human rights in Uganda, music as a tool for human rights engagement faces significant challenges. With an increase in the consciousness of the role of music in addressing the plight of the Ugandan people has also come government crackdown on music in Uganda. In December 2017, two musicians, David Mugema and Jonathan Muwanguzi, were charged with offensive communication under section 25 of the Computer Misuse Act for composing and singing a song titled *wumula mzee* (take a rest old man), which was distributed through social media (New Vision 2017). The song was interpreted as a protest against plans which were underway to extend President Museveni's 30-year rule over the country through amending the constitution to remove the age limit of 75 (New Vision 2017). In October 2018, another musician Moses Nsubuga aka Viboyo was arrested and charged with offensive communication under section 25 of the Computer Misuse Act over a song in which he used expletives to insult the president of the country and the speaker of parliament. The arresting detectives informed the media that 'in the song, he abused several leaders and tribes in Uganda which is illegal' (Bagala 2018). In June 2018 the Resident District Commissioner (RDC) of Kitgum district in northern Uganda banned radio stations, discotheques and other public places from playing a song by a popular artiste, Bosmic Otim, titled *mac Onywalo buru* which means 'fire produces ash'. The song lampooned the President and many leading politicians from the northern region of the country (Makumbi and Kalokwera 2018). The RDC claimed that the song was inciting people to violence.

The RDC's actions were condemned as they lacked any clear basis in law as RDCs do not have authority to make such bans (Daily Monitor 2018b). The actions of the Resident District Commissioner had a chilling effect on the use of music as an artistic expression intended to fight against human rights abuses.

However, the most prominent restriction on music has been demonstrated through attacks on one of the prominent music artists in Uganda called Robert Kyagulanyi (aka Bobi Wine). Robert Kyagulanyi in particular is noted for singing powerful emotive songs that capture the struggles of and injustices faced by the urban youth (Kaggwa 2018). In late 2017, the song *'Freedom'* by Bobi Wine which reveals how the Ugandan political opposition is fighting for the very same freedom Museveni fought for as a guerrilla in the 1980s was banned by the Uganda Communications Commission (UCC). Earlier in 2012, Robert Kyagulanyi released an immensely popular song titled *tugambire ku Jennifer* meaning 'Go tell Jennifer'. The song was addressed to Ms. Jennifer Musisi, then Executive Director of the Kampala Capital City Authority (KCCA). For months leading up to the release of the song KCCA had been harassing illegal street vendors and hawkers who had previously gone unmolested. The new measures were an effort to clean up the streets but had inadvertently led to mass joblessness as many of these illegal vendors had no other source of income (Musasizi 2012). Robert Kyagulanyi's song captured the injustice many felt that these people were facing with the line *'Tugambire Ku Jennifer akendeeze obukambwe'* (Go tell Jennifer to reduce on the toughness). True to form within days of release, UCC threatened radio stations that played the song. Nonetheless its popularity spread largely due to social media (Musasizi 2012).

3 Music, Human Rights and Artistic Expression in Uganda

Uganda is a party to several international and regional human rights instruments. Uganda is a dualist country and treaties; conventions, agreements or other international instruments signed by Uganda only have a binding force in Uganda after being domesticated by the Parliament (Constitution, Art.123). This is intended to secure the sovereignty of Uganda as a country. However, it has been argued that international law is and should be directly applicable in Uganda (Seelinger 2017). Seelinger argues that customary international law can be applied directly in Uganda (Seelinger 2017). In any case domestic law shall not conflict with international law. Article 1(3) of the United Nations Charter obliges all member states to promote and encourage respect for human rights and fundamental freedoms. These human rights are well spelt in the Universal Declaration of Human Rights (UDHR) (n.d.), the International Covenant on Civil and Political Rights (ICCPR), International Covenant on Economic, Social and Cultural Rights (ICESCR) and the African Charter on Human and Peoples Rights (ACHPR) among others.

Article 27 of the UDHR provides that everyone has the right "to enjoy the arts". Article 15(1) (a) of the ICESCR provides that everyone has the freedom to take part in cultural life. The authoritative interpretation of this provision is General comment No. 21 by the Committee on Economic, Social and Cultural Rights (CESCR 2009) which extends it to include the freedom of artistic expression. The Committee stated that taking part in cultural life included 'the right to seek and develop cultural knowledge and expressions and to share them with others, as well as to act creatively and take part in creative activity' (CESCR 2009). The Committee further interpreted the provision to include 'the right of everyone to be involved in creating the spiritual, material, intellectual and emotional expressions of the community' (CESCR 2009). Under article 15(3) of the ICESCR, states "undertake to respect the freedom indispensable for ...creative activity." The Committee has interpreted this right to include the right to "enjoy freedom of opinion, freedom of expression in the language or languages of their choice, and the right to seek, receive and impart information and ideas of all kinds and forms including art forms..." (CESCR 2009). Article 4 of ICESCR only permits "limitations as are determined by law only in so far as this may be compatible with the nature of these rights and solely for the purpose of promoting the general welfare in a democratic society." The Committee, while acknowledging that some limitation on the right to take part in cultural life might be necessary, emphasised that any such limitation "must pursue a legitimate aim, be compatible with the nature of this right and be strictly necessary for the promotion of general welfare in a democratic society, in accordance with article 4 of the Covenant" (CESCR 2009). Article 19 (2) of the ICCPR provides that freedom of expression includes the right to seek, receive and impart information and ideas of all kinds "in the form of art". The Committee in General Comment 34 stated that the right to freedom of expression includes cultural and artistic expression (Human Rights Committee 2011). Any regulation of broadcasting, publishing, performing or showcasing artistic works necessarily engages the right to freedom of expression. This is because by its very nature, regulation may be seen as a restriction on freedom of expression. It is therefore necessary that regulation be limited and controlled.

To limit interference with freedom of expression, regulation should be done by an independent body. Principle VII of the Declaration of Principles on Freedom of Expression in Africa (African Commission on Human and Peoples' Rights n.d.) provides that any public authority that exercises powers in the areas of broadcast or telecommunications regulation should be independent and adequately protected against interference, particularly of a political or economic nature. A joint declaration by the UN Special Rapporteur on Freedom of Opinion and Expression, the Organization for Security and Co-operation in Europe (OSCE) Representative on Freedom of the Media and the Organization of American States (OAS) Special Rapporteur on Freedom of Expression states that:

> All public authorities which exercise formal regulatory powers over the media should be protected against interference, particularly of a political or economic nature, including by an appointments process for members which is transparent, allows for public input and is not controlled by any particular political party (OAS; OSCE; UN 2003).

4 Conclusion

In a nutshell therefore, music can be used to shape the human rights narrative, scholarship and act as a way of using the voice to air human rights violations or to discourage such violations. Besides, music appeals to a big section of the Ugandan population, since much of it is sung in the local languages which helps promote human rights since the Government of Uganda (GoU) is yet to translate the Bill of Rights and other human rights instruments into over 65 indigenous languages of the communities of Uganda.

In emerging democracies like Uganda, artistic freedom of expression is key to holding governments with autocratic tendencies in check, challenging long established social norms, highlighting injustices of marginalised groups and expressing dissent. The effects of censorship or unjustified restrictions of the right to freedom of artistic expression and creativity are devastating. Restrictions on artistic expression result in social and economic losses, deprive artists of their means of expression and livelihood, create an unsafe environment for artists and their audiences, neuter debates on economic, social and political issues and limit the functioning of democracy.[1] Greater artistic freedom through the repealing or redrafting of laws such as the Computer Misuse Act can go a long way towards creating the right environment to harness music and other artistic talent as a tool for human rights engagement and advocacy.

Music can be used as a tool for engagement, and to curtail the perpetuation of dangerous stereotypes and propaganda that violate human rights, especially against the vulnerable societies in Uganda, including ethnic and religious minorities as well as women and children. Highlighting examples and drawing largely on native Ugandan music, this chapter notes the intersection between music as an art and human rights law in Uganda as an innovative pattern of thinking about human rights.

References

Abrahams F, Rowland M, Kohler K (2012) Music education behind bars: giving voice to the inmates and the students who teach them. Music Educators J 98:67–73

Achebe C (1975) The African writer and the Biafran cause. In: Achebe C (ed) Morning yet on creation day essays. Heinemann Educational, London

African Commission on Human and Peoples' Rights (n.d.) Declaration of principles on freedom of expression in Africa. Banjul, the Gambia: 32nd session, 17–23 Oct 2002

Allsup RE, Shieh E (2012) Social justice and music education: the call for a public pedagogy. Music Educators J 98(4):47–51

Anon (n.d.) Attorney-General v. David Tinyefuza, 1 (Supreme Court 1997)

Bagala A (2018) Singer Viboyo arrested for using obscene words to attack Museveni, Kadaga. http://www.monitor.co.ug/News/National/Viboyo-arrested-attacking-Museveni-Kadaga-new-song/688334-4792240-10pq5kcz/index.html. Retrieved from Daily Monitor

Barz G (2006) Singing for life: HIV/AIDS and music in Uganda. Routledge, New York

[1] Report of the Special Rapporteur in the field of cultural rights, A/HRC/23/34 at para 86.

Bast G, Carayannis G, Campbell D (2015) Introduction to Arts, Research, Innovation, and Society (ARIS). In: Bast G, Carayannis E, Campbell D (eds) Arts, Research, Innovation and Society. Springer International Publishers, Cham, p 1

Beausoleil E (2013) Political actors performance as democratic protest in anti-apartheid theater. In: Love NS, Matter M (eds) Doing democracy: activist art and cultural politics. State University of New York Press, Albany, pp 257–288

Big Eye (2016) Bobi Wine confirms his "Dembe" song was banned. https://bigeye.ug/bobi-wine-confirms-his-dembe-song-was-banned/

Big Eye (2017) MC Mariachi apologises to Muslims for ridiculing them. https://bigeye.ug/mariachi-apologises-to-muslims-for-ridiculing-them/

Breitinger E (2004) Uganda. In: Banham M (ed) A history of theatre in Africa. Cambridge University Press, Cambridge, pp 247–264

Carvalho JM (2013) "Strange fruit": music between violence and death. J Aesthetics Art Criticism 71:111–119

CESCR (2009) General comment No. 21, E/C.12/GC/21 21 December 2009. United Nations

Chimp Reports (2018) Lyrics: Ronald Mayinja Stings Museveni in new song. https://chimpreports.com/lyrics-ronald-mayinja-stings-museveni-in-new-song/

Curtis M, Bharucha J (2009) The minor third communicates sadness in speech, mirroring its use in music. Am Psychol Assoc 10(3):335–348

Daily Monitor (2018a) Porn committee warns singer Sheebah over 'indecent dressing'. http://www.monitor.co.ug/artsculture/Entertainment/Porn-committee-warns-singer-Sheebah-over-indecent-dressing/812796-4339962-gvu5wmz/index.html

Daily Monitor (2018b) RDC shouldn't ban song but take singer to court. http://www.monitor.co.ug/OpEd/Editorial/RDC-should-ban-song-take-singer-court-/689360-4597164-e1dtr0/index.html. Retrieved from Daily Monitor

Danaher W (2010) Music that will bring Back the dead? Resurrection, reconciliation, and restorative justice in post-apartheid South Africa. J Religious Ethics 38:115–141

Davis W (2007) Art and politics: psychoanalysis, ideology theatre. Pluto Press, London

Dunn CK (2011) "Know your rights": punk rock, globalization, and human rights. Ashgate Publishing Ltd, Surrey

Edge (2017a) Bobi Wine fumes, UCC denies banning his song 'Freedom'. https://edge.ug/2017/11/05/bobi-wine-fumes-ucc-denies-banning-his-song-freedom/

Edge (2017b) Museveni wants NRA heroes songs on school syllabus. https://edge.ug/2017/06/09/museveni-wants-nra-heroes-songs-on-school-syllabus/

Epstein HC (2017) Another fine mess: America, Uganda, and the war on terror. Columbia Global Reports

Friedman JC (2013) Songs for freedom: music and the struggle against apartheid. In: Malisa M, Malange N (eds) The Routledge history of social protest in popular music. Routledge, New York, pp 304–318

Gibbs J (2011) 'Together we go red soldiers': the revolution's first song. South East Asia Res 19:737–753

Gouge MC (2016) Human rights in play, transnational solidarity at work: creative playfulness and subversive storytelling among the Coalition of Immokalee Workers. Crit Sociol 42:861–875

Hellier-Tinoco R (2011) Power needs names: hegemony, folklorization, and viejitos dance of Michoacan, Mexico. In: Randall JA (ed) Music, power, and politics. Routledge, New York/London

Huffington Post (2010) Yes, Sevo! Ugandan President Yoweri Museveni has hit rap song. https://www.huffingtonpost.com/2010/11/05/yes-sevo-ugandan-presiden_n_779769.html

Human Rights Committee (2011) General comment no. 34, CCPR/C/GC/34, 12 September. United Nations

Insider (2018) Singer Mayinja claims was trapped to sing for NRM. https://theinsider.ug/index.php/2018/02/26/singer-mayinja-claims-was-trapped-to-sing-for-nrm/

Isabirye (2008) Philly Lutaaya: popular music and the fight against HIV/AIDS in Uganda. J Postcolonial Writing 44:29–35
Kaggwa A (2018) The politics in 10 of Bobi Wine's songs. http://www.monitor.co.ug/Magazines/PeoplePower/-politics-Bobi-Wine-songs-Kyagulanyi-Ghetto-Mayinja/689844-4749988-he1k75/. Retrieved from Daily Monitor
Kasasira (2006) Uganda Elections 2006: Musicians take over political campaigns. http://www.ugpulse.com/government/uganda-elections-2006-musicians-take-over-political-campaigns/292/ug.aspx. Retrieved from UG pulse
Kato (2017) Police explain why they blocked Bobi Wine's Kiryandongo music show. http://www.monitor.co.ug/News/National/Police-explain-blocked-Bobi-Wine-s-Kiryandongo-music-show/688334-4194770-ue93b6/index.html. Retrieved from Daily Monitor
Katumanga M (2007) Folk poetry as a weapon of struggle: analysis of the Chaka Mchaka resistance songs of the national resistance movement/army of Uganda. In: Njogu K, Maupeu H (eds) Songs and politics in Eastern Africa. African Book Collective, Dar es Salaam, pp 129–156
Khiddu-Makubuya E (1974) The concept of human rights in traditional Africa. Makerere Law J 1(1)
Kintu D (2018) The Ugandan morality crusade: the brutal campaign against homosexuality and pornography. McFarland & Company Publishers, Jefferson, NC
Kiryowa S (2004) Titi treads on forbidden ground. https://www.newvision.co.ug/new_vision/news/1098235/titi-treads-forbidden-ground. Retrieved from New Vision
Knepper P (2009) The 'white slave trade' and the music hall affair in 1930s Malta. J Contemp Hist 44:205–220
Legros D (2004) Indigenous peoples' self-determination and the broken tin kettle music of human rights and Liberal democracy. Florida J Int Law 16:579–600
Makumbi C, Kalokwera P (2018) Song critical of government big shots banned. http://www.monitor.co.ug/News/National/Song-critical-government-big-shots-banned/688334-4596014-qk4025/index.html. Retrieved from Daily Monitor
Masaba J (2017) Police bans arrests of the 'idle and disorderly'. https://www.newvision.co.ug/new_vision/news/1455593/police-bans-arrests-idle-disorderly
Mateus-Berr R (2015) In: Bast ECG (ed) Art and design as social fabric, in: arts, research, innovation and society. Springer International Publishers, Cham
Mohamed NK (2015) The September 11 generation, hip-hop and human rights. J Sociol 51:1039–1051
Mosongo E (2017) Bobi Wine's Freedom banned in Uganda. https://www.musicinafrica.net/magazine/bobi-wine%E2%80%99s-freedom-banned-uganda. Retrieved from Music in Africa
Musasizi S (2012) Tugambire ku Jennifer rubs govt the wrong way. https://www.observer.ug/component/content/article?id=21025:tugambire-ku-jennifer-rubs-govt-the-wrong-way. Retrieved from The Observer
New Vision (2017) Musicians charged for disturbing the President's peace. https://www.newvision.co.ug/new_vision/news/1467010/musicians-charged-disturbing-president-peace
New Vision (2018) Mayinja wages war against corruption. https://www.newvision.co.ug/new_vision/news/1335665/mayinja-wages-war-corruption
Nkwaya N (2013) Art work Africa: monitoring freedom of creative expression. Arterial Network Report, 87
OAS; OSCE; UN (2003) International mechanisms for promoting freedom of expression: joint declaration
Olwage G (2011) Discipline and Choralism: the birth of musical colonialism. In: Randall JA (ed) Music, power, and politics. Routledge, New York/London
Onoria H (2010) Jurisdiction ratione materiae of the Uganda human rights commission: making sense of the ambiguity in the jurisprudence. Afr Hum Rights Law J 10:53–77
Osofisan F (1998) The revolution as muse' drama as surreptitious insurrection in a post-colonial, military state. In: Boon R, Plastow J (eds) Theatre matters: performance and culture on the world stage. Cambridge University Press, Cambridge, pp 11–35
Putz-Plecko B (2015) Provocation as a constructive element in the arts and in education to Foster societal development and innovation: experience and knowledge as forms of social relations.

In: Bast GC (ed) Arts, Research, Innovation and Society. Springer International Publishers, Cham, p 197
Rajan D (2001–2002) Music licensing, performance rights societies, and moral rights for music: a need in the current U.S. music licensing scheme and a way to provide moral rights. Univ Baltimore Intellect Property Law J 10:1–23
Randall JA (2011) A censorship of forgetting: origins and origin myths of "Battle Hymn of the Republic". In: Randall JA (ed) Music, power, and politics. Routledge, New York/London, p 5
Reed T (2005) The art of protest: culture and activism from the civil rights movement to the streets of Seattle. University of Minnesota Press, Minneapolis
Saud AK (2007) Rep that Islam: the rhyme and reason of American Islamic hip hop. Muslim World 97:125–141
Schiesser G (2015) What is at stake: qu'est-ce que l'enjeu? Paradoxes: problematics: perspectives in artistic research today. In: Bast G, Carayannis E, Campbell D (eds) Arts, research, innovation and society. Springer International Publishers, Cham, p 197
Schumann (2008) The beat that beat apartheid: the role of music in the resistance against apartheid in South Africa. Stichproben. Wiener Zeitschrift für kritische Afrikastudien
Seelinger TK (2017) Uganda's case of Thomas Kwoyelo: Customary International Law on Trial. California Law Rev Online 8
Serubiri M (2012) Political music: Kadongo Kamu is dead. http://startjournal.org/2012/04/political-music-kadongo-kamu-is-dead/. Retrieved from START Journal of Arts and Culture
Shaheed F (2013) The right to freedom of artistic expression and creativity. http://www.houseforculture.eu/upload/Docs%20ACP/PresentationEuroParliament2Oct2013Shaheedspeech.pdf. Retrieved from European Parliament
Shirli G (2007) Singing against apartheid: ANC cultural groups and the international anti-apartheid struggle. J South Afr Stud 33:421–441
Ssempogo H (2006) 15 arrested over nude dancing. https://www.newvision.co.ug/new_vision/news/1134011/arrested-nude-dancing. Retrieved from New Vision
Steen A (2011) Long live the revolution? The changing spirit of Chinese rock. In: Peddie I (ed) Popular music and human rights. Ashgate Publishing Limited, Surrey, p 132
Swedenburg T (2011) Islamic hip-hip vs. Islamophobia. In: Mitchell T (ed) Global noise: rap and hip-hop outside America. Wesleyan University Press, Middletown, CT, pp 57–85
Sweers B (2011) The power of influence minds: German folk music during the Nazi era and after. In: Randall JA (ed) Music, power, and politics. Routledge, New York/London
Tiefenburn S (2005) The failure of the international laws of war and the role of art and story-telling as self-help remedy for restorative justice. Texas Wesleyan Law Rev 91:118
Tuhairwe J (2004) Panadol Wa Basajja arrested, police hunting for producer Didi. https://bigeye.ug/panadol-wa-basajja-arrested-police-hunting-producer-didi/. Retrieved from Big Eye
Turner B (2002) The problem of cultural relativism for the sociology of human rights: Weber, Schmitt and Strauss. J Hum Rights 1:587–605
Turner R (2003) Islam in the African-American experience. Indiana University Press, Bloomington
Turner R (2006) Constructing masculinity: interactions between Islam and African-American youth since C. Eric Lincoln, "The Black Muslims in America". Souls 8(4):31–44
URN (2012) Media council to ban songs with abusive content. https://ugandaradionetwork.com/story/media-council-to-ban-songs-with-abusive-content
Verily AH (2009) There is only one hip-hop Umma: Islam, cultural protest and urban marginality. Social Democr 18:107–126
Vivienne W (2015) Art, research and society: new ecology: the affective power. In: Bast G, Carayannis E, Campbell D (eds) Arts, research, innovation and society. Springer International Publishers, Cham, p 82
Waswa (2018) Police bans processions, politics at Kyarenga concert. https://chimpreports.com/police-bans-processions-politics-at-kyarenga-concert/. Retrieved from Nile Post
Wa-Thiongo N (1981) Writers in politics: essays. Heinemann, London

Wesaka A (2014a) City artiste convicted for erotic song. http://www.monitor.co.ug/News/National/City-artiste-convicted-for-erotic-song/-/688334/2507380/-/3bp2yiz/-/index.html. Retrieved from Daily Monitor
Wesaka A (2014b) Musician Panadol Wa' basajja released on bail, 2 December 2014. http://www.monitor.co.ug/artsculture/Entertainment/Musician-Panadol-Wa%2D%2Dbasajja-released-on-bail/812796-2542080-ri5v2kz/index.html. Retrieved from Daily Monitor
Wesonga N (2016) UCC denies banning Bobi Wine Dembe song. http://www.monitor.co.ug/News/National/UCC-denies-banning-Bobi-Wine-Dembe-song/688334-3020230-x8mwqf/index.html. Retrieved from Daily Monitor
World Bank (1997) Confronting AIDS: public priorities in a global epidemic: a World Bank policy research report. Oxford University Press, New York
Zhuk IS (2011) Fascist music from the west: anti-rock campaigns, problems of national identity, and human rights in the "Closed City" of soviet Ukraine. In: Peddie I (ed) Popular music and human rights. Ashgate Publishing Limited, Surrey, pp 147–184

Laws

Constitution of the Republic of Uganda, 1995 (as amended)
Copyright and Neighbouring Rights Act (CNRA) 2006
Declaration of Principles on Freedom of Expression in Africa, African Commission on Human and Peoples' Rights, 32nd Session, 17–23 October, 2002: Banjul, The Gambia
Treaty for the Establishment of the East African Community (EAC) 1999
Universal Declaration of Human Rights (UDHR)

The manufacturer's authorised representative in the EU is Springer Nature Customer Service Centre GmbH, Europaplatz 3, 69115 Heidelberg, Germany. If you have any concerns regarding our products, please contact ProductSafety@springernature.com

Printed and bound by CPI Group (UK) Ltd, Croydon, CR0 4YY
30/09/2026
02225607-0012